LEGENDS
— OF THE —
CELTS

FRANK
DELANEY

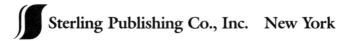

Sterling Publishing Co., Inc.   New York

LEGENDS
— OF THE —
CELTS

Library of Congress Cataloging-in-Publication Data

Delaney, Frank, 1942-
    Legends of the Celts / Frank Delaney.
        p.   cm.
    Reprint. Originally published: London : Hodder & Stoughton, 1989.
    Includes bibliographical references.
    ISBN 0-8069-8350-7
    1. Celts—Folklore. 2. Legends—Great Britain. 3. Legends—
Ireland. I. Title.
GR137.D45   1991
398.2'089'916—dc20   90-24605
                                            CIP

10 9 8 7 6 5 4 3 2 1

First paperback edition published in 1992 by
Sterling Publishing Company, Inc.
387 Park Avenue South, New York, N.Y. 10016
Originally published in Great Britain
by Hodder & Stoughton © 1989 by Frank Delaney
Manufactured in the United States of America
All rights reserved

Sterling ISBN 0-8069-8350-7 Trade
             0-8069-8351-5 Paper

For my son, Owen

by the same author:

James Joyce's Odyssey
Betjeman Country
The Celts
A Walk in the Dark Ages

fiction:

My Dark Rosaleen

verse:

Silver Apples, Golden Apples (ed.)

CONTENTS

INTRODUCTION

I

The legends in this book evolved from Celtic storytelling in Ireland and Britain. The stories have always been enthralling and entertaining. They possess all the beguiling forces of literature as a composing art – the colour, characterisation and incident; the intellectual, psychological and narrative enjoyabilities of fiction.

The writers, often monks, who as early as the eighth century AD, began to write them down, had presumably heard the stories in the telling. Could it be that these scribes, learned men, exposed already to the influences of Greece and Rome, and knowledgeable of the Bible, saw more in the stories than straightforward entertainment value? If novelists and poets, while reflecting the values and mores of their society, may also be seen to describe their world, why not the Celtic storytellers? We have knowledge of nineteenth-century Dorset from Hardy, London from Dickens, the bourgeoisie from Flaubert, before that Defoe and Fielding and Richardson, and so on: from novelists we may learn the past at least as atmospherically, and – invention of characters aside – as accurately in detail, as historians. The Celts themselves kept no records: on a ritual principle, they always refused to write down their laws and lore. Legend, descended orally and then in written fragments, is the fiction of the Celts.

The body of source material from which these stories have been selected is now regarded as the earliest Celtic 'literature'. As with the people whom they enshrine, the legends too have been excavated – from ancient manuscripts – and analysed.

LEGENDS OF THE CELTS

Despite a failure to consolidate, politically, in Europe, and losing any chance of doing so in the century before Christ, the Celts made a contribution to the culture of the continent which lasted in various significant ways for over two thousand years. They developed a distinctively expressive style which drew upon their own spiritual observations of the natural world, as well as the influences of the people with whom they traded. From these and other connections they made their lasting impact, visible in art, tangible in personality and imagination. With no ultimate political or nationalistic success, the extent to which their identity has depended and persisted is a tribute to their imaginative contribution.

'The unity of the Celts of antiquity,' observes the Irish scholar Professor Proinsias MacCana, 'was one of culture rather than of race.' Their storytelling, of which this collection forms only a portion, and chosen to represent their legends at their most vivid, was part of this flavour and unity.

Once they were a vaguely defined group, a presence rather than a firm state or civilisation. Now, history and archaeology combine to disclose the Celts in their own right. They were a peacock people, whose personal ornamentation denoted class, whose weapons indicated a capacity for emphatic aggressiveness. Ritualistic in their worship, imaginative in their art, they competed in physical contests and intellectual gaming; they were economically successful, enterprising and proud. The people recorded in the histories and found in the archaeological excavations are the same people who populate these legends – as if they intended their stories to immortalise them as accurately as the contents of their graves or the accounts of their historian neighbours.

Their distinctively vivid presence, one of the race pools in prehistoric and early medieval Europe, caused the Greeks to name them *Keltoi* – the strangers, the people who are different. During the millennium BC, Mediterranean writers, historians, travellers and others, including sailors and soldiers, observed and recorded them. With noticeable differences – in language, worship, social attitude and approach to life – they proved worthy of comment. From Herodotus in the fifth century BC to Julius Caesar in the first BC, a body of documentary work regarding the Celts gradually came into being. Fragmentary to begin with, then growing in scope, it traced a people who had tribal names, egregious behaviour, notable fierceness and pronounced social differences from those who wrote about them.

The late Dr T. G. E. Powell, who drew on linguistics, the early histories and his own discipline of prehistoric archaeology in his enquiries into the Celts, wrote:

> It is in fact clear that throughout the four centuries from Herodotus to Julius Caesar, the Celts were recognizable to their southern literate neighbours by their characteristic way of life, their political organization, and their appearance; factors, which, though easily misinterpreted, have ever remained the expression of strangeness between one population group and another.

Begin, then, with their display. Throughout the legends of the Celts we meet men of presence and women of great beauty. They dress to emphasise their appearance, they wear the finest of cloth in the brightest of colours. In one of the Welsh stories, *The Dream of the Emperor Maxen*, the Roman leader observes, in the palace of which he has dreamed and then visits, two young golden-haired boys wearing 'brocade made of jet black, thin headbands made of gold, and studded with shining gemstones and brilliant leather shoes strapped to their feet with straps of pure gold.' In the same scene an old man wears 'gold armlets and rings, as well as a thick gold torc round his neck,' while the girl 'wore white silk with gold brooches, a gold brocade coat and cloak fastened by a gem-encrusted brooch, her hair stayed in place under a band of gold studded with rubies and she wore a deep wide belt of gold.'

In *The Cattle Raid of Cooley*, when Ferdia girds for the battle with Cuchulainn, his clothing receives careful attention. 'He put on his most effective battle-dress, seven layers of silk, leather and stone covered by an apron of beaten iron and on his head an impregnable helmet encrusted with jewels and crystals.'

Elsewhere, clothing in all shapes and kinds performs a function of giving both mood and grandeur. In *The Dream of Rhonabwy*, when King Arthur is playing a board game while a sub-plot of mayhem takes place elsewhere, the characters who approach the king wear gaudy clothes. 'Messengers came to Arthur – one, wearing armour and a gold helmet with a leopard crest, sat on a beautiful grey horse swathed in thick crimson linen; another came on a white horse with one black leg, horse and rider covered in green and yellow mail topped by a gold helmet with a crest of a lion; a third rode up in flecked armour wearing a yellow helmet.' The entire story is marked by a predominance of costume, all denoting brilliance or turbulence or adventurousness.

When Culhwch rode off to have King Arthur cut his hair, 'He

dressed like a champion: two hounds loped beside him, each wore a collar studded with rubies and garnets, and he himself wore a voluminous purple cloak decorated at each corner with a crimson apple; an ivory hunting-horn joggled at his belt and his boots had been hammered from sheets of red gold.'

Of the ancient Celts, Strabo, in the first century, wrote:

> They wear ornaments of gold, torcs on their necks, and bracelets on their arms and wrists, while people of high rank wear dyed garments besprinkled with gold.

According to Diodorus Siculus in the same century:

> They accumulate large quantities of gold and make use of it for personal adornment, not only the women but also the men. For they wear bracelets on wrists and arms, and round their necks thick rings of solid gold, and they also wear fine finger-rings and even golden tunics . . . They wear a striking kind of clothing – tunics dyed and stained in various colours, and trousers . . . and they wear striped cloaks, fastened with buckles, thick in winter and light in summer, picked out with a variegated small check pattern. Their armour includes man-sized shields, decorated in individual fashion.

Archaeological proof has become copiously available. Many excavations have yielded beautiful artefacts of a type and purpose which might also have come straight from the legends. The graves of aristocrats have been identified by the remarkable objects interred with them. Within the last decade, one grave excavated in southern Germany disclosed a burial of extraordinary opulence and showiness. In *circa* 550 BC, the prince at Hochdorf, near Stuttgart, merited a huge festive funeral, a large, two-roomed tomb filled with textiles, flowers, a funerary cart bearing all the utensils for magnificent dining, a cauldron filled with over four hundred litres of mead and a series of drinking-horns for himself and the companions and guests he would host in the next world. To crown this display of his importance he had been festooned with gold, at his neck, his waist and his feet, and he wore gold armlets, bracelets and weapons. He might have stepped straight from one of the legends in this book, an Ulster prince, a Breton or Cornish knight, or a warrior in the 'Mabinogion'.

Multiple finds as far east as Silesia, as far west as Brittany and Ireland, confirm the tradition of glory; jewelled shields, gold torcs with intensive decoration, personal ornament, such as bracelets, rings, belts, hair clips, pins, harness-pieces for chariots and warriors' horses – details which so frequently colour the legends.

Hints of motifs in the stories and the details in the histories have also appeared archaeologically: the bull, the torcs, the figures wearing trousers on the Gundestrup cauldron found in Denmark; the Battersea Shield and the Snettisham Torc in the British Museum. All conform with descriptions of warrior apparel either in the histories or the legends or both – to such a degree that one hopes the connection between the historical writings and the archaeological evidence will in time be deliberately strengthened.

Weaponry, including the chariot, formed an important part of Celtic display. Swords, daggers, shields and spears found at Hallstatt and many other European sites, including Britain and Ireland, reveal evidence of fine craftsmanship in precious metals.

Setting off to win Olwen, Culhwch carried, '. . . his fiercest spear and his hardest sword, and to his back he strapped the widest shield he owned, the one with the huge centre boss and the fifty knobs round the perimeter, each knob the size of a wild boar's head.' The King of the Giants hurls three javelins at Culhwch and his companions, ferocious missiles which they turn back against him.

Diodorus Siculus observed:

Their armour includes man-sized shields, decorated in individual fashion. Some of these have projecting bronze animals of fine workmanship which serve for defence as well as decoration . . . Some have iron breast-plates of chain-mail while others fight naked, and for them the breast-plate given by Nature suffices. Instead of the short sword they carry long swords held by iron or bronze chains and hanging along their right flank. Some wear gold-plated or silver-plated belts around their tunics . . . the spears which they brandish in battle and which they call *lanciae* have iron heads a cubit or more in length and a little less than two palms in breadth; for their swords are as long as the javelins of other peoples and their javelins have points longer than swords. Some of their javelins are forged with a straight head, while some are spiral with breaks throughout their entire length, so that the blow not only cuts but also tears the flesh, and the recovery of the spear tears open the wound.

In both *The Cattle Raid of Cooley* and the Welsh story of Math, spears are wielded fearsome enough to pass through stone.

For several centuries, from the fifth century BC to the second century AD, many Celts interred their chieftain's or champion's chariot with him. This ritual element appears across a span of six centuries and a wide swathe of the continent, as far east as southern Russia, as far west as Britain. In the literature the chariot appears as late as the third century AD – in accounts of the attacks made by the *Caledonii*, a northern Scottish Celtic tribe, on the Romans.

Legendarily, the presence of the chariot frequently constitutes a thrilling ingredient. Cuchulainn dominates the early stages of the Tain battles from his chariot; his charioteer, Laeg, plays a character role; throughout the epic chariots form part of the contest, either in challenge, as when Cuchulainn obliges rivals to surmount obstacles he has laid down for them, or bearing new opponents to meet him – and taking their bodies away afterwards. In *The Champion's Portion* both Leary and Conall are humiliated when the giant in the meadow takes their chariots from them and Cuchulainn recovers them.

In Diodorus Siculus's account:

> For their journeys and in battle they use two-horse chariots, the chariot carrying both charioteer and chieftain. When they meet with cavalry in the battle they cast their javelins at the enemy and then, descending from the chariot, join battle with their swords.

The archaeology bears hard witness to a society that had achieved enough confidence and wealth to have moved up a stratum or two from the hunter–gatherer essentials of life. Their mythology charted that success. When perceived in Europe, in, say, the Danube valleys in the fifth century BC, or in Ireland ten centuries later, Celtic society had clear appurtenances that marked it down as self-contained and confident.

T. G. E. Powell summarised their economy thus:

> Apart from special opportunities in crafts, and trade, and indeed in pillage, the average Celtic tribe was mainly engaged in its own food production by agriculture, cattle raising, or both combined as mixed farming . . . From such material as is available from competent excavations, it would appear that in addition to cereal crops, mainly wheat and barley, the normal Celtic farm stocked cattle, swine and sheep.

Thus, in a story such as *The Champion's Portion*, Bricriu of the Poisoned Tongue can offer a Portion made of '. . . a seven-year-old boar, ripe and sweet, which since it was born had been fed only on sweetened porridge, oatmeal, fresh milk, nuts, wheat, meat and broth, according to the seasons. In addition he had a cow, seven years old too, who, since birth, had been fed only heather, herbs, corn and sweet meadow grass. And to accompany this cauldron full of wine, pigmeat and beef, one hundred wheat cakes had been cooked in honey, using a bushel of wheat to every four cakes.'

The legends of the Celts reflect the society in yet another significant way: in the matter of possessions. *The Cattle Raid of Cooley* was caused by a queen's envy of her king's possessions. Maeve discovers, in their pillow-talk, that Ailill owns a vital number more than she does. 'Then they counted their clothes, silks, brocades, linens, wools and cottons – Maeve had a slight edge over her husband in this department. He, however, won back that advantage – and more – when it came to what they raised on their farms. Here the trouble began in earnest. They each had beautiful animals whose fineness they measured as keenly as if selling them at market prices; they measured the height of their stallions, the girth of their rams, the weight of their boars and found that hand for hand, inch for inch, pound for pound, they did not differ in the overall total by as much as the weight or breadth of a sparrow's feather – until they came to the cattle. As they counted and measured Maeve began to get vexed, to exhibit a certain irritation, which finally burst forth in anger. Ailill, you see, had in his herds a wonderful bull, mighty and wide and enormously potent, and Maeve had nothing remotely like it.'

Possessions marked out Celtic society; the aristocracy had become great and wealthy through the acquisition of property and lands, hence the special stature of the warriors whose ferocity and prowess helped them to achieve their possessions. Time after time the legends tell of the quest for possessions, or the ennobling of a man by giving him a gift of land as in *The Wooing of Etain* where Aengus tricks Elkmar into surrendering his lands, and Elkmar therefore has to be compensated by being given other land.

Throughout these tales people feast frequently and extravagantly. Feasts and the invitations to them define a man's stature, both by the size of the feast and the quality of the food on display, and by the stature of the guests who attend, either happening by, or in response to a specific invitation.

Matters of great moment are decided or begin or break out at feasts. The tales regarding Bricriu and Mac DaTho both derive from the presence of the feast as an important entity in the social and hierarchical strata. Grainne seduces Diarmaid at a feast. The child that cries in the womb, who is to be Deirdre of the Sorrows, is first heard at a feast. The lovely Etain is born again as a human when she flies into a glass of mead at a feast. In the 'Mabinogion', marriage matters are settled and peace treaties agreed at feasts; guests, whether friend or foe, are appraised at feasts. Pwyll, Lord of Dyfed, first sees Rhiannon as he takes a walk between courses at a feast. He gains her hand at a feast. Feasts are used for treachery – Fergus, sent to guarantee the safe passages of Deirdre and the Sons of Usna, is decoyed away from his duties because he has given a bond never to refuse an invitation to a feast. Lugh declares his revenge on the Sons of Turenn at a feast; Bres is satirised by the poet to whom he has failed to give a feast. Branwen's fate is sealed at a feast.

From *The Countess of the Fountain*: 'Next morning, Owen, still tired from the welcoming celebrations, persuaded Arthur to linger and enjoy some hospitality. The feast which followed took three years to prepare, three months to eat and three weeks to recover from.'

> They invite strangers to their banquets, [observed Strabo] and only after the meal do they ask who they are and of what they stand in need. At dinner they are wont to be moved by chance remarks to wordy disputes and, after a challenge, to fight in single combat.

This fact alone forms the core of the story, *The Champion's Portion*, also known as *Bricriu's Feast*, in which a number of warriors contend for the dish or portion which so exceeds the other food on offer, both in quality and size, that it can only be fit for a champion. An Irish ethnographic scholar, Professor J. J. Tierney, in extrapolations from the ancient historian Posidonius, pointed out,

> When the hindquarters were served up, the bravest hero took the thigh-piece, and if another claimed it they stood up and fought in single combat to the death.

If the combatants brought together by Bricriu do not actually die, they nonetheless fight ferociously and in many different challenges.

Further historical examples seem to represent the legendary descriptions so accurately that one wonders whether the original storytellers were drawing upon the Mediterranean scribe, in the manner of Shakespeare upon Holinshed.

> When a large number dine together, they sit around in a circle with the most influential man in the centre . . . whether he surpass the others in warlike skill or nobility of family, or wealth. Beside him sits the host and next to either side the others in order of distinction. Their shieldsmen

stand behind them while their spearmen are seated in a circle and feast in common like their lords. The servers bear around the drink in terracotta or silver jars like spouted cups. The trenchers on which they serve the food are also of these materials, while with others they are made of bronze, or are woven or wooden baskets.

One feast is described as:

> . . . so great a quantity of food that for many days all who wished could enter and enjoy the feast prepared, being served without a break by the attendants.

And according to Strabo:

> They have large quantities of food together with milk and all kinds of meat, especially fresh and salt pork. Their pigs are allowed to run wild and are noted for their height, pugnacity and swiftness.

The Hochdorf excavations yielded a cart piled with enough knives and utensils for a long, continuous feast; a burial excavation in England revealed the remains of a leg of pork also buried to sustain the dead on their journey – in death as in life.

Posture also identified them:

> They are boasters and threateners and given to bombastic self-dramatization.

Diodorus Siculus did not mince his words.

> They had lyric poets whom they call 'Bards' . . . They sing to the accompaniment of instruments resembling lyres, sometimes a eulogy and sometimes a satire . . . they also have certain philosophers and theologians who are treated with special honour, whom they call 'Druids'.

Again, all these characteristics may be encountered among their legends. A Druid, Carbery, satirised a king, Bres, destroying his kingship in the earliest tales of Ireland. In the Welsh stories, men attempt to gain favour by pretending to the exalted position of bard. The Ulstermen listen with gravity to the Druid who pronounces on the child that will be born to be called 'Deirdre', the eventual ruin of Ulster.

LEGENDS OF THE CELTS

In short, the legends of the Celts recurrently, if unscientifically, bear out the evidence and confirm the views derived from history and archaeology. Only a society that had progressed hugely from the hunter–gatherer in the darkness of the forest, that knew the power of gold and ornament, that understood how such power is maintained by the setting-up of elaborate courtly structures, could produce such legends.

II

As well as tracing the factual connections between the history and archaeology (which, especially if attempting to confirm them scientifically, would make a fascinating lifetime's work) one of the most absorbing aspects of Celtic legends lies in making connections, both between the various branches themselves, and between the Celtic and other mythologies.

Taking the internal correspondences first, and beginning with the Irish tales, frequent cross-references occur. The opening story in this collection is drawn together, in the interests of cohesiveness, from the accounts in the twelfth-century 'Book of Invasions', in whose chronology (such as it is) the story of the Sons of Turenn belongs. Many incidents and characters reverberate in later stories.

For example, Tuan, one of the first survivors (*In the Beginning . . .*), turns himself into an eagle, then a hawk. The motif recurs among the Sons of Turenn who, by becoming birds, steal the apples in their quest. In the story of Math, young Llew turns into an eagle when his treacherous wife has him shot at by her lover.

Shouts resound. The sons of Turenn, as the final task in their quest, must give three shouts atop a hill. Said Culhwch, in pursuit of Olwen, 'If you don't let me in, I will shout three times. Each shout will echo as far as the next island and as high as the clouds, and the noise will empty the womb of any woman carrying a child and make barren all those who are not.' In *Llew and Llewellys*, one of the three plagues is a terrible shout. In *The Countess of the Fountain* Owen hears three shouts in the course of an evening – they signify the death of the black knight.

And doormen: Lugh meets the doorman who questions him at Tara; the Welsh hero Culhwch, in search of Arthur, also has his way barred by a doorman.

And dogs: Mac DaTho has a dog worth several armies; Cuchulainn, in *The Cattle Raid of Cooley*, gets his name from killing an indispensable hound. One of the tasks imposed upon the Sons of Turenn obliges them to steal an invaluably fierce dog.

And disguise: in another stretch of their quest, the Sons disguise themselves as poets to win one of the objects they seek, as do Gwydion and Gilvathy and their companions when they go to acquire the swine for Math; later in the same story Gwydion and young Llew 'told the watchman that two distinguished young bards from Glamorgan had come on a visit' as they attempt to outwit the woman who will neither name nor arm the young man.

In *The Champion's Portion*, other cross-references bring to light the importance of the society's structure and how wealth was measured. Bricriu builds a magnificent castle: among the Welsh stories, the Emperor Maxen sees in his dream equally magnificent buildings. So do the two riders who stick to the fountain in the story of Manawyddan: 'a fortress they had never seen before in that countryside which they thought they knew so well. This keep, high and sleek and powerful, had a superior kind of stonemasonry foreign to Manawyddan and Pryderi.'

Animals play many parts, cats and birds and boars – a white boar kills Diarmaid; a white boar leads the hunt where Pwyll and Rhiannon are stuck to the fountain. Giants abound; in *The Champion's Portion*, Cuchulainn defeats both the giant in the meadow and the ogre walking out of the sea – both creatures have already routed Leary and Conall. Owen in *The Countess of the Fountain* defeats a giant – admittedly with the help of a lion.

Enchanted mists descend: in the story *Cormac and his Cup of Gold*, a fog cuts Cormac off as he rides out to find his wife and son; a mist separates Pwyll from his hunting companions and he meets Arawn instead; a deep mist wipes clean all of Arberth as Pwyll and Manawyddan and their wives are out hunting.

Human considerations play an important part: Deirdre of the Sorrows was reared like Balor's daughter Eithne, locked away out of all sight of men, yet freed by a champion. In the case of Eithne, her father feared a prophecy that he would be killed by one of his own descendants, so he tried to ensure that he would not have any; in the event his own grandson Lugh killed him. In *Culhwch and Olwen*, the King of the Giants fears a similar prophecy and suffers its inevitable fate when Culhwch accomplishes all the tasks and wins Olwen.

The love stories of Diarmaid and Grainne, and of Deirdre and the

Sons of Usna, have correspondences with the Tristan and Iseult legend: in all cases a warrior or champion or knight cuckolds a king or senior person; revenge obsesses the deceived or cuckolded one, and pursuit, or poignant and violent end, takes place.

And an old romantic motif occurs at least twice – where Grainne dies, a yew tree springs from her grave and spreads its branches out across the countryside until it finds the branches from Diarmaid's. In Tintagel church, no matter how often King Mark cuts them down, two yew trees spring from the graves of Tristan and Iseult, either side of the nave, and intertwine. The same occurs in the Victorian rural ballad, 'Barbara Allen', also known as 'Sweet William'.

One of the most enduring attractions of mythology lies in comparisons across universal culture. In this the Celts also connect, sometimes in major chords, sometimes in minor, with the earliest strands of the Indians and Greeks, down to the later colloquial manifestations of story form, such as the Brothers Grimm. Obvious and pervasive archetypal motifs such as the Bull and the Quest recur, virility, or the search for self or meaning. Less powerfully, though yet enchanting, little flicks of detail arise, such as the moment when the Celts went in a delegation to Alexander the Great in 335 BC and told him they were afraid of one thing only – that the sky might fall; more than one commentator has pointed out the children's story of Henny Penny or Hen Pen who rushes to tell the king that the sky is going to fall.

Celtic mythology, deriving like all others from prehistoric belief which existed to provide religion, or the example of leadership or heroism, shared the fixed points relating to the great personal events – fertility, procreation, birth, threat, survival, death. The mobility of the prehistoric peoples meant communication of ideas, which, along with the universality of the human spirit, explains why an Egyptian legend such as that of Osiris, who ruled so wisely and guided his country's harvest, can have correspondences among the Irish, as with the king in *The Wooing of Etain*: 'Eochy ruled with prudence and justice, banning all lies and deceit. During his monarchy no rain fell, but the dews of the morning and evening watered the earth sufficiently to ensure a rich harvest each year.'

The sacredness of bulls in many mythologies is an unavoidable motif; in Ireland the bull of Cooley took on almost deific proportions as the search for him plunged the entire country into war, at which point the animal showed mythic vitality. 'He received encouragement from a source never far from such trouble – the war-goddess, the many-shaped Morrigan. Sometimes a bird, sometimes a beast, sometimes a wind, sometimes a woman, she now perched, as a black raven, on the bull's shoulder and, goading him, cried death and slaughter in his interests. The bull took off, on the rampage. Head down, he levelled all before him, his horns tearing a deep furrow in the earth. Everyone ran for their lives.' In Greek mythology, Poseidon gave Minos a gift of a great bull. But when Minos did not return the compliment by sacrificing the bull, Poseidon, in revenge, maddened the animal, who tore through the countryside terrorising the people.

Hunting motifs, not surprisingly, also appear liberally; Finn Mac-Cool and the Fianna hunted with hounds on the mountains and lakeshores of Ireland, as Artemis did on the slopes of Arcadia. In Artemis' case other connections come to mind: Math turned Gwydion and Gilvathy into a stag and a hind – Artemis turned Actaeon, who had seen her bathing, into a stag whose own hounds devoured him.

The outstanding male figures provide some of the most interesting cross-references. Apollo, son of Zeus, can be compared with Lugh, shining and multi-talented, also son of an all-powerful deity. Cuchulainn, the archetypal omnicompetent hero, bears comparison with Heracles (the Roman Hercules), capable of the same violent rages. In common with Heracles, Culhwch is given, accepts and accomplishes a series of extraordinarily difficult tasks, as with the Sons of Turenn. The warriors, such as the Fianna and the Red Branch Knights, share a notably deep bonding, the archetype of the Greek male ideal. Balor of the Baleful Eye was killed by a missile through his single eye, the same fate as that of the one-eyed Cyclops. The Keeper of the Woods in *The Countess of the Fountain* also had only a single eye.

In one notable sector of Greek mythology, the Twelve Labours of Heracles, several motifs appear which resonate among the Celts. The first two labours of Heracles involve the Lion of Nemea and the Hydra of Lerna: Owen, in *The Countess of the Fountain*, finds a serpent fighting a lion. Next came the Boar of Erymanthus, whom Heracles had to subdue and capture: a wild boar killed Diarmaid of the love-spot, and a white boar led the heroes of the Manawyddan story to their captivity.

The Birds of Stymphalus attacked from the sky and fed on human flesh; Heracles took them on with arrows; Cuchulainn's pastime was chasing birds on the wing; in *The Dream of Rhonabwy* the ravens finally attack from the sky, savaging the men in the camp.

The entire *Cattle Raid of Cooley* rings with echoes of 'The Stables of Augeas' and 'The Bull of Crete': the most outstanding of the Augean Bulls was, like the Brown Bull's rival, brilliant white.

The Hesperides, daughters of Hesperus and Atlas, guarded apples in a garden in the far corner of the world. As their first task, Lugh obliged the Sons of Turenn to acquire the apples which 'grew in the Garden of the Light over an ocean far off in the East.'

In one of Heracles' lesser tasks, Hesione, the daughter of the king of Ilium, had been chained to a rock, about to die; Owen in *The Countess of the Fountain* finds Luned imprisoned in a stone tomb.

The Celts and the Greeks also shared a motif of buildings; Poseidon lived in the depths of the Aegean in a magnificent palace constructed of gold, the sort of building Maxen approaches in his dream, or Bricriu builds for his feasts, or the Welsh riders find in the woods. Incidentally, Poseidon, like Manannan MacLir, the god of the sea, possessed horses capable of riding with equal facility over land and water.

All across the world ancient mythologies contain corresponding echoes and murmurs. In Chinese mythology hunters also go into the woods and have strange sights revealed to them in flashes of lightning. Men seeking wives see them bathing or at their toilet by the river: as Eochy's man saw Etain, so did the Chinese Cowherd who married the Heavenly Spinster. Great leaders seem taller than the mountains: when Bran from the Isle of the Mighty crosses the sea to avenge the Irish treatment of his sister Branwen, the swineherds think a mountain and a forest are moving: a Punjabi tale personifies the king of the mountains as the one with his head raised high and aloft.

In a Persian story, a hero called Zal falls in love with a maiden he has never met and, at the mere mention of her name, he shudders and almost swoons with passion. When Culhwch first heard the name of Olwen, the daughter of the King of the Giants: '. . . Amazingly, the lad trembled and blushed at this remark, as he felt a love pour through him for this girl he had never seen and of whom he had only, this moment, heard.'

The Indian mythology where, given the Indo-European root, connections may be expected, also flashes with Celtic light. A semi-malevolent Celtic god, the Daghda, habitually ate huge meals of porridge from an inexhaustible cauldron; the ogre, Khumbakarna, had to be provided with a vast meal twice a year at which he ate ten thousand sheep and ten thousand goats, washed down with four thousand bowls of an alcoholic beverage, drunk from the skull of a boar.

Krishna, as a baby, was fostered out clandestinely to the house of a cowherd; Culhwch was born in the hut of a swineherd and Pryderi, son of Pwyll and Rhiannon, was initially raised in the house of a farmer Tiernan who returned him to his rightful parents.

When Siddharta removed himself from the harem and became a monk, he reduced his body to a barely skeletal existence. In *The Countess of the Fountain*, Owen's appearance 'became like that of the small animals; he shrivelled and foraged with them in the under-growth . . . running half-naked and whimpering along the grass. He had become so emaciated that the blood in his veins could be seen, and his matted hair covered most of his body.' The same motif recurs in the twentieth century: in Thomas Mann's novel of medieval times, 'The Holy Sinner', the hero shrinks to the size of a hedgehog and lives a sub-human life of asceticism on top of a rock, where the Vatican legates eventually find him.

Mythology's tales, while they thrill and enchant, also teach and inspire; the characteristics of humanity contain lessons in themselves – goodness, evil, greed, generosity, vengefulness, forgiveness, devi-ousness, directness, violence, peace. And when then exaggerated and gilded so that mortals may have huge and magical models, terrific storytelling materialises. Therefore, the legends of the Celts perform the functions of all ancient 'fiction' – entertaining us, while stimulating thought and emotion, and with a finite, if large, range of devices.

III

Celtic mythology has long attracted those who want to retell it, bring it up to date. It is an understandable impulse: the stories are not only exciting in themselves, the exercise of retelling teaches implicitly many of the functions of story, characterisation, action, suspense, humour and daring. Furthermore, they have survived. The antiquity of Celtic legend has a provable, written record over a thousand years long. From the 'Dark Ages' of the early medieval period, through the political re-ordering of Europe, through the high monastic Middle Ages into the dynastic European and Elizabethan times, the late eighteenth and nineteenth centuries to the present day, writers of varying disciplines, some scholarly, some romantic, some interested in the roots of the story, some poetic, have experienced the urge to bring the stories forward again and for as many varied reasons.

Augusta Gregory, for example, dedicated her retelling of, among others, *The Cattle Raid of Cooley*, to the people of her locality, Kiltartan in the west of Ireland.

> My Dear Friends, when I began to gather these stories together, it is of you I was thinking, that you would like to have them and to be reading them. For although you have not to go far to get stories of Finn and Goll and Oisin from any old person in the place, there is very little of the history of Cuchulainn and his friends left in the memory of the people, but only that they were brave men and good fighters, and that Deirdre was beautiful. When I went looking for the stories in the old writings, I found that the Irish in them is too hard for any person to read that has not made a long study of it . . . I have told the whole story in plain and simple words, in the same way my old nurse Mary Sheridan used to be telling stories long ago and I a child at Roxburgh.

(There is, incidentally, more than a hint of Big House patronage in the language the Good Lady used. She deliberately employed a kind of patois which, she believed, the 'natives' generally spoke: the Irish relentlessly satirised this view of themselves – the style of language, scorned for its stage-Irishry, became known as 'the mist-that-does-be-on-the-bog', with a 'wisha' or a 'begorrah' thrown in.)

William Butler Yeats, in a preface to the same volume, called it:

> the best book that has ever come out of Ireland; for the stories which it tells are a chief part of Ireland's gift to the imagination of the world.

and insisted that Lady Gregory was well on the way to giving Ireland 'its 'Mabinogion', its 'Morte d'Arthur', its 'Nibelungenlied'. Yeats, who drew widely upon the mythology for his own poems and plays, then went on to observe:

> The Church, when it was most powerful, taught learned and unlearned to climb, as it were, to the great moral realities through hierarchies of Cherubim and Seraphim, through clouds of Saints and Angels who had all their precise duties and privileges. The storytellers of Ireland, perhaps of every primitive country, created as fine a fellowship . . . they created,

for learned and unlearned alike, a communion of heroes, a cloud of stalwart witnesses.

Small wonder that others, such as James Stephens and John Millington Synge, fascinated observers of the ancient lines of peasant heritage, also became retellers. The poet Thomas Kinsella remarked in his 1969 translation of the *Cattle Raid* that

> It seemed extraordinary that, for all the romanticised, fairy tale, versified, dramatised and bowdlerised versions of the Ulster cycle, there had never been a readable translation of the older version of the 'Tain', tidied a little and completed from other sources – nothing in English to give an idea of the story as we first have it.

Others had different reasons. Lady Charlotte Guest, when approaching the 'Mabinogion', sought to empower Wales and its literature with a great spiritual past. Having established

> the great, though indefinite antiquity of these tales, and of an origin which, if not indigenous [is] certainly derived from no European nation

she then concluded that

> the Cymric nation is not only . . . an early offshoot of the Indo-European family, and a people of unmixed descent, but that when driven out of their conquests by the later nations, the names and exploits of their heroes, and the composition of their bards, spread far and wide among the invaders, and affected intimately their tastes and literature for many centuries, and that it has strong claims to be considered the cradle of European romance.

This book is by no means a full collection of all the available legends of the Celts: it is a selection of several attractive stories, known and enjoyed since childhood. I simply wish to put them on display once again, to share them, and to test them: after at least a dozen centuries can the cores of these stories stand up, can they be read aloud, or internally, by adults or children, or both?

It seems as if they can. Furthermore, they have much in common with, much to contribute to, modern storytellers. Many of the stories being told today in the cinema and on television rely, or perhaps unconsciously draw upon, the same mix of imagery, action, magic, heroism. To take one such example, the popular fantasy genre rings loud with echoes of the sights and fights already thousands of years old in the Celtic mythology: impossibly brilliant heroes – for

LEGENDS OF THE CELTS

Cuchulainn read Conan the Barbarian – fighting evil forces in the shape of ogres, or huge armies, or dragons or vile witches and wizards – and, psychologically, the dark forces and fears within us all.

The characterisations in these legends have all the larger-than-life qualities which guarantee their own kind of drama. Any art director would glory in the castles and the costumes. Tension, intrigue, betrayal, beautiful women, amazingly accomplished warriors, chases, pursuits – the storytellers who wove these marvellous fabrics at firesides and in banqueting-halls must surely count as among the earliest of screenplay writers. And they barred no holds: they showed no embarrassment or difficulties with credibility as they wielded magic – their spells could hold entire populations in thrall. And they suspended time – a man may be gone out for a day's hunting, but, in the reality of his past life, not return for a hundred years.

To retell the legends of the Celts becomes a little like retelling the Bible, with many of the inherent dangers. Since childhood I had known a great many of the tales, especially the Irish legends – though, surprisingly, many of the Welsh ones too, and less surprisingly the Arthurian element. But I wanted to stay within a framework more formal than that of childhood memory and yet retain the colloquialism and entertainment.

Therefore, even though all of these stories contain my own embellishments, added in the tradition that every storyteller should take the story on further, I have, as far as possible, stayed faithful to the record in the legends, backed up by the histories and the archaeological evidence. I have also stayed as close as possible to accessibility, notably in the spellings of the words where, risking heresies, I anglicised. Some have not been suited to phonetics – no point whatsoever in writing Cuchulainn as 'Koo-Kullen' when Ulstermen themselves refer to him as 'Koo-Hooalenn'; likewise, Bricriu receives two different pronunciations in Ireland.

Essentially three original branches of Celtic mythology existed: the Continental, largely Gaulish, myths; the Irish tales, long present in the oral tradition and eventually transposed into literature; and the Welsh medieval contribution exemplified in what Lady Charlotte Guest imperfectly called 'The Mabinogion'. The last two continue in reasonably abundant record; the first, the Gaulish, has been gleaned largely from inscriptional evidence, some statuary and observations by contemporary scribes – as Professor MacCana puts it,

Gaulish literature, being purely oral, disappeared with the Gaulish language: we have it on Caesar's authority that the druids of Gaul considered it improper to commit their learning to writing . . . As a result, since mythology implies some sort of narrative or other, Gaulish mythology, properly speaking, is lost beyond recovery. There remains, of course, a considerable body of residual evidence, but, since by its very nature it is allusive rather than descriptive, or else is reported at second hand, the modern student is frequently in the uncomfortable position of having to work from the ambiguous towards the unknown.

In terms of storytelling, this leaves anyone wishing to provide a popular retelling with the two main choices, from Ireland and from Wales. The Arthurian romances have an acknowledged general correspondence with the Welsh literature and indeed 'leak' into the 'Mabinogion'.

My initial approach led me to choose quite simply 'the best stories'. Taking the Irish tales first, a clear and understood chronology already existed – beginning with the 'pure' mythology, the means by which the Irish gave themselves a 'history', that is to say a vivid and chronological account of the island's first inhabitants and their successive invaders and colonisers: this is represented by the section *In the Beginning* . . .

Next come the action-packed heroic stories relating to Ulster, tales which belong in Ireland's earliest documents, such as *The Champion's Portion* and *Mac Da Tho's Boar*. These are followed in Part One by the Fenian cycle, the stories of Finn MacCool and the Fianna, such as *Diarmaid and Grainne*. In due course they evolved in part to what Professor MacCana calls 'the integrated tradition', when Christianity informs the later legends, as in the case of Oisin's return from the magical Land of Eternal Youth.

In Section One I have also included two examples of the many unclassifiable and miscellaneous stories which belong in no neatly categorised sections, but which nevertheless belong to Celtic legend and contain much of the essential colour – *Cormac's Cup of Gold* and *The Wooing of Etain*. Both possess that unique Celtic characteristic, paradox allied to magic.

Part Two, *The Cattle Raid of Cooley*, is perhaps the greatest single saga in Celtic legend, according to Thomas Kinsella:

The nearest approach to a great epic that Ireland has produced. For parts of the narrative, and for some of the ancillary stories, achievements at the highest level of saga literature may fairly be claimed.

Found in large part in 'The Book of the Dun Cow', a twelfth-century manuscript compiled by the monks of Clonmacnoise on the banks of the River Shannon in the midlands of Ireland, it tells the epic story of a war between the provinces of Ulster and Connaught. The story is a valuable source of early Irish geography, as the war rages back and forth across the north-east and north-west and north midlands of Ireland.

The storytelling aspects of the *Cattle Raid* have as much fascination for a writer as the scholarly implications for students of early Ireland. The character of the hero Cuchulainn is built up from the observations of those warriors who have to face him. We learn about him from the unsympathetic side of the tale, that is to say, from his enemies; thereafter, we are permitted to see him in all his heroism but against the background painted by his enemies. Undoubtedly he possesses heroism and prowess of monumental proportions but he is never painted in terms of an unambiguously likeable hero. His character is that of a surly and arrogant man, whose brilliance in combat cannot be faulted, but whose personality leaves much to be desired.

Likewise the character of Maeve of Connaught comes over very clearly. She, a greedy and devious woman, causes this tremendous carnage and all throughout her ferocious, uncaring pursuit of her goal, the great bull of Cooley, she appears as an untrustworthy, immoral woman. Not only is her femininity never in doubt, but she actually exploits it to save her life when Cuchulainn finally encounters her in Maeve's Foul Place (known to this day, and visible in County Donegal, as the Poisoned Glen).

The *Cattle Raid* observes many of the principles that hallmark the greatest of adventure novels. From the clear and morally doubtful motivation of Maeve's greed, which gives the story its great impulse – that is, someone evil who wants something and who will stop at nothing to get it – we proceed via vivid characterisation to tremendous and wide-ranging action, involving heroism, skill, decision-making, the gap between aspiration and achievement, conflict, the bringing of the great hero to the brink of defeat, and satisfactory resolution.

In the intervals between passages of violent action, we hear the arguments and discussions which motivate the next phase of action. We encounter many small sub-plots, such as the stealing of Fergus's sword, or the bribing of Ferdia; we observe the deep moral conflicts provoked when unscrupulous people oblige others to behave dishonourably too – Ferdia does not wish to fight Cuchulainn, Fergus never will – and we see the objective panoramic view of the battlefield from the bed of Cuchulainn, as the war draws to a close. An analysis of the patterns in the *Cattle Raid* would establish connections between this ancient saga, which may well have been current at the time of Homer, and the best of modern adventure, spy or thriller writing.

Of Section Three, the 'Mabinogion', Dr Jeffrey Gantz writes in the Introduction to his 1976 translation:

> It has often been stated that the *Mabinogion* is a literary masterpiece. Its virtues are, in fact, so abundant that its flaws can be cheerfully and confidently owned . . . In the first place the demands of oral composition are such that some degree of inconsistency is inevitable – even Homer's work is not perfect in this respect. And secondly the manuscripts which we possess were not approved by the storytellers themselves; they rather resemble the bad quartos of a Shakespearian play, subjected to innumerable mishearings and misreadings. The Welsh storytellers' audience must have enjoyed a much higher level of artistry than is evident in the surviving manuscripts.

The 'much higher level of artistry' shines through; these stories, brilliant and often amusing, gorgeously dressed and thoughtful, cannot fail to inspire and entertain. The original 'Mabinogion', brought into the eponymous collection finalised in 1849 by Charlotte Guest, contained eleven stories, nine of which I have included here.

In the retelling of the Welsh stories, more perhaps than in any of the others, I granted myself very substantial storyteller's licence. This is not to say that the stories do not adhere to the traditional forms, or rather patterns of the narrative in a sequential way – they do, but in the Guest and other early translations, and even in Dr Gantz's, swathes of detail were included, which I have chosen to leave out, in the interests of the narrative's pace. For instance, when Culhwch asks Arthur for the hand in marriage of Olwen, daughter of the King of the Giants, he then invokes dozens of warriors whose names follow in a biblical litany.

Part Four is a retelling of one of the greatest stories in any culture or mythology, *Tristan and Iseult*. Its imagery may prove the most lasting of all: black sails, white sails; the lewd group of lepers crying out to be given Iseult for their pleasure; the lovers lying in the wood with Tristan's sword between them [since interpreted as a metaphor for both chastity and venereal disease]; its duplicitousness, such as the dwarf with the flour, or the vindicating deceit used by Iseult. Certainly it has the liveliest survival, still current in many forms, *pace* Wagner's opera and other different artistic treatments. For these reasons it makes a fittingly modern coda to older, more ferocious tales.

Celtic legend began as stories told, domestically or communally, to set up system and ritual so that people could live together, acquire history and dignity and learn how to deal with life. Each community that heard its stories was made to feel that it belonged to a wider system, a wider unconscious, that it was not alone, yet had a cultural individuality. The stories taught the hearers how to deal with enemies and temptation and jealousies and disasters, with sexual and marital intrigues and situations of terror. Thus, the motifs which all myth-ologies have in common, though different perhaps in style and expression, come from the same pool of human experience and need. (Though variations will be found between, say, the bull symbol as used in Mycenean or Greek myth and the 'Tain' legend of the Irish, the underlying message remains the same – that virility is powerful and necessary but if misused or improperly regarded it is a force for, or an agent of, destruction.)

A people's mythology, whether it be the most ancient Babylonian or the most modern 'urban legend', functions on many levels. It permits the incredible a place in the imagination; it may further explain and make accessible the inexplicable, or provide a system for humanity to check itself against. Myth employs, and depends upon, gods and heroes, figures greater and therefore more licensed than human beings. Myths grow out of a culture needing to identify itself, to tell itself its own history. When the Irishman, Charles Thomson, the 'powerful clerk' of Philadelphia, who contributed so much organisationally and politically to the founding of the American state, refused to write a history of the Revolution, and indeed tore up the archives he had so carefully kept, he did so on the grounds that he knew too much to feel able to tell the unvarnished truth. The forthcoming generations, he said, would need heroes.

The Celts used their mythology, moral, heroic, magical, to give themselves a history and a system for living. Consequently their stories could not but inspire, thrill and enchant, while exhibiting all the worst qualities of humankind – greed, vengefulness, deviousness, violence. In myth, as in life, they abundantly embraced both good-ness and badness and feared only boredom.

With these tales the Celts passed long winter nights. The bards who told them, and had an obligation to learn them as part of their long training, often took several days to tell such tales, and in the case of the longer ones, weeks and perhaps months. (This may explain sudden diversions and digressions, changes of tempo, scene and even character.) Kings and slaves heard them, as the images of battle and love and revenge flickered on the walls of castles, wooden houses with high pitched straw roofs, and thatched mud huts.

In other words, the legends of the Celts were, at one primary level, popular entertainment. My retelling of the stories in this book is intended to continue in that colloquial tradition in which one voice, perhaps evening after evening, engaged a fireside audience with tales that entertained and thrilled.

FRANK DELANEY
LONDON,
SUMMER, 1989.

PART ONE

Ireland, never Romanised and therefore, unlike Britain, free of major cultural change for hundreds of years after Christ, retained a lively and well-preserved store of early Celtic legend. Indeed, the origins of Ireland as a pre-Celtic nation survive mainly in the heroic literature created by the recently arrived Celts to give themselves a genealogy, a history and a national morale.

The Celts' arrival in Ireland is put generally by scholars as somewhere in the fourth/third century BC. This seems logical, given the typical European migrations of that time. Some of their invading predecessors, whose defeats by the Irish Celts form the island's earliest 'history', also seem, by virtue of their names, to have come from Celtic tribal territories on the continent of Europe. For example, the term 'Fir Bolg', name of an early occupant people, emerges in some interpretations as a version of 'Belgae', continental Celts who populated parts of Britain some centuries before Christ.

The earliest mythology of the Celts in Ireland bulks colourful and robust in the general canon of Celtic legend. Without an extensive 'bible' as such, in other words a book which explains the beginning of the world at large – they belonged to a totally oral tradition – Ireland, in a truly insular way, stood as its own universe and did not concern itself much with outside events.

The cycles of mythology which do some explaining of Irish origins range from the earliest pre-Celtic moments, belonging to Noah's children, to the arrival of the Christian evangelists of the fifth century. The pre-Celts included such 'founders' of Ireland as the Fir Bolgs and the magical people of the Goddess Danu. Next came the Ulster Cycle, ranging arbitrarily a century either side of Christ, and represented by those warriors such as Cuchulainn and the Red Branch Knights in the court of Conor MacNessa at Emhain Macha (near Armagh). Finally – excluding miscellaneous, not easily classifiable material – came the stories of Finn MacCool and the Fianna, the warriors of the Fenian Cycle. Always difficult to date precisely, these stories, as in the case of Oisin and his return from the Land of Eternal Youth, spill over into Christian myth directed by the monks in the Irish monasteries, who first wrote them down.

The tales in Part One, therefore, correspond roughly with that none-too-binding chronology.

IN THE BEGINNING . . .

he Book of Invasions says that the first invaders of Ireland, fifty-one women and three men, descended from Noah himself and all, bar one man, died in the Flood. This survivor, Fintan, having the gift of magic, turned himself into a salmon so that he could swim through the deluge. As the waters subsided he changed into an eagle, and then a hawk and flew high above the land watching the mountains and plains re-appear as the water ebbed away.

In the next invasion, Partholon and his wife, the beautiful but impure Delgnat, and their large retinue sailed in from the Atlantic. Partholon began by surveying the entire island and found that the country had three lakes, nine rivers and one plain. He gave orders to clear as many forests as would make three more plains and divert as many rivers as would make seven more lakes. Born out of necessity in this thirsty work, his people brewed ale – they also opened guest-houses and passed laws of title and property.

Unwittingly, Partholon became involved, within his own court, in Ireland's first full lawsuit. His wife, Delgnat, seduced Partholon's manservant, Topa, and her adultery became apparent in an unusual way. Partholon had had a special barrel of ale brewed for him by the best brewers in the country, exclusively for his consumption and that of his most favoured special guests and statesmen. One day, returning for a long and faraway inspection of his properties and lands, Partholon found the marks of two mouths on the long golden tap leading to the bung; the tap had magical properties which protected Partholon's ale by recording any attempt other than his to drink from the vat. Questioning, shrewdness and the help of the tap's magic led to the culprits – his wife and his manservant. Before all of his court Partholon charged her with adultery. She defended herself on the grounds that by going away for so long he had left her tantalisingly vulnerable, as if he had left his goods exposed to a thief, and that therefore he must share the blame with her. She won.

Throughout Partholon's reign, evil and shapeless beings, the Formorians, there in the air since time began, haunted the country. Time after time Partholon fought them off, though it took heroic deeds of arms and great military effort to keep them at bay. In the end he and his followers were wiped out not by the Formorians, but by a plague which left only one survivor, a man called Tuan, Partholon's nephew. As he watched his plagued countrymen fall down all across the Great Plain, Tuan fled to the mountains. Here he lived for over twenty years among the rocks, avoiding the wolves and the bears and protecting himself against the extremes of winter by hiding deep in the caves. From his hiding-places he saw how the cultivated fields returned to nature in the empty landscape. And so, with Tuan, the story of Partholon survived for posterity.

One winter's day from a high cave-mouth, this thin, unkempt and miserable hermit, with grey, tangled hair long uncut, witnessed the arrival of the next invaders. Nine people, a leader called Nemed with four men and four women, arrived in one boat, the remnants of a great fleet which had foundered in the oceans to the west. Thirty-one of the original thirty-two boats had been lost, sacrificing to the sea, or to disease, or to starvation, nine hundred and fifty-one others.

The nine Nemedians settled, prospered and multiplied. They set about a fresh cultivation of the island along Partholon's model, but cut down more forests and undergrowth, enough to open twelve further plains. By diverting rivers they created four new lakes, one of which bore the name of Nemed's wife, Macha. She, a seer, predicted, through dreams and visions, great events on that plain. These, as we shall see, did indeed come to pass – at the court of Emhain Macha, named after the place where they buried her.

Centuries went by. The Formorians still haunted the land, doing dark and evil tricks. Again and again the descendants of Nemed had to fight them. Apart from many vicious skirmishes, four great battles took place; the Nemedians won three – in the fourth, however, they were destroyed. The end came when the Nemedians broached the fort of the Formorians on the rocky isle of Tory, domain of the beastly spirits and their two kings off the north-west coast. Fergus of the Nemedians killed one king, but the other, his huge rage giving him extra magic, slaughtered, and then threw into the ocean, all but thirty of the Nemedians. Some of those who survived fled to the east including one family, led by a chief called Britan, who settled on the next island. This country eventually became known by his name. Others fled farther over the sea and fetched up in Greece, from where, in due course, they returned to Ireland in another invasion.

Among these new invaders were the Fir Bolgs, who had been reduced by ancient defeats to the role of servant race. They had been obliged to assist in the fertilisation of Greece by carrying, in their large leather bags, the rich earth from the fields up into rocky places where it was needed. The invasion also included two other groups, the Fir Domhnainn and the Gailion who are important because between them they created the five political divisions which eventually became the five provinces of Ireland – Munster in the south, Leinster in the east, Ulster in the north and Connacht in the west, with Meath, in the eastern midlands, as the overall administrative centre. Each province had a king, who lorded over several smaller kingships. One provincial king, Eochy the son of Erc, married a princess, Tailtiu, in whose honour, right up to the mid-twentieth century, the Irish held the Tailteann Games. Eochy ruled with prudence and justice, banning all lies and deceit. During his monarchy no rain fell, but the dews of the morning and evening watered the earth sufficiently to ensure a rich harvest each year.

When they settled in Ireland, the Fir Bolgs gradually threw off the servant role and in the cultivated plains and valleys lived a prosperous and unimpeded life. But the next invaders had special powers of magic which would prove powerful and long lasting. Descended, like the Britons, from the routed Nemedians, they came in from the isles of the north, not in boats or marching over land but wafting purposefully through the air as an army of spirits, alighting softly on the fields on the first day of May. They called themselves the Tuatha de Danaan, the people of the goddess Danu.

The Tuatha de Danaan brought with them their four great magical possessions: the Stone of Destiny which cried out when the lawful king touched it and which to this day stands on the Hill of Tara, the royal site of the palace of Meath, seat of the High Kings of Ireland; the flashing spear of their warrior-god Lugh which, once hurled, brought inevitable victory to his soldiers; the sword of Nuada from which nobody could hide or flee – it sought out all enemies and destroyed them; and the great cauldron of their all-powerful god, the Daghda – this cauldron not only satisfied his insatiable desires for porridge, it fed to bursting all who ate from it.

In an effort to maintain peace in the land, the Fir Bolgs made friendly overtures to the Tuatha de Danaan. However, early differences opened up, and jealousies emerged, especially over weapons. The newcomers carried light, beautifully crafted and decorated swords and spears, whereas those of the Fir Bolgs seemed cumbersome, crude and blunt. Before long they forgot about keeping peace and made war instead. The great battle between them took place at Moytura near the west coast. The Fir Bolgs lost heavily and the Danaans won all Ireland, except the western province of Connacht. Not all went the Danaans' way, however. In the battle the king of the Danaans, Nuada, lost his arm. This meant his abdication, because, according to Danaan law, the king should have no physical defect of any kind.

In Nuada's place they elected Bres, whose mother came of that evil, shapeless race, the Formorians. Bres turned out to be an oppressive, churlish individual ill-equipped to rule. Sitting at Tara, he managed the affairs of the island so badly that the Formorians regained some of the initiative and psychological advantage they had long ago lost to the Nemedians. Developing a successful guerrilla strategy, they began raiding the Danaan settlements. The Danaans realised they had to get rid of Bres – so the poet Carbery satirised him, a fate all men of any stature feared more than death.

Carbery had had an experience at Bres's hands which added venom to his rhymes. Unannounced and unknown, he had called at Bres's house, expecting, under Danaan law as a traveller, the same hospitality as if he were an announced king. Bres, however, did not even invite him to the general meal that evening. Instead the poet was shown to an unlit chamber with no comforts, where surly lackeys served him a late meal of oatcakes and beer that was sour.

Carbery's words sharpened to a fine and deadly point. He versified so savagely that Bres's face broke out in carbuncles at the shame. Amid the humiliation he was forced to renounce the kingship – he had broken sacred rules, of general hospitality and, in particular, of the welcoming of poets, and therefore showed no further fitness to rule. In the meantime, ex-king Nuada had employed one of the Danaans' magical silversmiths to fashion a new arm which, though made of shining silver, had such power and elegance that, instead of being blemished, his physique became enhanced and he resumed the High Kingship.

The deposed and banished Bres, with the aid of his mother, raised a Formorian army abroad and returned to attack the Danaans. From the shadows of the mountains in the crevices of the river-banks, other Formorians had always remained alert, watching for any opportunity to attack the Danaans, but powerless as yet against their magic. Now Bres enlisted their help too, and then finally approached the mightiest and most evil of the Formorians, the one-eyed Balor, known as Balor of the Baleful Eye. His ferocity terrorised all who heard of him: his great, oozing eye needed four men to lift its lid, and, when opened, everyone upon whom his gaze fell would die, reduced to powder.

Balor lived on Tory island, the point where in previous centuries the Nemedians had been routed. He had only one fear – of an ancient prophecy which said he would eventually be destroyed by a member of his own family, his grandson. Since he had only one child, a daughter, Eithne, he thought to subvert the prophecy. He imprisoned Eithne in a remote cave to the northerly, sunless side of Tory, putting her in the care of twelve serving-women. Though unseen, she grew up to be a great beauty and, never having encountered a man, she had no knowledge of gender.

One day, Kian, a local Danaan champion, from whose family Balor had thieved and who now sought revenge, disguised himself as a woman and after much talk and charming stratagem gained an entry to the cave. There he seduced Eithne, and, say the locals, all the twelve serving-women as well. All bore children, Eithne having triplets. When he heard this news, Balor, to be on the safe side and in case any of the children had been swapped around in an effort to protect them, took all the babies and hurled them into the sea. It is said, incidentally, that those who drowned became the ancestors of the seals, 'the people of the sea' – which is why young seals have the faces of baby humans. One of Eithne's babies escaped, though – even as an infant he had magical powers which enabled him to swim ashore. A blacksmith, his blood-uncle, as it happened, found him on the shore, took him in, gave him the name Lugh, raised him to manhood, educated him and taught him how to make weapons. Lugh grew into a great hero who would yet father the hero-god of Ireland, Cuchulainn.

Advised by the gods, Lugh offered himself as the saviour of the Danaan people. At the age of twenty-one he journeyed to Tara to greet the king, Nuada of the Silver Hand. The doorman barred his entrance until Lugh declared his occupation.

'I am a carpenter.'

'This place is full of carpenters,' said the doorman.

'I am a blacksmith,' said Lugh.

'We have one,' said the doorman, 'we don't need another.'

'I am a warrior.'

'We have several of those.'

'I am a musician.'

'And those.'

'I am a scholar.'

'By the dozen.'

'I am a poet.'

'Ditto.'

'I am a magician.'

'Those also.'

'I am a hero.'

'Who says?' The gatekeeper remained impassive, the gates impassable.

'But,' said Lugh, with his last gamble, 'do the Danaans have any one being in whom all these talents reside together?'

The ploy worked and Lugh entered Tara.

King Nuada of the Silver Hand had the capacity to recognise destiny and now, when he saw Lugh coming up the hall towards him, without hesitation he abdicated the kingship in his favour. In a farewell speech Nuada urged Lugh to take on the Formorians and defeat them, otherwise the island would remain forever unfree. Lugh accepted the challenge – the gods had fitted him for the part. When he walked the land, people thought the sun had risen that morning in the west so bright did his countenance shine. The gods gave him, as his own property, the skies and the fields and all in between. The Milky Way he wore as a silver chain around his neck, the rainbow formed his sling. He had a sword called the Answerer which could cleave through any armour, wall or weapon. His boat, the Wave Sweeper, needed no helmsman. Manannan MacLir, the god of the waves, gave him his own horse which galloped with equal ease over water or land.

So, finely equipped and encouraged in his new command by Nuada, Lugh bade the Danaans prepare for a great battle which would eventually, because of where it took place, be called the Second Battle of Moytura. He knew from the history of Ireland and from the Danaans' earlier experiences that the Formorians would be extraordinarily difficult to defeat. He needed extra magic – especially against Balor. And he needed men to go and get the weapons and goods which would guarantee that extra magic: how he acquired them becomes a story in itself.

It all began when Lugh dispatched his own beloved father, Kian, the champion who had seduced Balor's daughter, to Ulster to muster an army. Lugh's two uncles, Cu and Ceithin, were sent to the other provinces on the same business. Kian's family, however, had long conducted a feud against three brothers, Brian, Iuchar and Iucharba, the Sons of Turenn. As Kian was crossing the Plain of Muirhevna, near what today we call Dundalk, the Sons of Turenn intercepted him.

Kian had seen them coming. Apprehending the danger, he used his Danaan magic to change himself into a pig and joined a herd of swine grazing out on the plain. The Sons of Turenn, though, had seen Kian riding in the distance and, when he disappeared, they suspected sorcery, or at least trickery. They soon guessed that he had magicked himself and hidden among the pigs. Using his own magic, Brian changed his two young brothers, Iuchar and Iucharba, into dogs. When they smelt out the disguised pig, Brian threw his spear directly into the animal's chest. Kian's voice pleaded for mercy, and the triumphant brothers closed in. Then Kian, knowing his last moments had arrived, asked that he might be allowed to die in his own human form. The brothers preferred this – Brian said he found it more appealing to kill a man, especially Kian, than a pig.

As Kian stood there, with one last laugh he pointed out how he had outsmarted them. The debt of honour to be paid – and in blood – for the murder of a man, especially Kian, the father of Lugh, would hugely outweigh revenge for the death of a pig, and, for his father's murder, Lugh would exact truly extraordinary revenge. For a certainty the great Lugh would not rest until he had found his father's killers; he would divine the owners of the weapons from the shape of the dead man's wounds.

The Sons of Turenn then thought to cover their tracks. They threw down their weapons, replacing them with large rocks with which they stoned Kian to death so that his body became a pulped and unrecognisable heap. As the dark blood spurted out into the dust of the plain, the Sons danced in it, splashing it over their feet, shouting and exulting. At last they dug a deep hole in the clay into which they dropped Kian's body and over it they heaped a cairn of the very rocks they had used to kill him. They then rode off in delight.

While the murder of his father was taking place on the Plain of Muirhevna, Lugh had engaged in a rough and demanding skirmish with the Formorians. He found that even in the preoccupying heat of battle he could not get his father off his mind and worried that he had heard no word from him. He finally vanquished the last of that day's Formorians and, with a posse of soldiers, headed back to Tara. As they rode across the Plain of Muirhevna, Lugh heard a strange cry, both ferocious and sad, from a cairn of stones. As the stones continued their cry, they not only called Lugh's attention to the whereabouts of Kian's body, they also named the murderers. Lugh's men dismounted, clawed away the stones and with their bare hands exhumed Kian and held the broken corpse up to his son. Lugh, overcome, wept for seven hours and then, with a long passionate lament, he swore vengeance forever on all of the name Turenn.

With great reverence they reburied the body of Kian and after suitable chants and vows, Lugh, flanked by his men, returned to Tara. The victory celebration had begun and there, among the warriors who had reason to celebrate the day, sat the Sons of Turenn. They too, before they murdered Kian, had been victorious in skirmishes against the Formorians and in any case had the status of great favourites among the other warriors and the women of the court.

For his great part in the day's events, Lugh was awarded the Champion's Portion, but, before the night's entertainments began, he stood up and, as he started to speak, the assembly sensed that something as yet unknown to them had occurred, something awful. Lugh glared red-hot like a man on fire and his voice, usually sweet as a deep bell, at first quavered before gaining strength, as he began to ask rhetorical questions regarding the revenge demanded for a father's death. All the guests looked at each other in questioning surprise, while automatically and in unison affirming to Lugh the principle of the most savage revenge due for the death of a father. Even the treacherous Sons of Turenn joined in the chorus of agreement.

Having built up dramatically to the moment, Lugh then told them that his own father, Kian, known and loved at this table, had been murdered wickedly and cruelly that day, stoned to death by men too cowardly to use their weapons. Now he intended to exact a long, slow and bloody revenge. For every blow his father received, his own sword, the Answerer, would strike the culprits a hundred times, until each broken limb and bone of his father had been satisfied one by one. All agreed that such a method of revenge would contain nothing but justice, and praised his determination. Again the Sons of Turenn joined in the chorus.

Then the avenging fire lit Lugh from head to foot so brightly that
it bathed the entire banqueting-hall in a great glow. He raised himself
as high as if he stood on the table and, in a voice shaking with rage
and grief, told them that Kian's murderers sat in the same room as
guests. He drew his sword and pointed it at the Sons of Turenn.
The assembly sat, stunned. Silence, hot and terrified, fell on the
room. Lugh continued. His hands, he said, were more tied than he
would want them to be. He could not directly avenge his father's
death. Under the Danaans' laws of hospitality the murderers, guests
at the feast, could not, now that they had been named in the actual
hall, be attacked by him. The only revenge open to him would come
by way of a massive forfeit or fine.

Openly he called his magic down to work, but began by declaring
what seemed to everybody the most innocuous of fines. He asked
the Sons of Turenn merely to obtain for him three apples, a pigskin,
a spear, a pair of horses yoked to a chariot, seven pigs, a young
hound, a cooking-spit and finally three shouts to be given from a
hilltop. In face of a fine so apparently small the Sons of Turenn had
to accept, but the older men of the court, who knew Danaan magic,
raised fearful eyebrows. So did all the other diners when Lugh began
to recite the precise details of these objects which, he stressed again,
would prove so useful in battle against the Formorians.

The apples, to begin with, grew in the Garden of the Light over
an ocean far off in the East. Each apple, big as a baby's head and
wearing a skin of shining gold, cured all wounds and ailments. The
pigskin too, guarded fiercely in the exotic house of a distant southern
king, cured all wounds and ailments. The spear, which belonged in
a heavily fortified palace even farther away, had a point so ferociously
hot, and therefore so invincible, that it always stood in blocks of ice
in case it melted everything around it. The horses and chariot, again
in a remote royal court though entirely in the opposite direction,
and again fiercely protected, could outpace the wind over land or
water. The seven swine, owned by the King of the Golden Pillars,
had the gift of magical regeneration: no matter how often they were
killed and eaten they re-appeared the following day. The young dog
owned by the King of the East terrified every other beast in the
world. The cooking-spit belonged to the underwater women of an
island so deep in the sea that it could not be reached. The three
shouts must echo on a chosen hill to the north of Tara, a hill owned
by a king and his three princes with whom the late Kian had been
fostered and trained as a champion. In honour of his death that court,
without ever knowing of the forfeit Lugh now imposed on the Sons

of Turenn, had pledged to prevent to the death anyone from ever shouting on their hilltop.

Now nothing in this enchanted society worked out simply. The Sons of Turenn had their own magic and they gladly took on Lugh's forfeits. First they went in search of the golden apples and when they found that the lovely rich gardens where they hung were a protected bower, the brothers turned themselves into hawks. Swooping down out of the noon sun and hurling themselves on the property, they swept up, in mid-flight, an apple each and travelled so far out to sea that none of the birds of prey employed to protect the apples could catch them. Thus they completed their first task.

Next the pigskin – and to seize this they appeared before its royal owner as poets in their own right: like all Danaans they had the gift of verse and song. In front of the throne they chanted a long and brilliant poem in this king's praise, and, when he offered them a reward, they asked for the pigskin. He said he felt he must refuse them but as an observance of the hospitality laws he suggested the volume of the pigskin in gold. While this bullion was being counted out, the three brothers seized the pigskin itself and fought their way ferociously out of the castle. In the fracas Brian slew the king, all three Sons of Turenn suffered terrible wounds but, once they had completed their escape and could rest, the magic pigskin did its work and cured them instantly.

As the third year of their quest began, the brothers went in search of the red-hot spear and, after long enquiry, found the palace where the spear stood in an ice-pit. Again the brothers presented themselves as poets; again they acclaimed the king who owned the spear; again they asked for it as their payment. This time their host showed none of the courtliness of the king who owned the pigskin. This king saw through their poetic device, curtly refused, and ordered his men to throw them out. The brothers drew the short swords they wore concealed under their poets' clothes and in the hand-to-hand fighting which broke out, the king jumped from his throne and ran down the steps of the throne-room to join in. As the king attacked, Brian threw one of the golden apples at him and broke his skull. Appalled, the king's soldiers drew back as Brian retrieved the apple. Together the brothers rushed across the courtyard, stormed the heavily guarded ice-house, tore the spear from the huge blocks in which it stood, and with it hacked their escape.

To seek the horses and chariot the brothers disguised themselves as mercenaries. On finding the king who owned the chariot, they described themselves as 'unique and powerful'; after all, they had an invincible spear and a pigskin that could heal all wounds received in battle. During the entire seven weeks in which they stood on guard duty they never once glimpsed – or even heard tell of – either the horses or the chariot. Knowing that by now they had proved their worth as sentries they then told the king that they would no longer guard him unless he showed them the possessions whose fame they had heard in every land.

The king laid on an exhibition for them – his charioteer drove brilliantly around the courtyard and then out through the castle gate and over the lake travelling like the wind. As it drove back into the castle for one last circuit, Brian of Turenn, quicker than a ray of sunlight, vaulted into the chariot and killed the charioteer. He circled one more time, threw out the dead body, and, when his two brothers jumped on the shafts of the chariot, drove off.

All these deeds made the Sons of Turenn famous throughout the world and when they came to the kingdom of the Golden Pillars, the king surrendered the seven magic swine without a fight. Further, it transpired that it was this king's own daughter and her husband who owned the golden hound. Thus the Sons of Turenn received an introduction. Not that it did much good – the three brothers still had to fight a fierce battle for the dog and won it only when it looked as if they would wholly destroy this man's army. And so the brothers completed their sixth task.

However far away the Sons of Turenn might have felt, Lugh with his magical powers had kept them under observation. As the war against the Formorians intensified he urgently required the magical objects they had seized. By throwing a spell over the Sons of Turenn, he brought them back to Ireland where, confused by Lugh's wizardry, they handed up the vital objects thinking their tasks had been accomplished and that the forfeit could now be lifted. Lugh, however, then reminded them that two of the original eight assignments had still to be completed: they had not yet captured the cooking-spit from the sea-bed, nor had he heard them give their three shouts.

Screwing up some more optimism they embarked on those last two tasks. Brian donned a magical water-suit made of leaves and lilies and in it he enchanted the one hundred and fifty water-maidens who guarded the cooking-spit. They gave it up to him with pleasure and he and his brothers brought it home to Lugh.

Now came the final task – the three shouts – and on the hill of King Michan, an ancient and beloved comrade-in-arms of the slain Kian. Slowly the Sons of Turenn walked up the hill. Michan greeted them as a king greets visitors with all the due hospitality. Having established their intentions, however, he forbade them their shouts and battle commenced. Never had the Sons of Turenn been involved in a fiercer fight. Shields rang, swords flashed and sparked as chunks of metal flew in the air, blood flowed down the hillside. Brian, always a superb fighter, slaughtered Michan with a blow that split the king's head in half, from crown to throat, and then man against man the king's three sons fought the three Sons of Turenn. The battle took on colossal dimensions as both sides brought their magic into the fight, raging and rampaging across the mountains and the sea and the sky until finally the Sons of Turenn killed the Sons of Michan. Now they could raise their three shouts – feebly, owing to their gaping wounds – on the Hill of Michan. They had fulfilled all the terms of Lugh's epic forfeits and now they could be freed from their bond. They had paid, in their opinion, for the death of Kian.

Turenn, their father, begged Lugh to lend him the magic pigskin so that his sons, dying of their wounds, might be saved. Lugh denied him – better he said, in the greatest traditions of warriorhood, that they should die now and be remembered for their glory; better a short brilliant life than a long tedious one. He spoke disingenuously: he had no intention of forgiving his father's murderers and so the Sons of Turenn died.

Equipped now with all the magical items brought back by the Sons of Turenn, Lugh led the Danaans against the Formorians in the Second Battle of Moytura. Even then he needed more magic weaponry and he called upon the skills of the three greatest Danaan craftsmen. One, with three blows of a hammer, made a spear; the second craftsman threw a handle towards it and the handle fitted immediately; and the third merely aimed his tongs at the place where the handle and the point joined and the rivets flew through the air and stuck fast into place.

In the afternoon, when the sun had just slipped from the highest point in the sky and the morale of the Formorians, these evil flapping phantoms, had sunk to its lowest they brought forth their greatest and most dreaded creature, their ruler, Balor of the Baleful Eye. A phalanx of men went before him until he had moved into the position from which he could see the greatest number of Danaan troops. Then, standing two on either side, his four attendants, huge, muscular men, used all their strength and lifted the Baleful eyelid. In a moment all within sight, Danaan warriors of the greatest prowess, even Nuada of the Silver Arm, died under the gaze of the eye. All except Lugh, who watched from afar – he had taken himself well out of the range of Balor's gaze. When the Baleful Eye drooped in rest Lugh rushed forward on his horse that could outrun the wind and just as the eye began to re-open he hurled a stone from his sling into the heart of the eye. The stone travelled on, into the very core of Balor's brain and he died. The prophecy had come true – Balor died at the hand of his grandson.

Thus, at the Second Battle of Moytura, ended the evil reign of the Formorians, and the great day swiftly entered the permanent repertoire of the bards. Their verses recounted how the battlefield had rolled with noise like thunder as the shields of the enemy broke asunder, how the wind had sung as the spears and javelins hurtled through the air and how the swords had flashed like the forked lightning thrown down by the fingers of the gods.

Thereafter, the people of the goddess Danu ruled the island peacefully for many hundreds of years.

Then, one day, on the first of May, a platoon of tall and beautiful men landed on a shore in the south-west. Warriors all, they had come from Spain, sons of the king, Mil, and they defeated every attack made upon them by the Danaans. Finally both sides made peace, deciding to divide the country between them. All below the ground was given to the Danaans. They still live down there, spirits beneath the earth; they still have their magic and they still practise their wizardry and tell stories drawn from the memories of the old days. All of Ireland above the ground was thenceforth ruled by the tall warriors from Spain, the Milesians – or, as we now know them, the Celts.

THE CHAMPION'S PORTION

he man they called Bricriu of the Poisoned Tongue, a chieftain in Ulster, decided to build the most impressive house imaginable especially for accommodating his guests. He had a powerful, selfish motive – by having such a place everyone who ever came to see him would go away saying what a wonderful host, what a fabulous fellow and so on. In fact Bricriu already had a mucky reputation as a boaster and a stirrer of trouble.

Bricriu embarked upon his great plan by first giving himself a deadline. He invited everyone to a great feast knowing that he had a year and a day to prepare for it. To house it, he set about his great building project, which he researched by looking at every other palace in Ireland. He took particular architectural inspiration from the magnificent Red Branch garrison and palace at Emhain Macha near Armagh which housed the crack troops, knights and household guard of the king of Ulster, Conor MacNessa. And then he deliberately set out to surpass all the edifices he had seen. With master planners and master builders he built a beautiful palatial compound abundant in columns and façades and carved decorations and pediments and architraves and long, shady colonnades, a gleaming place, unforgettable. The bad manners he might display by eventually outshining his king who, after all, lived not far away, never occurred to him.

Oddly enough, despite his vulgarity, Bricriu brought it off – the building had both taste and style, so much so that architects from many foreign courts came to see its innovations and general impression of sleek wealth. Everything had been created to give the impression of relaxed opulence. Bricriu and his wife arranged for the private apartments to be divided by partitions thirty feet high, and these they decorated multitudinously with gold and gold leaf. He even had a private suite built for the occasion when the king would visit: this stood high above all the others, a wonderful penthouse decorated with gold and silver and jewels, as bright by night, through the gleams from the gems, as by day. These private apartments formed an inner court; around its perimeter the architects had arranged an outer court of twelve further suites for those particular warriors who formed the king's private guard when he travelled to meet his subjects. The building materials cost a fortune – the best marble and granite that quarries could provide. The labour force became the biggest ever drawn together for any single building project in the country: for example, the plans provided for several hundred pillars and each pillar needed a team of oxen and seven of Ulster's strongest workmen to raise it in place.

Whatever Bricriu's claims to want only the best for his guests, he nevertheless had every intention of promoting his own place in society. In his castle he also built a special suite for himself and his wife, which he further packed with ornaments and the richest hides and furs; the tapestries and coverlets had just as many jewels as those in the king's room and Bricriu's suite had one detail to be found nowhere else in the castle or indeed anywhere else in Ireland – glass windows. One of these had been inserted in the walls at an angle whereby Bricriu could see every coming and going in the castle courtyard and the great hall without rising from his couch.

Happily for Bricriu, the building contractors beat the deadline for the building of the palace. They laid out the castle in the most lavish way; great swathes of saffron and blue tumbled down from the high walls and billowed in the breeze; the long oak table gleamed with the gold, silver and glass. Armies of servants shook out fresh linen in the fields around the castle in preparation for the rooms and the beds. And in the final six weeks, in poured the vast supplies of food and drink.

As the guests began to arrive, bringing with them word that the king had set out, Bricriu left the splendid building to meet the royal entourage and, as the custom decreed, to issue his formal invitations to the king and the warriors of the household guard. The party had not, however, travelled as far towards him as he anticipated – they had been delayed shortly after leaving their own palace. Eventually he found the king and his entourage of Ulstermen at a great fair in Emhain Macha a few hours' ride away, where they received him cordially, inviting him to join them for luncheon in the Red Branch pavilion.

Seated beside the king of Ulster, the famous Conor MacNessa, Bricriu issued the invitation to his own great feast. He told them a little of the hospitality he could offer them and for once the men of Ulster neither smiled nor scowled at the words coming from Bricriu's poisoned tongue. Conor, just as formally, replied that he would most certainly love to come, provided his chieftains would accompany him. At this they, all powerful men, asked for time to discuss the invitation among themselves. They rose from the table, held a brief conference in a corner of the pavilion and when they came back they told the king privately that they must refuse. Bricriu, they said, once he got them there, would exploit the laws of hospitality and provoke arguments designed to turn them against each other. Bricriu, they said, was known to be happiest when causing fights, the bigger the better – not for nothing, they pointed out, had he been given the nickname 'Poisoned Tongue'.

Bricriu overheard and turned on them, begging the king's pardon.

'If you don't come,' he said, 'I will do something much worse. I will go out and deliberately incite all the kings and all the chiefs and all the warriors, young and old, and turn them all against each other and against you and that will create a much greater carnage. And for what reason? Because you are too churlish to accept my hospitality.'

The king understood both points of view, but intervened for the sake of restoring dignity and calm.

'Bricriu,' he said, giving the other man a respect nobody usually felt for him, 'threats like that will have the opposite effect. People won't come to your feast if you threaten them.'

Bricriu, instead of calming down, stirred himself up further.

'Fine. Fine.' He began to shout. 'Then I will turn every son in Ulster murderously against his father. And I will turn all the brothers of Ulster murderously against their brothers. And I will turn all your daughters murderously upon their mothers. And failing all of that, if you still won't come to my feast, I will provoke the right breast of every Ulster woman to clatter against the left, so that both breasts turn sour to the taste and coarse to the touch. Now will you come?'

The chieftains, taken aback at his vehemence, had another quick conference and came back to the table.

'All right,' said their spokesman, 'we may have been churlish and bad-mannered to turn down such an invitation, but we still have to consider your reputation for making trouble with that tongue of yours and this is what we have decided. We will come to your feast provided you don't mind if we form a committee to safeguard our attendance.'

'Agreed,' said Bricriu.

There and then they formed their committee. One of the chieftains on it, Ailill's son, said, 'Now – a couple of things: first of all, Bricriu should give us hostages as an earnest of his good intentions, and, secondly, the moment the feast has begun, the moment the first course has been served, eight of our best swordsmen should escort him from the table and make sure he stays in his own apartment, because if he is kept away from the table neither he nor that poisoned tongue of his can do any damage.' The committee then delegated Conor MacNessa's son to take these points to Bricriu who, somewhat to their surprise, accepted these terms.

Bricriu, however, now found himself in a bind. A major intention in holding this feast in the first place had been to stir up trouble. He liked nothing better than causing rows among Ulstermen – they had a famous bitter streak in them. On this occasion he had spent long hours scheming how exactly to turn them against each other and, as an added edge, he now had to work out a method which would not cost him the lives of the hostages. His experience served him well – a pastmaster at working out how to irritate people, he decided to exploit the customary and usually good-humoured argument as to which of the many warriors should take the Champion's Portion. This time-honoured ritual granted the largest helping of meat – often it came as a specially prepared dish – to the indisputably strongest and bravest warrior.

As they all settled down again to enjoy lunch, Bricriu left his position by the side of his host, King Conor. Through the door of the pavilion, he had seen Leary, a notable hero who had enjoyed many victories over the Ulster warriors and who relished the way Bricriu could provoke them. He guessed therefore that Bricriu had some scheme afoot. Bricriu raised with him the Champion's Portion and who should have the rights to it at Emhain Macha. Bricriu suggested that it should always, without fear of contradiction, be Leary's.

'In fact,' he said to Leary, 'if you take my advice, I can make sure you will not only always have the Champion's Portion, you will have the upper hand over every Ulsterman. And you know what that will lead to – eventually it will make you the most powerful champion in all Ireland.'

When Leary asked him how he imagined this could be achieved,

Bricriu began to describe the Champion's Portion at his own forthcoming feast. To begin with he had chosen a huge pot, large enough to contain three big Ulstermen. By now the servants had filled it with a strong red wine. On top of that Bricriu had a seven-year-old boar, ripe and sweet, which, since it was born, had been fed only on sweetened porridge, oatmeal, fresh milk, nuts, wheat, meat and broth, according to the seasons. In addition he had a cow, seven years old too, who, since birth, had been fed only heather, herbs, corn and sweet meadow grass. And to accompany this cauldron full of wine, pigmeat and beef, one hundred wheat cakes had been cooked in honey, using a bushel of wheat to every four cakes.

'Now that,' said Bricriu, a boast never far from his lips, 'is what I call a Champion's Portion.'

'I'll go along with that,' said Leary.

And Bricriu continued: 'At the feast, when the crucial moment comes, make sure your charioteer jumps up and claims the Champion's Portion as yours by right.'

'And if there's any contradiction about it,' said Leary, 'the blood will flow.'

Bricriu, in his element, wandered through the fair until he met separately two other warriors who might similarly expect to get the Champion's Portion more or less automatically. First of all, he found Conall and saluted him with great flattery. He pointed out Conall's record in the defence of Ulster – not only had he been the star warrior of Ulster's youth, he also provided, single-handedly, the pathfinding and flank protection for every cattle raid mounted from Ulster's borders.

'Logically,' said Bricriu in his most silken voice, 'you should always have the Champion's Portion in Ulster.'

'I expect nothing more and nothing less,' said Conall.

Bricriu finally approached the greatest of them all, Cuchulainn, than whom no greater hero had ever existed, with the possible exception of Cuchulainn's magical father, Lugh. Bricriu took the same line as he had done with Conall and Leary – masses of flattery, praising Cuchulainn's exploits in battle, his popularity with women, his guardianship of Ulster.

'When you come to my feast,' he said, 'I suppose I am to assume that the Champion's Portion is always, automatically, yours?'

Cuchulainn, never a man to say much, growled: 'Only a man who wants to lose his head would challenge that right.'

And so Bricriu had done it again: he had laid careful plans which would set three of the greatest warriors in the world at each other's throats and he would not even be in the room when it happened. Now he wandered happily through the fair, chatting here and there, the perfect guest, and by the time he came back to King Conor in his pavilion his grin was huge.

Late that evening, after a long and enjoyable ride in which they diverted themselves with skirmishes of hunting, King Conor and his Ulstermen arrived on the hill overlooking Bricriu's castle. What they saw staggered them; somewhat grudgingly they admitted that they had never seen such a beautiful estate as this one gleaming in the valley below. The evening sun caught the saffron banners bulging in the wind; the colonnades looked dignified and inviting; the waters from the three high fountains sparkled.

They rode down to the gates, Bricriu, all smiles, leading the way, though careful not to outride the king. He accepted Conor's compliments with the air of a statesman and, as the others joined in at the back of the entourage, they even wondered among themselves whether Bricriu of the Poisoned Tongue had begun to improve at last. They observed everything, the exotic birds and animals, the detail of the gardens, the arrangements of the flowers along the long borders. Bricriu's general staff had been training for months to form a splendid welcoming party and already it looked as if Bricriu's hospitality would outdo everyone in Ireland.

As each man dismounted, whether king, prince, chieftain or warrior, a beautiful servant-girl conducted him to the splendid apartments; in the traditional style of such visits the men and women separated. The men went into the first inner court around King Conor MacNessa, the women into the other identical court where the queen would stay. Down below in the courtyard the music began; a piper tuned up, followed by another and another until soon twenty-four pipers, the castle consort of musicians, played at full blast. Some guests, excited early by the gaiety of it all, began to dance.

Shortly after this the king and his warriors, including Leary, Conall and Cuchulainn, assembled on the landing outside the royal suite and formed the dinner procession. Dressed in rich blue and white brocade, the king walked gravely down the wide, stone staircase and into the hall, his warriors, two-by-two behind him, dressed in orange and lime-green brocade. The other guests, friends and neighbours of Bricriu and his wife, gasped to see these famous men whose exploits had become legends.

Bricriu made a short address of welcome and his many servants hovered at the door of the kitchen, waiting for the sign to serve the first course. And, as the eight swordsmen materialised at Bricriu's side, he kept his promise to the committee of chieftains and prepared to leave the hall. As he left, with a flourish of his hand he pointed to the huge bronze cauldron and said dramatically, 'The Champion's Portion, a magnificent one too. Wine, beef, pork – all of the highest quality. Award it wisely – and only to the very best warrior in Ulster.' With this fuse thus lit, he went happily to his rooms where he could watch everything through his angled glass window without himself being seen.

When the first course had been eaten and praised, and as the servants cleared its debris away, the plot began to click in exactly the way Bricriu had planned. A charioteer, recognisable by his uniform, stood up and said, 'I claim the Champion's Portion for Leary. Hey! Bring that cauldron over here for my master.' Across from him another, Conall's charioteer, did likewise, only more vehemently and, inevitably, the most famous charioteer there, Cuchulainn's, did the same, aggravating matters by adding, 'He is the most accomplished of all the Ulster warriors.'

As the other two charioteers and their masters jumped up unsheathing their short swords – long swords being prohibited at table – Ailill's son, on the *ad hoc* committee of chieftains, groaned and said to the others, 'Bricriu of the Poisoned Tongue. He doesn't even have to be here to cause trouble. He started it before he left.'

In the middle of the room the charioteers glared at each other nose to nose while Leary and Conall yelled insults at each other. Cuchulainn merely grunted, and his cool demeanour united Leary and Conall against him.

The charioteers, having set the formalities for the fight, sat down again and the three champions went at each other. Ulster society always loved watching a tough fight and in this case they got value for money. So high did the sword-blades' sparks fly that the rafters threatened to catch fire; flying spear-edges gouged holes in the roof; the guests coughed and choked in the clouds of enamel powder the fighters knocked off each other's shields.

This kind of fracas, usually well controlled, often broke out at a feast, but to the older, wiser men, including the king, this one had a different, nastier undercurrent. They put it down to the malice with which Bricriu had calculated everything and this then gave rise to anger, because the scheming had resulted in Cuchulainn being unfairly outnumbered two to one. The king, now the host in Bricriu's absence, stopped the fight and ordered the men to lay their swords on the table in front of him. Even this they could not do without squabbling as to whose sword should be nearest King Conor. Eventually, for the sake of peace, he allowed them to sheathe their swords and told them to sit down, which they did as meekly as young boys. All discussion of the Champion's Portion then stood suspended; the king ruled that the matter should be adjudicated next day rather than fought over. In the meantime he ordered that the Champion's Portion should be divided amongst all present, a punishment, as he thought, for Bricriu and his scheming. He could not have known that Bricriu had even better Champion's Portions lined up. And Bricriu's boasts proved true – the mixture of wine, pork and beef and cakes with honey could not be bettered, not even by the king's cook at Armagh.

Bricriu had watched every move and moment. He felt disgruntled that more trouble had not broken out, so sitting there on his couch by his window sucking his teeth, he wondered what new mischief he could mix. His mind worked hard – he hadn't been called the Poisoned Tongue for nothing. So – he would provoke the ladies. At that moment, Fidelma, the wife of Leary, walked across the court-yard below followed by fifty considerable women all of whom had taken strong drink. Bricriu called down to her, and she waved up and stopped to listen.

'Fidelma – hey, what a woman you are,' he cried, 'bright as a bead, so elegant, such good blood in you. You know what my opinion is, Fidelma?'

'What is it Bricriu?' she asked, flattered, though 'sober' she would not have passed the time of day with Bricriu.

'I'll tell you, Fidelma, it is this. Every woman should be made to walk behind you. No other female should be allowed to precede you into the court of Ulster. I mean this in your own right, not just in your capacity as Leary's wife. Are you listening to me? Every woman in Ulster – no, every woman in Ireland – should be glad to walk in your wake and they should be honoured to have the privilege. Right?'

He had touched a nerve and he knew it. For a start Fidelma always resented being introduced as Leary's wife. Secondly, the sorest point among the women of Ulster had always been who should walk first into the court. It had never been settled, it never looked like being settled and the argument sat on the surface of their society like a mighty sore boil.

Bricriu hammered his point home.

'Now,' he called down, 'this is my feast, so tonight you must make sure – and this is my express invitation – you must make sure to enter my court at the head of all the other women – lead them in. For ever afterwards no-one can deny you your rightful place as first woman of Ulster.'

Fidelma nodded her head in gracious agreement, her stature rising visibly. She acknowledged Bricriu's invitation in a queenly way and, turning around, she led her women out from the courtyard to the third ridge in the distance, the point from which all ladies, court and visiting, traditionally began their procession to the feast. Bricriu knew he had plunged a red-hot point into that turbulent question – he only had to sit back now and enjoy the results.

As Fidelma and her retinue disappeared into the shadows outside the brightly lit courtyard, another troop of fifty drinking women marched into the yard from a different direction, led by Lendar, wife of Conall. Bricriu called down to her too, laying on the same syrupy blandishments.

'Lendar, how has it come about that you possess such beauty? You are so beautiful that it doesn't seem fair to any other woman – no wonder so many men are secretly in love with you. I wonder if you would allow your beauty to honour my feast by entering the court first tonight and thereby claiming your rightful place as the foremost of all the women of Ulster?' Again the Poisoned Tongue flicked right on to the target: Lendar possessed enormous vanity and she wanted nothing more than to be regarded as the leading woman in Ulster because of her great beauty. She swallowed his multicoloured flattery and with her fifty women headed for the same hill as Fidelma to prepare the stately entrance to the court. Finally Emer appeared, Cuchulainn's woman, a tough lady at the head of her fifty, equally tough, companions.

'Emer,' called down Bricriu, 'Emer.'

She stopped, looked up askance at him; she had no time for this coarse boaster but being his guest she had to acknowledge him. When she heard his words, though, she perked up. Bricriu had the knack of getting right to the most tender corner of her vanity, and now he told Emer that she outshone the stars in the sky, that she had the secret of eternal youth, that her beauty and elegance made Fidelma and Lendar look like upstarts.

'I look forward to watching you, their unrivalled leader, parade the women of Ulster into my feast tonight – just as I enjoy your husband's stature as the leading warrior.' Emer turned and headed for the earthen banks from which she would begin the procession into the court – she had no idea that her rivals had already assembled their followers there too.

Three parallel processions therefore formed up – with dignity initially: the slow, stately walk of noblewomen. None of their three leaders now walking side-by-side had any notion that they had each been provoked by Bricriu. As they drew nearer the palace, their competitive edges sharpened, their speed quickened correspondingly and their stateliness began to unravel. Well before they got to the castle precincts they had all hoisted and bunched their skirts waist-high, running hell-for-leather – the ground even shook under them, so much so that inside the castle the guests thought an attack had begun. Then Ailill's son, twigging what had happened, clapped a hand to his forehead and shouted, 'That bastard Bricriu. He's done it again.' He recalled that when initially they had refused to come to the feast Bricriu had, among other things, threatened to set the women of Ulster against each other.

In the nick of time the servants in the hall, assisted by the soldiers, got the door closed, keeping out the monstrous regiment, and the men at the feast sat back and laughed in relief. That, however, coincided with the moment when Emer, Cuchulainn's wife, the swiftest woman in Ulster, arrived. She ordered the doorkeepers to open up immediately – glancing over her shoulder to check whether Lendar and Fidelma were now in sight. At which point their two husbands inside the hall, Conall and Leary, rose – no way would either allow Cuchulainn's wife to upstage theirs. Cuchulainn, though bored with all this, rose too, and went to open the door before Leary and Conall. King Conor MacNessa, increasingly irritated with all this mischief, banged his silver sceptre against the bronze arm of his chair, a noise like a gong. Everybody sat down again, wondering what to do next in this farcical mêlée. The champions took matters into their own hands by agreeing among themselves to fight not with swords but with words. And how! Back and forth across the long tables, elaborate, embroidered insults flew – questioning their bravery, the characters of their wives, the quality of their family origins.

It all grew too much for Conall and Leary; they jumped up, and, as if to establish their Champion's credentials, with huge blows of their sword-hilts, knocked down two of the columns in Bricriu's façade – which let Fidelma and Lendar into the hall with all their followers. Cuchulainn, still bored, mocked this effort and stirred himself enough to lift that entire side of the building so high that those inside could see the stars in the sky. Through this opening Emer marched like a creature on fire. She swept the others aside and led her own retinue up the length of the hall to where the king sat –

by which time the gangs of women following Fidelma and Lendar had no option but to fall in behind her.

Cuchulainn then let go the side of the palace which he had been holding up in the air. It plunged several feet into the ground, tilting the whole building so severely that Bricriu and his wife in their own apartments were tipped out of the window and thrown on a huge midden, there for the palace dogs to start sniffing and licking them.

Bricriu, certain that his wonderful house had been invaded by ferocious enemies, picked himself up and charged to the main door. He had a job getting in, the doormen hardly recognized him – the filth from the dump he had fallen on clung to his head and clothing. He raced along the corridors into the hall where the most uproarious shouting and laughing went on, and arguing and mock wrestling, quite out of control – even the king seemed much too roisterous for a man in his position. Bricriu jumped on the table and yelled, 'Listen, you black misfortunate sons of Ulster, listen! You don't know how to behave, you are little better than pigs. Right, I'm placing you under a bond. See this house – it means more to me than life itself and you will not eat or drink or close an eye here until you restore it to the immaculate condition in which you found it. And I mean immaculate.'

Oddly enough they listened to him with a degree of respect. They even made an effort to get the house back to rights – but they failed. The chieftains held another of their quick conferences, and concluded that the man who broke it should fix it, Cuchulainn himself. In any case all of them put together could not restore the columns or colonnades which had been shattered when the wall dropped several feet below its foundations.

Cuchulainn, still muttering, strolled over to the ruined wall. He spread his hands wide enough to get a grip, so wide that a chariot and pair could have galloped through. At the first attempt nothing much happened and the murmur of doubt ran around the room. He heard the silence of the Ulstermen and saw the half-sneering, 'I-told-you-so' look on Bricriu's face; this proved too much. Cuchulainn stood back and let his famous war tremors stir: in such a state a drop of flaming blood like a tiny sphere appeared on the point of each strand of his hair – these then seemed to carpet his pulsing skull. He raised his arms above his head, turning them like a chariot wheel while opening his body wide and high to galvanise all his energy. With a deep, slow and savage grunt he lifted the whole superstructure of the house far above his head leaving all the guests open under the sky and then, with great precision and phenomenal strength, he put the walls back exactly where they had belonged with the delicacy of a jeweller. Not even the builder, even upon the closest scrutiny, would detect that anything had been disturbed. Cuchulainn muttered all the way back to his place at table.

The assembled company, marvelling, followed suit and returned to their banquet, somewhat quiet to begin with, as they discussed in low, amazed tones what they had just seen. All around the great hall whispers rose – 'But did you notice the moment when . . .?' and 'I heard that he did something similar some years ago . . .' and 'If I hadn't been here myself I wouldn't have thought . . .' and so on. Bricriu, pulling the last of the cabbage stalks away from his clothes and trying to wash his face with a clean corner of his sleeve, puffed himself out as if he had done the job himself.

Gradually the hall settled back and now the feast had become greatly adorned by the presence of so many beautiful women from the retinues who had come through and under the disturbed walls. The king, Conor MacNessa, let all his charm appear and glowed with benign good manners. He spoke to his right and he spoke to his left, thanking every servant who came near him, a beacon of wisdom and goodwill. But how long could such a good mood last wherever Ulstermen and other Irishmen gather – especially with Bricriu of the Poisoned Tongue among them and the Champion's Portion still a matter of contention? Within the hour the women, who still had Bricriu's compliments ringing in their heads, began to spark off each other, little digs, then open competitiveness, which, regrettably took the dangerous form of praising their respective husbands. Even though King Conor and then her own husband, Cuchulainn, told her to shut up, Emer became the worst offender, needling the wives of Leary and Conall. Eventually, on the far side of the table – which indicates how loudly Emer had been talking – Conall rose to his feet and said, 'If your husband has genuine capabilities – not the sleight-of-hand trickery he has just shown us – why doesn't he prove it himself instead of having a woman mouthing on his behalf? I wonder what he's like in single combat, eh?'

Cuchulainn groaned. 'Now look what you've done,' he called over to Emer. 'Why didn't you keep your mouth shut when you were told?' He turned to the king pleading exhaustion: only that very morning he had been dragged all over the entire country by a wild stallion he had caught and had a hard job trying to break in. Conor MacNessa only smiled – he knew that where the honour of Ulstermen came into question he could not have a better defender on his side. Then the king drew attention to some unfinished business – meaning who should have the Champion's Portion. Ailill's son called out that an independent judge, an outsider, was needed, to which Conor and all three heroes agreed. However, before they could decide on the right sort of person, the would-be Champions started to quarrel all over again and fling insults at each other; when Cuchulainn asked Leary why he didn't have a decent chariot, instead of the heavy and slow job he rode around in, everybody laughed. Conor alone knew what Cuchulainn – no fool either, he also had muscles in his brain – stirred. Leary rose to the bait and rushed out of the hall with his charioteer to show everyone what great feats his chariot could do.

They shot out through Bricriu's great gates like a wild, hot wind, Leary shouting and waving, and, within minutes, shrank to a dot of dust on the far landscape. Heading for the mountains, whose high passes and impassable tracks tested a charioteer's skill and a chariot's flexibility, they hurtled across rough terrain until a heavy fog came down and forced them to a halt. The charioteer unyoked the horses and allowed them to idle through a meadow, waiting for the air to clear.

Out of the mist a giant arrived, not a pleasant sight. He had a mat of tight, black hair, coarse as uncut grass. He wore a stained and undistinguished tunic under which his huge behind heaved. In his fat, slobbery mouth short, spiky teeth showed out of sick-looking gums; a permanent drip hesitated from the end of his nose; above his watery red swollen eyes he had a forehead as wrinkled as an old leather bag; over his shoulder he carried a wooden club the size of a millwheel's axle.

'Who owns the horses?' he asked the charioteer.

The man replied with pride, 'My master Leary, the great warrior.'

'Ye-iii,' cried the giant, 'get your legs out of here!' and belted the charioteer a really serious blow with his club.

Leary strode forward. 'Oi, dung-head! Who do you think you are? What are you doing to my charioteer?'

'The same as I'll do to you, chicken, and to all trespassers. Out of my fine pastures. Go on. Out.'

'Hit me, so,' said Leary and they went at it: the charioteer had to step back two fields in case he got another thump, by accident this time.

Leary, no slouch or weed, stood little chance against this massive, smelly ogre, and, to his shame, he had to turn and run for his life, leaving behind his horses, his gear and even his charioteer, a fact which did not go down too well with that already disgruntled servant. Eventually word got back to the palace, but they hardly laughed – they knew that if Leary had been unable to contend with somebody or something, then a formidable opponent had surely turned up.

Next day Conall arose, cleared his head and headed out in the same direction, up into the mountains. The same thing happened, same sunshine turning to thick mist, same meadow with buttercups and sweet grass to graze the horses – and the same giant, same devastating blow aimed at Conall's charioteer. Conall, likewise, had a go at the black-haired giant and likewise had to run.

On the third day Cuchulainn set out and landed in an identical predicament – the heavy fog, the green meadow, the charioteer, the dirty ogre. After long hours heaving back and forth across the mountain, into rivers and mud and bending each other over rocks, Cuchulainn subdued the giant, held him tight by the mat of coarse black hair (unpleasant to the touch; more than a hint of slime in it) and made the giant give in. Cuchulainn then retrieved those horses, chariots and weapons the others had lost. With a wide, smug grin he headed back to the feast and in front of all the guests made an elaborate performance of graciously returning their weapons and chariots and charioteers to Leary and Conall.

Bricriu, thrilled at the thought of what he could stir out of this, happily awarded Cuchulainn the Champion's Portion. Just as the applause died down, both Conall and Leary shouted their objections. Leary claimed that the fog had been a put-up job, called down by Cuchulainn's friends from the underworld to deny him, the westerner, a fair opportunity of winning the Champion's Portion. Conall agreed with him, saying that Cuchulainn would never have won it if he had not had powerful friends among the spirits. Curiously enough, the logic of this slipped by unquestioned – nobody observed that Cuchulainn had been stopped by the same mist. Instead the assembly in Bricriu's hall returned to the earlier suggestion that an independent judge should decide both the allocation of the Champion's Portion and settle the never-ending arguments of the women; now they decided the name of the person – King Ailill over in the west, whose son sat at Bricriu's feast.

From Bricriu's castle, caravans of assembled guests set out for Ailill's. Cuchulainn, however, did not leave immediately; he hung around for a while, enjoying the admiration of the women, not something which pleased his own woman, Emer, too greatly. He juggled for them all, and did magic tricks involving apples, javelins and knives, nine of everything, and they squealed and applauded. Eventually and with asperity, his charioteer, who also looked after Cuchulainn's business arrangements, hustled his master out and on to the road so that the others would not beat him to the Champion's Portion.

Cuchulainn knew his own measure of speed and sure enough he travelled so fast that he easily caught up with the others. Here indeed was a mighty and impressive caravan – a king at their head, with various courtiers riding nearby, all dressed in vivid saffrons and blues and crimsons, pennants streaming from their spears, horses all jingling and flashing in their jewelled harness-pieces. They also possessed considerable force – their procession made such a racket that the people through whose lands they passed thought an earth-quake had begun. And ahead, in the great castle of Queen Maeve and King Ailill, weapons rattled in their racks on the walls – in fact the castle might have alerted its garrison, but for the sharpness of Princess Findabar who climbed to the ramparts to locate the source of the great noise.

As the girl stood there, Maeve asked her what could she see.

Findabar called down the stairs, 'Mother, I behold a chariot coming towards us at great speed.'

'What is it like?' answered Maeve.

'There are two horses,' said the girl, 'both superb. They have grey coats and manes, their tails fly in the wind. They have broad chests and fierce nostrils, they are dappled and spotted, and their pointed ears rise like spearheads high above their long necks.'

'And the chariot?' asked Maeve.

'Beautiful. Beautiful. Made of highly polished wood, the best. The wheels are black and must be well oiled they run so freely. The reins have been woven in yellow braid by an artist, the chariot-yolk has been beaten out of silver.'

'But who rides in this chariot?' cried Maeve.

'I don't know – but he's some remarkable man,' replied the daughter. 'He has streaked hair, ranging from dark brown to gold and bright yellow, and he keeps it in place with three headbands indicating his warriorhood. He wears a brilliant scarlet tunic, bor-dered with gold and silver, he has a bright shield on his arm and there's a flock of wild birds high in the sky above following him.'

Maeve exclaimed, 'But that's Leary! He's terrifying. If he's coming here out of anger we will all be slaughtered.'

'Wait, wait,' cried Findabar. 'Mother, I see another chariot.'

'What is that one like?' asked Maeve.

'Brilliant. Brilliant. Two horses, one the colour of copper with a shining white face, enormous strides devouring the ground, leaping across rivers. I can actually see its hooves flashing in the light. The other horse – and there's nothing between them for speed – has a bright red coat and plaited black mane and a high vicious mouth snarling with strength. There's foam dripping from its teeth.'

'And the chariot?' asked Maeve.

'Timber again, but marvellous, and it has silver poles and the reins have fringes and yellow tassels.'

'And the warrior in it?' asked Maeve.

'Big fellow, very big, Mother. Strong. Distinguished-looking, too – he has long, shining hair braided to the neck, he gleams with sweat and he wears a cloak of red and deep blue. He wears a shield bordered with bronze and carries a spear which seems on fire. And above his head too there's a flock of wild birds wheeling.'

'Now that,' said Maeve, 'is Conall. I hope he comes in friendship, because if he doesn't he will fillet us as if we were fish from the river.'

'Hold! Hold on!' shouted the girl in even greater excitement. 'There's a third.'

'A third what?'

'Mother! They are followed by a third chariot.'

'Quick. Tell me what it is like. Every detail.' Maeve hopped from foot to foot at the bottom of the narrow stone steps leading up to the ramparts.

'Oh, wonderful! Wonderful!' shouted the daughter. 'This is the most wonderful of them all. For a start, one of the horses has a lovely, firm, grey coat, with a long curled mane which flaps up and down in regular movements as it speeds along. Broad hooves like wide blades and it carves slices from the fields. Yes, there are the birds overhead too but it outpaces them. The other horse could not be more different, yet equally remarkable. A harder animal, built more tightly, with elegant strides of long legs, a swift and controlled creature.'

'And the chariot, the chariot?' called out Maeve.

'The best yet,' said the girl, 'made by true masters, none of your timber here – this has a body of copper built in a high arching curve, iron wheels bound by handmade bands, and the yoke of beaten gold is catching the light, and the charioteer holds the long, wide, yellow braids of the reins.'

'And the man in the chariot?'

'Mother,' said Findabar, beside herself with excitement, 'I have never laid eyes on a more gorgeous man. He is both sad and ferocious. He has profound eyes, and they look as if somebody set fire to them or filled them with gemstones in all the colours of a dragon's eyes. He has the widest chest I have ever seen in a man, I can see it gleaming through the opening in his red tunic. And his agility – look! He is actually leaping as he goes along, up above his chariot like a salmon at a waterfall. Oh, Mother – who is he?'

Maeve replied, 'Daughter dear, that is the most mighty warrior in the world, that is Cuchulainn. We might be just about able to contain the first two, but if he doesn't come here in peace, his anger will grind us to powder.'

Maeve put on her diplomatic mood, and called her retinue of fifty waiting-women. They did hurried things to their appearances and went to the castle door. Just beside it they arranged three tall urns of cool water from the well, one for each of the warriors. Now the stately procession of Ulstermen came into view out of the dust-clouds. In the distance, the castle staff could see them approaching slowly across the plain. It did not, however, look like an invasion and Maeve invoked the hospitality of the castle.

To begin with, she offered each of the three warriors a grand apartment, and the choicest of her fifty women. Cuchulainn, however, found Maeve's daughter leading him by the hand to the room she herself had prepared for him. When the rest of the party arrived, they inspected this marvellous palace of a castle and found it splendid (Bricriu, incidentally, had included it in his tour of inspection before he briefed his architects.) The high-vaulted roof had a bronze ceiling through which could be seen the oaken rafters; the partitions between the apartments had been made from yew inlaid with copper, most of the walls had been made of oak. The royal apartments at the very centre reeked with wealth and magnificence; in Ailill's own office stood a long silver rod leaning against one wall and reaching to the roof, the wand of authority which he used to keep his castle and kingdom under control. Musicians came in, playing reed pipes and strings, and the food appeared. In the lavish custom of the west, they feasted and caroused for three days and three nights.

All the while, however, the great question hung in the air: the reason why they had come. Irish laws of hospitality decreed that business could never be discussed until at least three days of eating and drinking had passed. At last Ailill enquired of the Ulstermen what had brought them there; when they told him, though, he refused to adjudicate on the question of the Champion's Portion. They pressed him, saying that they had ridden all this way to get his judgment – Conor MacNessa even urged him as king to king. Ailill replied that at least he needed more time to think, and therefore they gave him three more days and nights. The greater party had to return to Ulster, but Leary, Conall and Cuchulainn stayed behind to watch the deliberations – and undertake any trials Ailill might specify in order to settle the matter.

Indeed a test materialised that very night, as the men sat down to dine. From a cave nearby erupted three wild cats, three magical animals called forth by the Druids. The cats, making a horrifying noise and showing claws as long and shiny as razors, headed straight for the food of the warriors. Leary and Conall, who both hated cats, said in unison, 'I'm getting out of here,' and jumped to the rafters where they stayed, looking down as the cats ate their food. Cuchulainn ate on, did not even lift his head, just sat there munching and picking meat off bones. When one of the cats, a big ugly thing, dared approach his plate he fetched it a ferocious swipe with his short sword. The sword skidded off the cat's neck and he hit it again. Now the other cats approached. Cuchulainn tried, but he could not budge them: the beasts sat there, denying him food and sleep all night, although every time they made any kind of move or sound he belted them again. At the first light of dawn the cats disappeared, back to their cave which could be seen in the distance from the castle window.

Ailill, advised by the Druids, judged that on this trial alone Cuchulainn should have the Champion's Portion. Conall and Leary, climbing down from the rafters and rubbing the stiffness from their bodies, told him that the contest should revolve around humans, not animals.

This threw Ailill into one of his quandaries of indecisiveness, sleepless nights, worried days, back and forth. Maeve chided him for his vacillation and then tried to influence his decision.

'Think of the three in terms of gold,' she said. 'Leary counts as bronze. See Conall as white gold. I'd say Cuchulainn was powerful, red gold.' She then sent to their rooms for the three men, one at a time.

'Now, Leary,' she said. 'You are the great hero, and you must be the champion of Ireland. I seal this award to you – here, take this cup.' She handed him a beautiful bronze goblet with a white bird portrayed on the bottom. 'This cup will prove to the Ulstermen that you have been chosen here as the undisputed champion. Say a word to no-one. Hide the cup until the right moment at the feast. Then rise, hold the cup high above your head, show them the bird. That will prove that my husband and I have awarded you the Champion's Portion.' She filled the cup with a deep red wine and Leary, standing before her throne, drained it at one gulp and belched.

'For one hundred years,' she said to him, 'not a soul will dispute your championship of Ulster.'

Then Maeve sent for Conall, and said exactly the same things to him, the only difference being that his vessel was made of white gold and had a portrait of a golden bird on the bottom. Maeve told him too that he would be undisputed champion of Ulster, etc., etc., and he too drained his cup and took it away with him, under strict instructions not to show it to anyone until the end of the feast, when he would be awarded the Champion's Portion.

Cuchulainn would not answer when Maeve sent for him. The footman found him busy at a board game, truculent and muttering, unwilling to be disturbed. He actually threw a piece from the game at the messenger and hit him right in the centre of the forehead. The man barely made it back to Maeve, gasped out his story and dropped to the floor – dead. Maeve went to Cuchulainn – still at his board game – and tried flattery. She put her arms around him and openly offered him the Champion's Portion.

'Liar,' he said. 'Two-faced bitch.'

'No. On my oath.'

'That's not worth a lot, I'd say.'

'No,' she protested. 'You have to be awarded the prize, not only in Ulster but the whole country. It stands to reason, Cuchulainn – your strength, your looks, your energy.'

'H'm,' he said, but he went along with this. He should not have done – he should have stayed with his first instinct; Maeve should have been married to Bricriu, pity to spoil two houses between them.

Cuchulainn, yawning, walked with Maeve to the throne room, where, in front of Ailill, she handed to him a cup made of rich red gold, and the bird at the bottom had been fashioned from jewels. They filled the cup for him with their best wine; he drank it at one gulp. They flattered him some more, saying how wonderful his wife Emer seemed, certainly the foremost among Ulster women. Cuchulainn, though not impervious to such compliments, took his leave and went back to his board game.

The following afternoon, the young bucks at the court, out on the sward in front of the walls, were vying with each other at feats and tricks. One of their games sought to establish who could pitch a chariot wheel the highest. Leary and Conall joined in and did well;

each threw it just about half-way up the wall or, with a supreme effort, just to the top; the youths applauded them ironically. Then, when Cuchulainn threw the wheel right over the highest turret he mistook their applause – genuine this time for irony. Irritated, he decided to stage something really spectacular to shut them up. He approached the nearest group of fifty women who were sitting on the grass watching these young limbs gleaming about the place and he asked them for their sewing needles. These he arranged in the palms of his two hands and one by one threw each needle high in the air. Like little javelins he aimed the point of each one into the eye of the one before it, until they shone in a chain across the sky. Then, dismantling the chain, he caught each needle individually as it fell to the ground, gave the needles back to the women, stuck his tongue out at the assembled youths, and at Leary and Conall, and walked away.

No good conclusion came out of the palace of Maeve and Ailill, who then directed them to another royal house where the judgment would continue. Remember, each one of the champions knew nothing of Maeve's trickery and each one therefore thought he, and he alone, had been secretly awarded the championship. In this other house the king, nonetheless, told them he had to test them and he sent them out, one at a time, into the night to meet the spirits. At the first chilly brush with the malevolent hosts of the air, Leary ran off terror-stricken, literally jumping out of his clothes with fright, and leaving his garments and his weapons on the ground. When Conall did the same, Cuchulainn fell about with laughter and told everybody how scared the other two had been.

Then, on the third night, his turn came and he, predictably, stood his ground. The spirits, though, stripped him naked, trussed him like a dead boar and then, whirling around in the air above his still body, began to mock him, the one kind of attack Cuchulainn could not stand. He let go his war tremors, the magic, fiery vibrations in him which neither god nor man could withstand, and burst his bonds. Up on his feet he grabbed and savaged the ghosts, tearing them apart with his bare hands and filling the air with a misty vapour of their blood. What could the king of that household say? Cuchulainn, without doubt, should have the Champion's Portion. No, not proof enough for Conall and Leary – again they said that Cuchulainn's influence with the underworld had helped to make the ghosts give way more easily.

So they travelled to yet another house for judgment, with Cuchulainn by now thoroughly bored with the whole caper. This king himself greeted them, and began to tell them of his pride in a great and combative horse that he owned. He challenged them to a duel, with horses. Leary went first – the king's horse routed Leary's and the king had his sword-hand poised to do the same to Leary himself, when the warrior turned his back like a coward and ran back to Bricriu's feast, where he told the Ulstermen that this wild king had killed the other two. Conall, in a similar fix, also decamped to Bricriu's feast and told everyone the mad king had now killed Cuchulainn. A lie – Cuchulainn easily overcame the king, tied him in a bundle on the floor of his chariot and drove him back to Bricriu's. Great cheering broke out at his appearance, much to the embarrassment of Leary and Conall.

Still the matter of the Champion's Portion had not been satisfactorily settled – it became clear that the award, when finally decided, would have to prove utterly beyond dispute. They all sat down to feast again, among them this time Cuchulainn's father, and the contrary issue of the Champion's Portion continued.

'We'll have to choose some other candidate altogether,' suggested one guest. 'After all, these three have now come back from being judged at length, and they haven't a thing to show what Ailill or anybody else thought of them.'

'Oi!' Leary roared to his feet and held aloft his bronze cup so that everyone could see the silver bird on the base – proof, he shouted, of his unchallengeable right to the Champion's Portion. Conall jumped up too, yelling and waving his white gold cup – clearly superior, he said, to Leary's bronze cup and therefore he claimed the right. Cuchulainn stood up slowly, held high his cup made of deep red gold with the jewelled bird on it and did not even bother to claim – just looked around him without saying a word. He displayed such utter superiority, both in himself and in the cup, that King Conor MacNessa and the others unanimously awarded Cuchulainn the Champion's Portion.

Leary hit the roof. He roared his head off, saying that Cuchulainn had actually bought the cup from Maeve – to avoid being disgraced. Up rose Conall saying the same, and yet again all three drew their swords and had to be ordered by King Conor to put them away. After much argument they agreed to be judged one more time, this time at the house of a man called Buda. He, a shrewd old fellow, said he plainly felt unable to judge men who would not accept the judgment of Conor, and then Ailill and Maeve, and then another, and another, so he sent them one step further, to a mystic he knew who lived by a lake, a seer of great and Protean powers. This character could turn himself into any spiritual shape necessary to settle any dispute, even between gods. The sorcerer agreed to judge them on one condition – that they accepted his judgment as final and to this they had to give their word of honour as warriors and heroes.

'Right,' he said, 'this is how I will go about it. Just as you have given your word of honour about accepting my judgment as final, I will strike a bargain with you and you must keep it.'

'Yes,' they said, Leary and Conall a little apprehensively, Cuchulainn aggressively – now utterly fed up with all of this, he simply wanted to hunt.

'Here you are,' said the mystic. 'This is my axe. Today you cut off my head. Tomorrow I cut off yours.'

He handed the hatchet, a fearsome object, to Leary. Then the sorcerer laid his neck on the stone step outside his house and Leary chopped his head off. The seer rose, picked up his head, shoved it under his arm, slung the axe over his shoulder and wandered off down to his lakeshore, telling Leary to return tomorrow without fail. As dawn broke, no Leary appeared: he had by now gone far away and had no intention of coming back.

The mystic shrugged, turned to Conall, handed him the axe and lay down with his head on the stone step. Conall chopped off his head. The seer got up, same as before, collected his head and his hatchet and drifted off down to the lake contemplatively, turning back on the way and reminding Conall to return at dawn. As the clouds grew pink over the lake next morning Conall could not be found: he had hidden in tall, thick reeds a long way off.

When it came to Cuchulainn's turn, he arrived punctually without fuss and lay down. The seer swung the hatchet three times and dealt three massive blows. Three times the huge toothed blade bounced off Cuchulainn's neck. Cuchulainn shook himself, rose and the seer embraced him saying, 'Now that's an end of it. No dispute – the Champion's Portion's for you.'

Nobody seemed one bit surprised – though they should have been, and disgusted – when back at the feast Leary and Conall refused to accept the mystic's judgment. Rather wearily, and to Cuchulainn's intense anger, one more judgment was arranged. This time they drove in their chariots to another royal house whose king, away at war in Scythia, had instructed his wife to make these heroes welcome. In line with the hospitality of the household, she had them washed and pampered, fed and watered and shown to their splendid bedrooms. Then she issued the test her husband had left behind. Each night one of them, youngest first, had to stand sentry on the castle ramparts and, in the king's absence, be prepared to defend the castle and all in it to the death.

Leary took watch the first night. Nothing stirred until the darkest hour before dawn when he heard a quick rumble in the gloom. Looking west he saw, walking up out of the sea, water dripping from him, a mad-looking giant, a huge and fearsome figure, head reaching nearly to the clouds, legs wide enough apart to sail a ship through. In his hands he carried several missiles – the trunks of oak trees, each one sharpened to a blackened point. These he began to fling at Leary as if they were little darts. Leary dodged them and with his massive strength threw his spear, which only bounced off the giant. The giant then picked up Leary as a man picks up a ball, and began to grind the warrior around in the palms of his hands like a woman testing corn at a millstone. After a few agonising minutes of this, he then dropped the unconscious warrior over the ramparts into the rubbish pit just inside the castle walls and strolled off into the ocean again, huge and black against the blue morning sky.

Conall took the next night's watch, patrolled quietly through the hours of darkness and then, just before dawn, suffered the same gruelling fate as Leary. This time the giant spat in his own hands before rubbing Conall through his palms and nearly drowning the warrior in the process.

On the third night, when Cuchulainn took watch, he divined something that neither of the other two had seen: local enemies had begun to gather in droves for a massive attack on the castle. He saw them off, beheading nine of them at a time and displaying their blood-dripping heads on the arms of his chair. The fates threw another challenge at him – a monster in the lake set to eat every man, woman and child, every horse, dog and bird. The creature arose, dark and awful and towering high above the castle, looking down into it. Cuchulainn roused himself from his exhaustion and leaped way up, on to the monster's neck. He pulled the beast's head back, stuck his arm down the red throat and tore out the heart. With his sword he then cut the heaving monster up into tiny pieces of meat and tossed them to the castle hounds and curs.

At last dawn broke and Cuchulainn felt that his night's labours had come to a successful end. As he walked along the ramparts to feed and rest, the giant appeared, striding dripping out of the waves, bigger than the monster. He unleashed his tree-trunk darts at Cuchulainn who boxed them aside. Then, as with Leary and Conall, he reached down and tried to snatch up Cuchulainn in his hands.

Cuchulainn dodged him and with his huge salmon leap hung in the air above the giant's head, sword in hand.

The giant went down on one knee and pleaded for his life.

'Only on my conditions,' said Cuchulainn.

'Yes, yes, anything. What are they?'

'I want complete, unchallenged, acknowledged domination over all the warriors, not just of Ulster but of the entire country, so that I never again have to go through this nonsense of the Champion's Portion.'

'I agree.'

'And I want the same position for my wife Emer – foremost among the womenfolk.'

'I couldn't agree more.' And the giant vanished. Cuchulainn did not bother walking down the steps from the ramparts – he jumped, like a swooping bird, over the castle wall and landed right inside the heart of the keep. As the celebrations began, the owner of the castle, the king, returning from the Scythian wars, bore trophies from the local armies that Cuchulainn had slain nine at a time.

'Who did this?' he asked. They told him.

'That's it,' he said. 'That's it. There can be no more argument. No argument whatsoever. Who, in the entire countryside, could equal such a warrior? Give the Champion's Portion to Cuchulainn. And give his wife the corresponding stature among the women.' Leary and Conall had to endure hearing all of this, and to their further chagrin, the king showered Cuchulainn with coins and jewels and the three warriors left for the court of Ulster.

Incredible as it may seem, after all such varied proof, Leary and Conall still disputed Cuchulainn's right to the Champion's Portion. This time they argued successfully that the judgments had all been made outside Ulster where different principles applied. Cuchulainn looked disgusted – he had been promised by the giant he defeated that this would not happen – and took no interest whatsoever in the arguments.

Leary and Conall did not, however, have the luck they wished for, because a test then began inside Ulster which would decide the business for all time. A filthy ogre appeared, one sunny evening, as they all rested after a day at the sports. He stood double the height of any Ulsterman, triple the thickness, quadruple the girth; he had fingers as thick as a man's thigh. His yellow eyes burned and smoked like sulphurous cauldrons; his face had a dirty brown colour. In one hand he carried an enormous pointed tree trunk, in the other a great axe sharp enough to shave with.

He walked right up through the court hall, and took his position standing in front of the fire. After some timid enquiries from various chieftains he stated his business. He had searched the world, he said, for a warrior honourable enough to keep a bargain. This bargain, it transpired, resembled the challenge thrown down by the lakeside seer.

'Is there any man here,' asked the ogre, 'who will come forward that I may cut off his head tonight and he can cut mine off tomorrow?'

One man stood up and amid laughter said, 'I will keep a bargain with you – I'll cut off your head tonight and you can cut off mine tomorrow night.'

'Well,' said the ogre, 'if that's the best the yellow-bellied men of Ulster can come up with, go ahead.' And he lay down with his neck on the table. The warrior who had spoken took the ogre's axe, the blade of which was as wide as a man's height, and swung it so hard that it cut through the ogre's neck and stuck in the table underneath him. The head rolled off and great spouts of blood thick as a dragon's spittle splashed the walls, the floors, the roof and the guests. The head rolled towards the fire, the ogre picked it up, collected his axe and left.

He came back the following night.

'Where is he?' – but the warrior had reneged and disappeared. Someone had to abate this dishonour, so King Conor MacNessa, irked at the cowardice, suggested the three men still contesting the Champion's Portion.

Leary stepped forward, though everyone should have known from his previous behaviour with the lakeside mystic that he would never keep such a bargain. He pulled the same stunt as before – cut off the ogre's head, and vanished when it came to his own neck. Conall, next night, did the same – upon which the giant's rage threatened to bring down not just the house but the very sky itself. By now the women had also gathered to hear the ogre mock what he called 'the cowardly Red Branch Knights' (the king's most feared and honourable regiment) and all the men of Ulster. Soon he had the women joining in, taunting their menfolk.

Cuchulainn stood up. He did not want to be included in the taunts, or lumped together with the others. He grabbed the axe and cut off the ogre's head so hard that it bounced off the ceiling and on the way down Cuchulainn swung at it again and with one blow split it into tiny fragments. The ogre gathered all of these in the lap of his tunic, picked up his axe, and strolled away.

The following day nobody could talk of anything else in the

palace. Would Cuchulainn shirk the other half of the bargain as the others had done? Would he put his neck on the block? The court hall could not hold all the people who wanted to watch the feast that night.

Punctually the ogre arrived.

'Where is he?' he asked, again straddling the huge fireplace with his enormous legs, his eyes burning like filthy yellow pools of flame.

'Here I am,' said Cuchulainn.

'Aha. I see you're whispering tonight,' said the ogre. 'Fear of death, eh?'

'Fear of nothing,' said Cuchulainn, and promptly knelt down by the table and offered his neck to the axe blade. The blade, however, being so wide, needed a larger target and the ogre asked Cuchulainn to stretch out his neck a lot further.

'Don't needle me,' said Cuchulainn, 'hit me quickly – in the same way I cut your head off. Or so help me I will stretch myself as long as a crane bird and peck you from the skies.'

'Go on. Stretch yourself, stretch yourself,' said the ogre. 'I have no room to hit you.'

Cuchulainn stretched his wiry body until his ribs nearly came apart to the width of a man's foot and he elongated his neck like a heron's or a swan's. The ogre swung the huge axe whose handle had the thickness of three oaks. The blade now nicked the rafters as he raised it higher and higher. Down it flashed, in full view of the court, making the noise of thunder and the gleam of lightning, and when it hit Cuchulainn's neck it bounced – the giant had reversed the blade.

'Up you get, Cuchulainn,' said the ogre. 'You're a hero. A true champion must have honour as well as strength and bravery and you have all three, unlike those cowards around you who cannot keep a bargain, who are as weak as water and who run away when they can't handle a problem. Here and now, I award you, with no more disputes, the Champion's Portion. Added to that, Emer, your lady wife, has the right to raise her glass first of all the women of Ulster.' The ogre glared at them all. 'If anyone here dares – ever – to dispute one word of this judgment I will shorten his life there and then.' To Conor MacNessa he said, 'On a king's honour, and you know how serious that is, you must acknowledge this and protect it.'

The ogre began to change shape and before their eyes stood first of all the lakeside seer, and then the king whose castle Cuchulainn had defended so valiantly; sick of the Ulstermen's dithering he had turned up at the Red Branch Knights' palace to see his judgments effected. Cuchulainn shook his hand, then took the Champion's Portion. Emer, in front of all the others, led all the women into the drinking-hall and sat beside her husband concealing her immodest glee with great difficulty. Leary and Conall sulked, defeated and disgraced. The others, jeering, lobbed small bits of meat at them and, after a while, their two wives got up and left the feast, thoroughly ashamed.

As for Bricriu, though his feast was declared a great success, and though everyone admired his wonderful palace, a work of architectural genius, they all gave as wide a berth as possible to his Poisoned Tongue – which never improved and eventually cost him the social esteem he so desperately craved.

CORMAC'S CUP OF GOLD

ne morning in May, as the cobwebs glistened with jewels of mist, King Cormac stood on the earthen walls of Tara. Out on the plains of his royal meath, the green of the early corn waved to the breeze's patterns across the fields. Looking to the north-west, he saw a curious figure approaching on foot from the direction of the river Boyne, a warrior by the look of him, dressed in the brilliant style to which only warriors, princes and kings were entitled. He wore cloth-of-gold brocade edged with broad bands of purple and his short crimson brocade cloak, which flapped a little behind him so quickly did he stride, had a saffron lining.

On his right shoulder he bore, at an angle, a branch made of beautiful beaten silver with three golden apples hanging from it as if they had grown there. When this branch shook as he stepped along in his high prancing gait, the apples made music. Cormac knew instinctively that this sound would make all ailing people sleep peacefully: wounded warriors; women in the labour of childbirth; people with palsy or old soldiers whose aches had caught up with them.

The warrior saluted formally as he approached Cormac and then spoke with confidence and with obvious, though not obsequious, respect.

'I come from a country where only truth may be spoken, where nothing ages or decays, where melancholy, envy, hate or conceit do not exist.'

Cormac replied, 'This trebles your ready welcome at my court.' The stranger bowed according to the etiquette due to a High King, the men clasped wrists and both immediately and spontaneously offered friendship. Cormac, in the ritual which permitted a king or host to ask any visitor for the gift of such valuables as he carried, asked the stranger for the silver branch with the golden apples. Unquestioning, the man agreed, but only on condition that the king grant him three wishes. Cormac, understanding the game, said, 'Of course', at which the stranger disappeared.

Cormac walked down the steps from the ramparts and strolled back into the palace. Inside the courtyard, he shook the silver branch. When the golden apples tinkled, the entire royal household fell asleep.

After a year and a day, and on exactly the same kind of sunlit morning, the brilliantly clad warrior reappeared on the ramparts at Tara, wearing stripes of red to match the evening sky and pink to match the dawn.

Cormac, delighted to see him, asked, 'Tell me, do I have the privilege of granting you your three wishes?'

The stranger bowed.

'Yes, and my first wish honours three people, you, me and your daughter, whose hand I want in marriage.'

The king clapped his hands in delight and when the royal women protested – who was this man? what was his breeding? – Cormac, smiling like a boy, shook the branch and they were pacified into sleep.

A month later, on a morning of wind and sun, with the air on Tara exhilarating, the stranger returned, wearing the deep blue of the sea and the soft white of the early clouds.

'I hope,' said Conor, 'that I now shall have the privilege of granting you the remaining wishes.'

'One at a time,' said the stranger, 'nothing to excess. But you're right. I have come to claim the second wish. This time it honours three of us again. This time I want you to foster your young son on me.'

The king happily agreed, but the lad had proved a great favourite among the women at the court who spent a lot of time combing his hair and making a pet of him. Once more Cormac subdued the family disquiet by shaking the silver bough. Once again they all fell asleep. Useful item, this.

One year and one day later, the mysterious warrior returned, clothed this time in the green of the young corn and the bright saffron-gold of the sun at noon.

'I have come to claim my third and last wish – your wife.'

The king – rueful this time, for he loved his wife – had no choice but to agree. It proved too much for him and, when the stranger left the ramparts, accompanied by the queen who looked back just once in sorrow and puzzlement, the king mustered his own followers and set out in pursuit. Suddenly, from the sea, a deep mist floated in at great speed, cutting off the members of the party from each other.

King Cormac found himself isolated, entirely alone on a wide moor. He led his horse gently up a defile, avoiding the thorn bushes which caught the edge of his gold cloak, and there, at the end of the pathway, as suddenly and unreally as in a dream, stood a mighty fort with walls of shining metal. He dismounted and hitched his horse to a short stone pillar beneath the walls. As he walked forward, a door swung open slowly. He had entered a house made entirely of silver; the roof, he noticed, had been only half thatched – with the feathers of white birds – and a small army of thatchers worked with huge armfuls of more feathers to complete the job. But every time they tried to peg down a new piece of thatch, and then clip it into place with long willow rods the length of a man's forearm, the wind blew away the feathers.

By the great fireplace a man crouched and heaved on a huge fire a tree – trunk, branches, roots – all of which burnt to ashes in the few moments while he went away to get another tree which he hauled through a door in the back: he seemed to perform this task every half-minute or so. Out through the back door of this chaotic silver house, Cormac could see a great palace of four citadels – banners and pennants flying at each corner. In the courtyard stood a circle of nine gnarled hazel trees, dropping their nuts into a silver pool in which swam five salmon snapping at each nut as it fell. Five wide streams, reflecting the light, flowed from the pool in a sound that made bright melodies.

Inside this palace Cormac found two people sitting on large oaken chairs – a champion and a beautiful woman. Neither showed any surprise at the arrival of the king. Their servants had prepared a bath for Cormac, of water warmed by stones that appeared magically as he called for more heat. At that moment through the doorway came a powerful and churlish man carrying an axe, a club and a small pig. With the axe he killed the pig and split the wooden club, and then cut the pig into four parts and tossed it into a large bubbling cauldron. Throughout this performance, the man protested that the pig would never be properly cooked until four truths were told, one for each of the pig's four quarters. So the man himself told a tale, followed by the beautiful woman; so did the warrior, and, as they did so, three quarters of the pig cooked beautifully. Then they turned, looked at the king, and waited.

Cormac told the story of how his wife had vanished and he told it eloquently. This completed the cooking of the pig, ready to be eaten. When they served his portion to the king, he objected, saying he never ate a meal without an entourage of at least fifty people. The warrior rose from his chair and sang a song that lulled the king to sleep. When he awoke fifty warriors stood around him, and foremost in the company stood his loving wife, daughter and son, restored to him.

They all feasted merrily amid much music. During dinner, Cormac, the perfect guest, admired his host's exquisite drinking chalice, made of simple beaten gold. The warrior said, 'All its wonder does not lie in its beauty. It has its own soul.'

'How do you mean?' asked Cormac.

'If three lies be told it will break in three parts. If three truths are told, it will then be restored.' The warrior told three lies, and the cup, with little crashes, splintered in three before their eyes. He said to Cormac, 'Look – now I will make it whole again; your son has not seen a woman, and neither your wife nor daughter has seen a man, since they left Tara.' At that the cup came back together again with three loud musical rings and stood restored, handsome as before.

Cormac said, 'But how can all of this be?'

His host replied, 'I am not a mortal, I am Manannan MacLir, the god of the sea, and I sent the sea-mist. I have lured you here that you may view the Land of Promise.' He revealed himself as the warrior who had pranced across the fields that sunny morning to the ramparts at Tara.

'I favour you and I guard your sleep,' Manannan announced, and gave the king the Golden Cup 'for Truth' to go with the Silver Branch 'for Pleasantness'.

Slowly, and with an air of finality, the god explained the riddles of the palace.

'The thatchers with the feathers represent poets who tried to hoard wealth; oh, such a futile thing to do – the world blows the wealth of poets away. The spring pool in the courtyard – that is the sparkling fount of all knowledge and the five streams that flow from it are the same as the five senses of seeing, hearing, smell, taste and touch, which flow from the mind and soul and through which knowledge is garnered. To drink from the well itself will do you good in soul and heart, but to drink from the streams guarantees excellence in the things you most want.'

Manannan clapped his hands, the musicians played a last march and a last lament and a last lullaby. The household stood, bowed to the king and everyone retired after this great feast and evening of wonders.

Next morning the king found himself rubbing the sleep out of his eyes – not in the bed to which, surely, he had gone the night before, but on the high green ramparts of Tara. Had he dreamed it all? There, in the distance, were his wife and daughter and son, and the palace seemed its normal, early morning self.

But as he stirred himself, blinked, stretched and sat up, he saw nearby on the ground, gleaming in the early light, the golden cup, and beside it, the silver branch with the dear little ringing gold apples.

MAC DATHO'S BOAR

ong ago in the province of Leinster lived a king called Mac DaTho. He owned two possessions which gave him great pride – a hound of such ferocity that he, solely, protected all the family lands, and a tame boar reared for the table which, for seven years and seven days had been fed only on the milk of sixty specially dedicated cows. By now this boar had grown into a magnificent creature, large enough – Mac DaTho's original intention – to furnish a year-long feast.

His hound, though, attracted more attention than the pig – imagine the power it gave the man who owned it, a dog as good as ten armies? Almost daily, from one source or another, at home or abroad, King Mac DaTho got offers; two of the most significant – and persistent – of these came from the court of King Ailill and Queen Maeve in the west and from King Conor MacNessa in Ulster. The more Conor bid, the more Maeve and Ailill outbid him.

Mac DaTho took all this attention with his natural nobility. A generous man, he graciously received visitors in the great hostel he had built to exhibit his command of hospitality. The magical figure of seven dominated the architecture – seven gates, seven doors, seven hearths and seven cauldrons always full of steaming beef and pork. As Mac DaTho said, 'Just as we have seven openings in our heads, two eyes, two ears, two nostrils and a mouth, so shall my guests have seven openings through which to receive hospitality.' And the management of the place lived up to this ambition – for instance, it was considered insulting to the host for a guest to walk past one of the cauldrons and not to eat.

One day it became apparent that the bidding for the hound had intensified: strife threatened between Conor's Ulster and Maeve's province of Connacht. When the messengers from both kingdoms arrived, Mac DaTho straightaway received them in audience.

'I am instructed,' began the messenger from Maeve and Ailill, 'to tell you that a hundred and sixty prime dairy cows shall be yours today – they are waiting over the hill there, to be driven into your paddocks – with a prize chariot drawn by the two best horses in the western provinces. And I am further instructed to say that the same again will be given to you annually for your lifetime and that of your generations down to your grandson.'

'Wonderful friendship and secure alliance, jewellery and cattle every year forever,' offered the envoy from Conor MacNessa and Ulster, who may well have been listening at a crack in the wall – the messengers, experienced court diplomats, had been given a certain amount of discretion in their offers.

How difficult it became for Mac DaTho, never a decisive man at the best of times. Confusion broke out all over him, sleepless nights, tossing and turning, loss of appetite. His queen said to him, 'Come on. Eat up. What's the matter with you? All this lovely food?' He said not a word, and – a thoughtful woman – she moved him with a poem, saying that these uninvited offers had placed Mac DaTho in a predicament. On the one hand, if Conor felt in-sulted by Mac DaTho's answer he would attack, and on the other hand, if Ailill and Maeve did not get the hound, one of their famous warriors would come and assassinate Mac DaTho and his wife.

'Right,' she said, 'this is what you do. Give the dog to them both,' she said, 'and let them fight it out. Keep out of it.'

He wailed a little, and then he screwed himself up and came forth again, feeling refreshed and more assured. The delegates from the west and from Ulster had stayed on to enjoy the renowned hospitality of this elegant and gifted court presided over by such a nice man. Mac DaTho ordered more wine and much more music and then, after all had feasted well and had begun to loll about, he beckoned the ambassador from the west to one side.

'As you can perceive,' he began a little pompously, 'I have rarely had such a demanding decision to make. But, all things considered, I have decided to accept the offer from your king and queen, Ailill and Maeve. Go back and tell them to come here with their best regiments in full ceremonial battledress to honour the giving of the hound. Their greatest warriors must attend the receiving of such an extraordinary animal.' The western legate, a shrewd man, gave thanks in the most perfectly judged elaboration and then, calling his delegation around him, rode from the castle immediately, though the time had passed midnight, to rush home with the good news.

When they had gone, Mac DaTho retired from the aftermath of the feast to his private chambers and from there asked to see the Ulster delegation. 'I have taken my decision,' he said – by now he felt a trifle jumpy, this part needed nerve – 'though you must have perceived how long and hard I had to deliberate – a most difficult decision this one.' The Ulster ambassador nodded, respectfully but not obsequiously, his beard wagging a little with the movement. Mac DaTho, who loved such respect, continued in a slightly more pompous voice and manner than before.

'And I have agreed to accept your offer. King Conor MacNessa, whose friendship I value, shall have my wonderful hound. Go back and tell him so, with my warmest compliments, and ask him to come and fetch it. But –' he raised a finger '– he must bring here, to this castle, and mass them on the plain in front, his finest armies. This is a hound that must be honoured.' He then named the day – the same that he had chosen for Maeve and Ailill's delegation.

Four weeks later, on the appointed morning, they arrived, resplendent and colourful; they came from different directions and converged on the wide sward that stretched in front of and below the castle. The men from the north wore red and white, the men from the west vivid blue, and their pennants fluttered from their spears. Mac DaTho, his queen at his side, offered them a welcome at the gates and invited them into the castle courtyard. The men of Ulster ranked themselves along one side of the wide yard and the men of the west on the other: between them the fountains danced in the sunlight. They dismounted and went indoors to a great feast for which Mac DaTho had slaughtered his magnificent boar; servants wheeled it into the banqueting-hall and it lay there garnished by forty huge cows who lay across it. King Ailill and King Conor MacNessa sat either side of King Mac DaTho.

'Some pig,' admired Conor.

Ailill remarked, 'But how shall we divide it fairly?'

Bricriu of the Poisoned Tongue saw a chance to stir things up.

'When you get so many warriors from different provinces under one roof,' he said, 'there is only one way – by open contest, hand-to-hand.'

Regrettably, Conor and Ailill both rose to the bait; each beckoned their best warriors and the familiar ritual began, the taunting in order to whip up the necessary rage. Ferocious belting then broke out and, at the end of the day, only one warrior remained standing or uncut or undefeated – Cet, from Ailill's and Maeve's court. He therefore won the right to hang his weapons on the wall higher than anybody else; then he reached for the carving-knife and said, 'Unless you can find a warrior who can best me, I am going to carve this pig – now.'

This sickened the Ulstermen, because they knew Cet's worth and because they had nobody in the room to match him at that moment. They could only sit there and watch. King Conor MacNessa could not bear it at all – Cet had begun to gloat a little – and he called over his warrior Leary.

'Listen. Do something. Do anything. I can't stand this. I can't stand just sitting here, watching him carve that wonderful animal.'

Leary scratched his armpit and said in a fairly brazen voice, 'Look – it isn't right that Cet gets to carve King Mac DaTho's boar.'

Cet looked up.

'Go 'way out of that!' he said with a huge sarcastic grin on his face. 'Listen to you and the mouth on you! Explain one thing to me, Leary, you headstrong dolt. How is it, Leary, that Ulster keeps on threatening to invade us in the west, you even come as far as the border, and yet when I go out to meet you – you give a sad little wave, and then you turn tail and head for home? The last time you even abandoned your chariot, leaving your charioteer to look after himself while you ran. And is that how you propose to stop me carving this?'

Another voice cut in, from a tall good-looking fair-haired warrior.

'I agree with Leary. Come on, Cet, why should you have been given this honour?'

'Who might this be?' asked Cet, as scornful as he had been of Leary.

'Aengus,' cried the Ulstermen, 'a great warrior.'

'I doubt it,' said Cet. 'I knew his father, I cut his hand off one afternoon when I was doing nothing else. I doubt whether his son could realistically challenge me.'

As Cet warmed to this theme his impatience grew. 'Right. Is there or isn't there a contest? Are you going to take me on or are you like all the Ulster breed, all talk? Otherwise I'll get on with the carving in earnest. I'm hungry.'

Another warrior offered himself.

'Who are you?' asked Cet.

'Owen of Fernmag.'

'Ah, listen to him,' said Cet, laughing so hard he broke down wheezing. 'I stole your cattle – off your own land. Look at you, you one-eyed simpleton. Tell them how you lost that eye. I'll tell them. When you challenged me I put a spear through your eye. That's how. And you want to lose the other eye now, is that it?'

When Owen sat down sheepishly, Cet asked. 'Any more, any others? Roll up, roll up, roll up.'

Three more came forward. Cet insulted and dismissed each one of them – he had either beheaded their colleagues or seriously damaged them and their relatives; sure enough they all had fingers or ears or eyes missing. Eventually, no more warriors came forward, so, to the huge enjoyment of his colleagues, Cet went on to drown the Ulstermen generally in contempt and abuse. When finally they were reduced to sullen embarrassment, he rose, in a heroic pose above the pig, ready to carve unchallenged.

The door crashed open. A shout echoed through the hall.

'Oi! Get yourself out of there!' And in burst the warrior Conall, one of Ulster's toughest men.

'What do you think you are doing, Cet? You may be the most brave and generous fighter, adept with spear or javelin, brilliant with sword or razor-shield, but you're not going to carve Mac DaTho's boar.' The Ulstermen cheered. Conall and Cet looked at each other and whooped in recognition of equals.

Cet's greeting also rang with admiration. 'Heart like a rock, passion of a mountain lion, eye clear as the glint of ice, a true champion who bears his many wounds – and he's going to get a few more shortly I can see – with such bravery.'

Conall's reply conveyed similar respect.

'Well, Cet, you who have the graceful bearing of a swan, the rage of the ocean, the fortitude of a bull. When we fight the world will know of it forever, will speak of these two lions whose fighting spirit and prowess becomes an example to all. Now – shift away from that boar, put down that carving-knife. What right do you have to wield it anyway? Here, give it to me, I'll carve if you don't mind.'

They could hardly be heard above the cheers of the Ulstermen; Mac DaTho and his wife sat wide-eyed at the honour of this august meeting between two such warriors actually taking place beneath their very own roof. Cet rebuffed Conall and elbowed him out of the way; Conall then made his declaration.

'Cet, since I first took formal arms as a registered and invested warrior of Ulster, not a single day has gone by without my killing one of your yellow-faced countrymen. Not a night has passed in which I did not sleep with the bloody head of a westerner dripping under my bed.'

'Then,' said Cet, beginning to have second thoughts, 'you might well be a better warrior than me. You're a nice man certainly. I'll tell you one thing though – if Hanlon were here you might change your tune.'

'Hanlon is here,' said Conall, reaching behind his back at the waist and hauling from the skull-bag at his belt the blood-spattered head of Hanlon.

'All right,' said Cet, looking uncomfortable, to say the least – the usual good colour had forsaken his face – 'sure, I'm not that partial to pork anyway,' and slowly retreated until he found the place where he had been sitting, and gingerly subsided.

As Conall began to carve Mac DaTho's boar, all of Ulster's warriors stood and cheered him. The men of Maeve and Ailill, though, began to throw things, bread at first, then little lumps of other food, then spoons, then goblets and finally arrows, so that the Ulstermen had to gather in a phalanx around Conall to protect him with their shields.

Conall, a huge grin across his hairy face, did great carving. According to custom, with a nod from his host Mac DaTho, and then his own king, Conor, he began to eat, to show them how it was done. First he leaned half-way across the table to take the boar's stomach in his mouth. Now it would have taken nine men to haul the carved meat from the belly, yet Conall chewed and sucked it dry in a matter of minutes. Laughing, with a gesture that smacked suspiciously of contempt, he handed the pig's front feet to the westerners as their share: *en route* he held them out in front of him as if they were his own paws and waggled them at the warriors.

They drew their swords and the fight began, on and off the table, rolling under it, overturning chairs, knocking the rushlights off the pillars, reeling and belting and sawing with blades. So much blood flowed that it swished into rivulets and ran down the sloping stone floor out into the passage-way, the fight flowing after it until warriors were locked in arms all over the hostel courtyard. Men were thrown into the fountains, hanged off railings and stakes, chased along battlements, they kicked each other and gouged each other and all done with a huge roistering enjoyment that left arms hanging on fences, eyes bouncing along the ground, ears flapping on the table, and bodies on the floor being licked by the castle dogs.

Speaking of dogs, Mac DaTho appeared, with his famous hound on a leash. The dog, a sleepy enough article, smelt the blood, perked up, looked around and opted for the Ulstermen, whom he then helped in their rout of the westerners. These fled, Cet included, and the hound followed them, biting off their horses' tails, chomping through their chariot shafts, taking the heels and ankles and feet, and sometimes buttocks, off their soldiers.

Out of the castle yard they raced, across the sward now slippery with blood, heading west to get away from this carnage. The dog, who seemed to grow larger with each bite he took – and he swallowed everything he bit – dealt out the most appalling damage. From the moment he saw a soldier he could not be fought off. He chased men and chariots and horses and showed no regard for age, rank or infirmity. This was the dog they had heard of, better than any army, and now he proved it.

The most dramatic moment came, however, when the hound attacked the chariot of Maeve and Ailill. Their charioteer, a noted hero, struck out and decapitated the animal, whose head got stuck on the chariot pole. Headless, the dog lolloped along beside the chariot for several yards. The charioteer whirled into the bushes and lay there in ambush for the pursuing Ulstermen. To attract their attention he kicked the hound's head, all blood and brains, into the middle of the road.

Next, Conor MacNessa's charioteer, in full flight, pulled up headlong in his tracks. But wasn't this the head of the hound they had all come for? At that moment the charioteer roared out of the bushes and blocked the king's chariot. By threats he 'persuaded' the king to give him a job back in Ulster at the court in Emhain Macha. He even got Conor – not difficult, he held a sword at his throat – to have someone tell the women of Ulster that he, the charioteer, must be hailed as their darling.

The charioteer spent the best year of his life at the Ulster court before going back to the west driving two of the king's horses, each wearing a golden bridle. And Mac DaTho and his wife lived on without anything else much happening to them – which was just as well, since they had eaten their famous boar and had lost their famous dog.

THE WOOING OF ETAIN

ar away and long ago there lived a magical king by name of Eochy. He had immense powers: like a god he controlled the weather and the seasons, the rain and the warmth, and could therefore guarantee how the crops grew and the size of the harvest – in consequence, it paid to keep in with him. Sometimes, though, Eochy did not use his powers in entirely admirable ways. For example, he coveted a woman, a somewhat remarkable creature, called Eithne, who lived near the famous burial shrine on the banks of the river Boyne. This woman had a husband, a chieftain called Elkmar, upon whom Eochy used his powers unscrupulously. To get him out of the way Elkmar was sent off on a military and diplomatic mission and then, to make sure he would not come home too early, Eochy removed from him any perception of time, morning, noon or night; he also took away Elkmar's appetite so that he could not regulate his life according to hunger and thirst.

Out of this seduction, Eochy and Eithne bred a son. They called him Aengus and, with great care and discretion, Eochy fostered the infant on another king, Midir. This transaction obviously had to be completed before Elkmar returned. Under Eochy's spell he had been gone nine months but thought it only a few hours – no day, no night, no meal times.

Anyone who observed the boy Aengus growing up could see that he came of an unusual and gifted parentage. Without effort he emerged as the natural leader of the other boys and girls fostered at Midir's palace. He had his vulnerabilities, though: one day his bright little world collapsed in tears and confusion when another boy taunted him with being a foundling. The child ran for comfort to the throne-room where Midir, of whom Aengus was a favourite, consoled the boy, calmed him down and the him with the truth of his lineage. Aengus, drying his displaying his inherent bravery, asked to meet his real father.

Midir, always one to follow the impulses of nature, took him to meet Eochy. The boy responded a little warily; not so the father – Eochy greeted the boy with warmth and delight and they began, in the custom of their society, to settle the boy's future. Lands had to be allotted, possessions, leadership to be acknowledged. Eochy then had to tell Aengus that his inheritance had not yet fallen vacant, that Elkmar, the husband of the boy's mother Eithne, still ruled that tract of land along the Boyne.

At this restriction Aengus kicked up a fuss, so Eochy taught the boy a trick to get control of Elkmar's territory.

'Pick your moment to visit Elkmar. If you catch him while he's watching the sports, he won't be carrying any arms. Threaten to kill him unless he lets you rule his land for a day and a night.'

It worked – Elkmar, caught on the hop, had no option. However, when he came to reclaim his lands, Aengus would not give them up. They called upon Eochy to settle this dispute; treacherous, this, as Aengus had already agreed the next stage of the proceedings with Eochy, who judged that since Elkmar had valued his life above his land, then he had forfeited his territorial rights. Eochy compensated Elkmar by giving him other lands of equal value, and thereby ensured that his natural son, Aengus, had obtained a kingdom of his own.

A year later, Midir called to see Aengus by the Boyne. At the very moment of his arrival a fierce quarrel broke out among the boys on the playing-fields, and, while trying to act as peacemaker, Midir was struck badly in the eye by a thorny branch. Aengus sent messengers to gather every great doctor in the province and managed to have the eye repaired fully. He then prevailed upon Midir to spend a year's recuperation with him, to which Midir agreed, on one condition – that he be rewarded with the most beautiful woman in the whole country.

Now, at that time too, there lived in Ireland a king called Ailill, a man of some renown, though not as wealthy or powerful as the kings of the Boyne. Ailill had a daughter called Etain, of whom everybody spoke – 'A princess by name and a princess by nature,' they said, and she had extraordinary beauty. Much talk of Etain went on in the courts of the Boyne, and, in the outcome of the debate, all the men decided that Etain fitted the description specified in Midir's reward. Aengus journeyed north to ask for her hand on behalf of Midir, but Etain's father refused. He said that if he allowed his daughter to go, and if they then treated her badly, he had neither the power nor the resources to avenge any such dishonour.

The discussion continued most courteously. Aengus began to offer money; Ailill began to bargain. He told Aengus that he would negotiate with him if Aengus would provide sufficient labour to drain twelve of Ailill's great bogs and to level twelve of Ailill's forests. Aengus agreed and by magic had it accomplished in one night. Next morning though, Ailill held out for more – this time he asked Aengus to change the course of twelve great rivers and turn them from his lands to the sea so that his moors could become arable.

'Done,' said Aengus, and it was.

Ailill had one more demand – Etain's weight in gold and silver. This completed the transactions for her hand, and so Etain, this girl of gracious birth whose radiant beauty and incomparable grace made her the fairest maiden in all the land, sat up on the horse behind Aengus and he rode away to bring her to Midir. Messengers raced ahead and by the time they arrived Midir had decked himself out splendidly. He had brushed out his long golden hair and put on his slim golden headband. Wearing his purple tunic he stood heroically at the gate of the castle holding a spear of pointed bronze and a large circular shield ornamented with jewels. His shining, grey eyes sparkled as he began the wooing of Etain.

How did they describe her? The poets had scarcely enough words. Eyes vivid as blossom, eyebrows as black as a beetle's shell, teeth like twin rows of pearls in her mouth. Her long hair, woven into tresses, had a little golden ball at the point of each strand. The skin of her cheek had the colour of the foxglove, her lips had the red of the rowanberry, each slender arm had the soft whiteness of snow. She had the high fluid neck of a swan and thighs smooth and white and silky as the foam of a wave.

Etain, too, fell in love at first sight. The very moment the welcoming feast had ended, the couple went to Midir's bed. On the following morning they set off back to Midir's country. The besotted man had given little clear thought to such an excursion; he seemed to forget completely that at home he had a wife, Queen Fuamnach. In fact, throughout this entire affair he never once gave any impression to anyone that he was already married. Fuamnach, not unexpectedly, roasted with jealousy when she saw them riding towards the castle, Etain's hands around Midir's waist. This jealousy increased a hundredfold when, closer at hand, she saw how beautiful Etain was and how Midir mooned over her.

Fuamnach pretended friendship, even encouraging Midir to take Etain on a tour of all his lands and possessions.

'Show them off,' she said, 'show them off to Etain.'

But by the time they got back to the house, Fuamnach had a spell ready. First she touched Etain with a gem-tipped wand, turning her into a pool of water which lay in Fuamnach's hands. Then she made the pool suck itself up into a spout which became a great maggot, and this in turn developed into a wonderful flying insect, a butterfly really, bright mauve and heliotrope in colour which grew to the size of a man's head, with eyes like jewels.

The beat of the Etain-insect's wings filled the air with lovely whirring music. And if the dust which powdered its wings cascaded down upon any sick human, then that person recovered immediately.

Midir, distraught, recognised the butterfly as his beloved and lovely Etain. Although his own magic could not draw her back to him in female form, he managed to have her fly alongside him always. However sad he felt, he derived some contentment from the presence of this beautiful purple creature who, in the air always just above and little to the right of his head, lulled him with her humming. Fuamnach, fearing Midir's wrath, had run from the castle when she saw the spell taking effect. Now, hearing of Midir's sadness rather than anger, she returned, and, when she saw how the king and the insect went everywhere together, she raised a jealous tempest which for seven years blew Etain the butterfly round and about the land-scape, anywhere but near Midir or his friends. Day and night, the wind did not abate for a moment, neither a lull nor a pall, and Etain never rested all this time, because the endless storm con-stantly prevented her from alighting on a tree or a hillock or a stone.

One day the storm unwittingly blew Etain on to the land of Aengus and altered her fortunes for the better. When she crashed against his cloak, Aengus, through his own magic, recognised the battered and bruised, but still lovely, purple butterfly as Etain. He took her into the safety of his house and concealed her within his warm and elegant chamber, where, in time, her spirits revived. His magic had an edge over that of Fuamnach, and unlike Midir, he was able to change Etain back to her womanly form, though only at night. Aengus fell in love with her as passionately as Midir had done, wooed her with an equal fervour and their nights were filled with music and love. Thus restored, the beautiful Etain spent from each sunset to each sunrise in the arms and bed of Aengus and in the morning she reverted to butterfly form.

This happy arrangement did not last long – Queen Fuamnach came driving through and once more her harsh gale blew like a cold white force and drove the beautiful insect out of the house. For a further seven years Etain endured buffeting up and down the land from mountain to glen, from valley to plain. At last the tempest drove her with unbearable force against the roof of a northern palace belonging to Etar the Hero – whose wife, a fecund woman, had at that moment raised a cup of honeymead to her lips. With an uncontrollable gulp, the woman swallowed the butterfly Etain, who then swam down into her womb where she changed form again, turning into a human. And so, a thousand and twelve years after her first birth, Etain was reborn, a mortal's child this time, but no less beautiful than the shy girl who had so obsessed Midir, then Aengus.

In the meantime Aengus, who had been on a visit to Midir when Fuamnach cast her second spell, returned. Learning that Etain had been driven out again by the same high wind, he pursued Fuamnach, killed her and bore her severed head, hanging from his saddle, back with him to the Boyne.

Etain, now the daughter of Etar the Hero, grew up alongside the girls and women of the palace. So distinguished did she become, and so remarkable in her beauty, that fifty chieftains had fostered their daughters there in order to have them reared near Etain, that they might have the privilege of attending her. She, with a natural grace, took it all in her stride and never allowed it to spoil her. Then one day, as they all bathed in the river-mouth, a warrior rode by, magnificently dressed, carrying a huge round silver shield which reflected the sun. His long yellow hair flowed freely except for the gold band that bound it to his forehead, and he carried a spear with five points. He stopped his high roan horse, looked with his dark eyes at the girls as they bathed, and then sang a song which both recognised and praised Etain. With the women and girls giggling, Etain finally acknowledged his tribute and he rode away, back to the court of his king, Eochy.

What he had seen enabled the warrior to bring good news. Eochy, now the most powerful king of all, not only wanted a queen for himself – he needed one, because his people wished him to secure the succession in their kingdom. For some time his envoys had roamed the land looking for a girl who would make a suitable queen. Now this warrior, a most trusted man, brought back word of Etain's beauty.

Eochy went to see for himself. He encountered Etain near the same water as she washed and combed out her hair with the girls of the court in attendance. In her right hand Etain held up a wide comb of bright silver decorated with gold. The silver bowl in which she washed her face had large ornamented handles in the shapes of four jewelled birds and round the rim flocked clusters of jewels thick as mushrooms. In her left hand she admired herself in a large oval mirror which, when she needed both hands, she hung on a tree.

With much gaiety the girls dressed her – in a bright purple cloak, beneath which they had put on another gown, white fringed with silver. An outer mantle had been drawn modestly closed at her breast with a long, golden jewelled pin. The entire ensemble was protected with a hooded tunic of a glossy green, red and gold embroidered brocade cloth. The men in King Eochy's party, gathered round him on their horses, gasped, whistled quietly and threw amazed looks at each other. Eochy said nothing for several minutes, then stunned by her great beauty, dismounted, walked over to her.

So began the wooing of Etain by which she became the queen of Tara. Their wedding, when Eochy crowned her and paid her the homage of a king to his queen, had never been equalled – not even, they said, among the gods.

Soon after, as so often happened in their complex society, trouble – of a passionate kind – arose. King Eochy's younger brother fell deeply in love with Etain from the moment he saw her as she walked into the long hall at Tara. From that instant he could do nothing further with his life except pine for her – and pine he did: he paled, he wasted; he even seemed as if he had chosen to die. The court doctor examined him and pronounced a diagnosis of two lethal pangs – love and jealousy. Nothing to be done: the young prince simply lay in his house, dying by the day.

Not long afterwards, Eochy had to undertake a tour of his kingdom – he had already delayed too long. None too happy he set out, and as he left he noticed, not for the first time, that Etain wept over her young brother-in-law's mysterious illness. Her anxiety took a different turn when she noticed that he seemed specifically to improve on those days she visited. She questioned him as to what had caused his terrible illness. He evaded her – fed her riddles and metaphors. She pressed. Finally his passion burst out of him like an explosion. He told her that his love for her had commandeered him completely, had poured over him like a wild flood-tide, and that now only one more thing would cure him, a night in her arms.

Etain, completely disconcerted, agreed, but only for the sake of the young man's recovery. Imagine her dilemma – she loved her husband, who loved his brother, who loved her, and all of equal passions: how could such a circle be broken? She decided to give the prince his dearest wish, though on condition of the greatest discretion, and they made an assignation well away from Tara. On the eve of their tryst, however, he fell into a coma from which he did not wake in time to meet Etain. He did not yet know it but he had fallen victim to a spell woven by the magical Midir who interposed himself in the young man's place and assumed his shape. In this guise he presented a deliberately sad, uninterested and cold attitude to Etain – who still thought she was seeing her young brother-in-law. This, not unexpectedly, reduced her ardour and concern. Altogether, this state of affairs happened three times and not once did Etain know that this shape, this young man in front of her, seemingly the young prince on whom she had taken pity, was being impersonated by Midir. Even though the true young man woke up from Midir's spell each night, he never did so in time to meet Etain out on the hillside and he never discovered what had been happening to him.

Eventually Midir revealed to Etain that he, Midir, had assumed her brother-in-law's shape for the purpose of meeting her. He told her of her history before she became the daughter of Etar the Hero. Midir outlined the story of Fuamnach's witchcraft, and the great seven-year gales and the large, humming, mauve-and-heliotrope butterfly. He told her of the great times a thousand and more years ago, when the beautiful Etain of those days also had the reputation of being the most wondrous beauty in all the land. He then revealed to Etain that he had cast this spell so that he, Midir, could make this approach. Finally he invited her to accompany him back to his palace, to fly with him to the Land of Youth, to everlasting life.

'Fair woman, will you travel by my side to a glorious country where music plays?' Midir had the gift of incomparable poetry. 'In that land the hair becomes as the petal of the primrose, and the body assumes the colour of snow. Sweet gentle streams flow through the countryside, there is honeymead and flowing wine; the people are incomparable and unblemished, love has no sin, no guilt. Woman, if you will come with me to meet my fine people, you shall have a crown of gold and myrtle upon your head, and honey, wines, ales, sweet new milk, beers, shall all be yours there, lovely woman.'

At first Etain refused to leave her palace, her people and her king: she did not know this stranger nor his family. Eventually she allowed herself to be talked into it, but only if her husband, Eochy, could be persuaded into letting her go. Midir smiled – and vanished.

One bright morning not long afterwards, a young and glamorous stranger, colourfully dressed, materialised by the side of King Eochy on the ramparts at Tara. Tucked under his arm he carried a silver board game with pieces made of gold and jewels. He introduced himself as Midir who had come to challenge the king's well-known skill at the game, an invitation that Eochy could not resist.

They declared stakes – fifty dappled horses fleet as deer and fifty enamelled bridles; from the first throw of the first game Eochy won. Next morning, galloping as a herd down the sward before the castle, the horses appeared. In the dust of their wake, Midir materialised again. They declared new stakes – fifty swords with golden hafts, fifty white cows and their fifty white calves, fifty gelded sheep, each wether with three horns, fifty daggers with ivory hilts, fifty flecked cloaks.

Eochy won them all with every throw of the game. But when his foster-father, a shrewd old chieftain who lived at the castle, saw these new riches, he warned Eochy to watch out – any man who could afford to gamble such possessions had great riches: great riches meant great power and Eochy should therefore tie him down with excessive forfeits or demanding labours. Eochy took the advice and when next Midir lost, Eochy, as payment, ordered him to cut down seven great forests, reclaim seven hundred acres of bogland and make seven causeways through them. Midir accomplished all of this in one day, and, no matter what major labours Eochy thereafter imposed on him, Midir achieved them all with brilliant swiftness.

Midir could see very well that he had been tricked into improving Eochy's kingdom. Concealing his anger, he threw one last game and, as the dice clattered and rolled, asked that the stakes be at the pleasure of the winner. Midir won and demanded to kiss Queen Etain on the mouth. The king, though disgruntled, pretended to agree and told Midir that a month hence he could collect his prize.

On the due day when Midir, more strikingly dressed than ever, arrived on the hill across the Boyne from Tara, he saw in the distance the enormous garrison Eochy had mustered to bar his entry. Still, it did not matter whether a thousand or a hundred thousand warriors had gathered – they could not match Midir's magic. Deep in the heart of the palace, as a great feast got under way with Etain serving the wine and Eochy thinking they were safe and secure, the guests, who had followed the board games all the way through, saw, to their amazement, Midir walking up through the middle of this banquet, gleaming in face and armour.

Midir took his weapons in his left hand and with his right he clasped Etain round the waist. Like birds they rose, above the tables – she even had to drop a wine flagon as she rose: it clattered on the table-top and then rolled to the floor. Through the little skylight in the roof of the palace they flew and outside the soldiers patrolling the ramparts saw, against the moon, a pair of swans. The swans circled once, then flew south to Slievenamon, the Mountain of the Women, through whose portals Midir and Etain entered Midir's own country, the Land of Youth.

Fury broke out at Tara. In the angry days that followed, Eochy's Druid finally waved three wands of yew, and traced Midir and Etain to Midir's palace. All royal business suspended, for nine years Eochy and his men laid siege but, as fast as they damaged Midir's castle, he repaired it with his magic. There came a day when Midir managed to persuade Eochy to cease hostilities. He appeared before Eochy and promised that he would restore Etain to Tara. Eochy accepted but immediately fifty women materialised, each single one of them identical to Etain. Eochy thought to test them by having each one pour wine, as he had long known that only Etain could pour wine perfectly. One of the women seemed to get it right, and despite some reservations he chose her – in any case she satisfied his honour. Much jubilation broke out when it transpired that the king had at last rescued his wife from the clutches of the faery host and, content enough, Eochy took this version of Etain back with him to Tara.

Midir, though, had not yet finished tormenting Eochy whom, by now, he had come to hate for the humiliations of the board game forfeits. He arrived in Tara one day – magically as usual – and informed Eochy that when she flew away with him that night, Etain had been carrying a child. Furthermore, this child, Eochy's very own daughter, had been the one chosen out of the fifty identical women by Eochy – so that the woman who now lived with him as his wife was, in fact, his daughter. To cap it all, Eochy's wife-daughter then bore a daughter. He found all of this unendurable, threw her out and told his men to take the child away to feed to the wild animals. The men left Eochy's child in the kennels of a house not far from Tara, whose owners had gone out for the day. When these good folk returned they rescued the little fair-haired girl and raised her well.

In time she, like her famous mother, grew beautiful, though human only. She even married a hero and bore him a hero, and thus began the breeding of a long line of Celtic champions. In this way, the legendary wooing of Etain, though once mischievous and magical, came to a profitable, if human, conclusion.

DEIRDRE AND THE SONS OF USNA

In the great times long ago, Phelim, son of Dall, held first rank as a storyteller at the court of King Conor MacNessa of Ulster. Phelim's rank gave him power and riches: few other bards had the nerve, status or permission to receive the king in their own homes and give a feast in his honour.

Now, throughout one such feast at Phelim Mac-Dall's, his pregnant wife moved among the guests, according to custom, pouring wine, calling servants to attend to the food, should a warrior want for anything. Very important people had gathered for this feast, not only the king himself, but his Chief Druid, Cathba, a number of visiting bards and many, many distinguished warriors, both resident and visiting. At the end of the evening, as Phelim's wife walked slowly down the centre of the banqueting-room, with all the wine now ceremonially poured, the child in her womb screamed. Everyone heard the cry – it echoed through the hall, an ear-piercing shriek which made the drinking cups ring in echo. The women gathered round her, thinking her time was due, and proceeded to escort her to the women's quarters. The men, disturbed by the eeriness of the cry, the like of which nobody had ever heard before, rose in agitation: they almost fought, so greatly did they feel disturbed, so much terror and unease did that strange, infant cry provoke. Gravely, the king asked Phelim – who agreed – that the wife should be invited back into the banqueting-hall for some interpretation of the cry's significance.

She, a noblewoman in her own right, spoke quietly, addressing her remarks, as decreed proper in the presence of the king, to the Chief Druid.

'I cannot find the fluent words to answer my husband's questions. All I can say is that no woman can assess the eventual nature of the child she carries in her womb.'

Everybody nodded, considering this an answer of suitable dignity and wisdom. The Druid called for silence and after some contemplation offered a prediction.

He began by describing the child which the wife of Phelim Mac-Dall would shortly bear. A girl of flaxen hair and eyes of grey and green, he said, with cheeks the colour of the foxglove and bright red lips. This child already screaming in the womb would become a woman of great beauty and invite the courtship of kings and the envy of queens. He foresaw great slaughter on her behalf, great controversy, which would split Ulster man against man.

'I will name her now,' continued the Druid. 'She will have the name of Deirdre and because her fame and looks will cause so much to be destroyed, and because all of Ulster will suffer owing to her beauty, we will end up calling her Deirdre of the Sorrows. On her account, three of Ulster's most glorious sons will be forced into exile. On her account, great misfortune will spread through this court and kingship. Families will divide and fall, warrior will turn upon charioteer, vows will be broken like rotten wood. Deirdre of the Sorrows will bring prolonged sorrow and bitterness to Ulster.'

His words fell like deadly missiles on the assembled company and thus, when the woman gave birth, many of the chieftains felt the baby girl should be slaughtered there and then. The women objected fiercely – try and take a cub from a she-wolf or a lamb from a ewe – and gathered round Phelim MacDall's wife, who bore all of this agony as graciously as anyone could while enduring the pangs of childbirth.

Ultimately King Conor intervened and resolved the problem – in an unusual way. He declared that he would prevent the predictions from coming true by personally taking charge of Deirdre, by seeing that while being reared she was kept out of trouble, and by then marrying her himself; under his control she could cause no havoc. The Druid looked doubtful, but realised that his king's divine assertions should not be questioned.

King Conor MacNessa kept his word – as far as he could. First of all he observed the tradition of fostering, and thereby bestowed a great honour on Phelim and his family. Rarely did the king foster anyone's child, and, when he did, only those of the most distinguished subjects. Secondly, he owned a remote castle deep in the woods to which he dispatched the infant. There she would be raised by a trusted retainer, a middle-aged nurse of great commonsense, called Lavarcham.

On good days, those with relaxed court duties, the king rode out to this demesne to see the child, Deirdre. And indeed she seemed to grow even more beautiful than the Druid had prophesied. Conor, by now no longer young, expressed satisfaction that his plan progressed so well. He even let it be known publicly that he could hardly wait until Deirdre came of marriageable age – by which time she would never, thanks to Conor's plans, have seen another man.

It did not work out like that. One winter's day an innocent event took place that changed the lives and fate of thousands. Below the ramparts on which Deirdre and Lavarcham had been standing enjoying the falling snowflakes, a servant killed a calf. Shortly afterwards a raven landed and pecked at the blood staining the snow. Deirdre called out to Lavarcham, with whom she had just been discussing men and her intended marriage to the king:

'Look at these colours. I love them. I wonder if men ever have such colours in their countenances – hair black as the raven, cheeks red with health, skin snow-white – or are they all like the king, grey and weary and wrinkled?'

Lavarcham sighed; as a woman with much experience of life she had often speculated whether a day might come when all Conor's plans would fall apart at the inevitable touch of human nature. Then – though she should not have said so – she declared that she knew just such a young man, by name of Naoise, who dwelt quite near. He and his two brothers, Ardan and Ainle, held cherished places as young warriors at King Conor MacNessa's court. The renowned Sons of Usna, they excelled at charioteering and ball-playing. Members of one of the three houses of Ulster's Knights, Lavarcham called them 'the strongest and most distinguished among the Knights of the Red Branch', and, as she said these words, she shivered: she had heard the Druid's prophecies – 'Three of Ulster's most glorious sons will be forced into exile'. She had stood in the court on that night years ago when the child screamed in the womb: 'Families will divide and fall,' the Druid had intoned, 'warrior will turn upon charioteer.'

Too late now – Lavarcham could not go back, and her words about Naoise and his brothers had cast the die. She tried to withdraw her words about the Sons of Usna, but Deirdre begged and begged. Eventually Lavarcham agreed to act as go-between – in truth she, both a practical and romantic woman, did not want her beloved Deirdre to be confined in marriage with any old man, king or otherwise. Her resistance broke a little further and then a little further again, and then toppled, and, in womanly conspiracy, arranged for Deirdre first to see Naoise, and then to meet him.

In the first stage of the plan, Deirdre disguised herself and sauntered past the ramparts on which Naoise was known to practise his singing. Those who had heard him said that his voice made the cows give more and richer milk, made the birds try harder to sing sweeter, made every mortal who heard it sit more tranquilly. As Deirdre walked by, Naoise stopped singing and looked at her. Sharp banter took place between them and suddenly Naoise recognised Deirdre as the famous recluse who, since birth, had been spoken for by the besotted old king. Tricky this, though the whispers round the court had long suggested that she would much prefer a young bull. In his own interests, therefore, he decided not to acknowledge her, nor she him. She strolled off and he began to sing again. Next day, though, Deirdre urgently dispatched Lavarcham to find Naoise.

By then the mutual flame had ignited – he, stunned by her beauty, she, captivated by what she had asked for, the white of the snow, the red of the blood, the blue-black of the raven, colours she saw in Naoise's face and hair. The young couple sat down, shaking with nerves and emotion, and began to talk. They exchanged little enough love-talk – the practical had to intervene. Both lovers anticipated King Conor MacNessa's anger; both, Naoise in particular, understood fully his power to express it.

In the upshot, Deirdre asked Naoise to take her safely away. He summoned his two brothers, and that night, hiding in a group of fifty men and fifty women and fifty beasts, the Sons of Usna smuggled Deirdre out of Ulster. They got a head start of several days before Conor discovered they had gone – at which point he drew together his crack troops, the best dogs, the fastest horses; then began one of the most famous pursuits in the history of Ireland.

For years Deirdre and the Sons of Usna lived the life of fugitives. Up and down the land they travelled, with Conor always in pursuit, permanently enraged at having lost his carefully tended prize. To this day, people will point out the places, under dolmens and high rocks, in deep woods and caves, where the lovers hid and slept. The brothers, expert hunters since boyhood, fed them all well off the wild, and, when the weather turned too harsh, they stole and roasted cattle. Many people took risks and hid them, sympathetic to the romance of the two beautiful young people fleeing an old and bitter man. Eventually though, Conor's knot tightened; the four, with just enough luck left to find a boat, fled to Scotland.

Life then improved immediately. The Sons of Usna, whose reputation had already been well known abroad, received appointments as honoured mercenary soldiers in the royal army. The King of Scotland, however, also saw Deirdre and fell for her – though in fairness she gave him no encouragement. He thought to win her by default – he gave the brothers ever more difficult and dangerous assignments, both to take them away from her whom they protected so diligently, and in the hope that they would be killed. They perceived his plans, discussed the situation and decided to flee again. They had already reconnoitred a remote and rocky glen that offered them more than shelter and fortification – it gave them a base from which they consolidated, and in due course they carved themselves a sliver of territorial power up and down the west of Scotland.

Through all these long years King Conor MacNessa remained baleful. He never recovered from losing Deirdre: hard to tell which hurt more – the loss, the sexual jealousy, or losing out to the young bull, Naoise. This fact, he knew, must have given amusement to many of the young warriors at his court. Conor brooded much of his life away in this fashion, figuring out revenge.

His chance came when the senior Ulstermen at his court came to him and argued that such great warriors as the Sons of Usna rightly belonged in Ulster. They should be at home serving their own people, not banished to a Scottish glen where, shame of shame, they might eventually die in exile. They insisted that Conor should pardon them, show his regal nobility and magnanimity. He appeared to concur and negotiations began.

At first the Ulster delegates could not even get near the three brothers, who had good reason to distrust anyone with an Ulster accent. Eventually, in formal talks they agreed to come home – in truth they longed to – and then they asked for specific, named guarantors. These included former colleagues, members of the Red Branch Knights, most prominently Fergus Mac Roy. He, who had assumed the leadership of the Red Branch, had a reputation for sincere speech and honesty, a man who honoured his obligations more diligently than any other knight in Ulster. Upon his word the Sons of Usna, and their beautiful charge Deirdre, could return in total safety. King Conor MacNessa, though, did not possess the same sincerity – he, no matter who gave the guarantees, still wanted

Deirdre, still wanted to exact the bloodiest revenge on the Sons of Usna.

All negotiations completed, all preparations made, all escorts arranged, the great morning broke when the four exiles stepped once more on the shore of Ulster and kissed the ground fervently. Back at the court in Emhain Macha, some of the Knights had prepared a brilliant welcome and the king, though inwardly seething, had made no attempt to stop it – it stood to his interest to permit the most natural of appearances. He had, in any case, hatched an imaginative plot which soon began to work. Fergus Mac Roy, as the chief guarantor and their oldest friend, had been there to greet the Sons of Usna: tears fell as they embraced. Then, along the triumphant way local chieftains, men of influence and power, began to put into practice the plot to which Conor had primed or bribed them.

One of the oldest bonds upon Fergus forbade him to refuse the hospitality of any chieftain through whose land he passed. Initially he led the party so fast that he could not be trapped under any such bond but one chieftain intercepted him and, carrying out Conor's treacherous wishes, obliged Fergus to dine with him. The Sons of Usna could not join in because, during the negotiations, though puzzled, they had agreed to the king's clause that the first food to their mouths in Ireland would come from Conor's own table. Foolishly they had taken this to mean some kind of public reparation.

Now the trap began to close. As Fergus went off to observe his bond and eat with the man who had invited him, they likewise observed theirs and abstained from food until they reached the court of Ulster. Thus their ways parted – though Fergus did appoint his sons to travel in his stead. And so without their major guarantor the Sons of Usna, Deirdre between them, rode on to the palace of King Conor MacNessa at Emhain Macha.

As they entered the last leg of the journey and slowed to a walk, Deirdre, who had always had qualms about King Conor's 'truce', recounted to her husband and his brothers her dream of the previous night. She had seen, she said, three birds flying from the direction of Conor's court with, in each of their beaks, a glistening drop of honey. They circled to drop the honey on the three sons of Usna, but, when it fell upon them, it turned to three drops of blood. Almost in tears she then interpreted the dream: the honeyed promises of Conor turning inevitably to the blood of the three brothers. Naoise consoled her with the reminder that no king in Ireland would dare break a promise given to Fergus Mac Roy. But as they rounded the edge of the escarpment and rode down towards the palace,

Deirdre's anxiety turned to horror when, in the air above Naoise's head, she saw a halo of dripping blood.

The travellers received a respectful though cautious welcome from the courtiers. Conor did not appear – his chamberlain brought word that an official reception would take place the following noon. By way of precaution, the four travellers initially refused the food of the king, saying they would eat when Fergus caught up with them; to pass this time they began to play chess. The king, brooding in his throne-room that night, sent for Lavarcham, ancient now, and asked her to investigate whether Deirdre had remained as beautiful as ever. Lavarcham, in floods of tears, embraced the woman she had nursed since infancy and had missed daily ever since. She bore out Deirdre's premonitions by saying that the castle gossip foretold treachery. To buy time for their escape, Lavarcham went back and told King Conor that, owing to flight and the rigours of exile, Deirdre had lost her looks but that Naoise and the brothers seemed fiercer than ever.

Conor, though, had sent a separate spy, a curious man with Norse blood by name of Trendhorn. By now the Sons of Usna had barricaded their quarters in the villa of the Red Branch Knights. Trendhorn climbed along the roof to get to the skylight. Deirdre saw him and screamed – Naoise threw a silver chess-piece upwards with such accuracy that it put out one of Trendhorn's eyes. He scrambled back and with blood streaming down one side of his face, told the king that Naoise with Deirdre more lovely than ever sat there as if they owned Ulster.

Morning came. The Sons of Usna, with a little protection from those Red Branch Knights who had made up their minds, went out on the sward before the palace. By now the rumours had spread and nobody believed any longer that Conor would hold a ceremonial welcome. Instead, the huge crowd anticipated a savage confrontation, to be heightened by Fergus arriving in fury at having been tricked. Working women in their brightest checks and plaids alongside noblewomen in their brocades lined the high earthen ramparts. Conor's household regiment had formed ranks in the open space when in walked Naoise and Deirdre, followed by Ardan and Ainle; their escort of the previous night, the sons of Fergus, brought up the rear. Standing in a row, they looked all around at the huge silent crowd arrayed in the sunlight. Suddenly Conor appeared, a small golden crown on his head, riding out from behind a high wooden partition. He signalled and soldiers seized Deirdre, tied her hands before her, and dragged her, as if she were an animal, to the king's side. Still no sign of Fergus Mac Roy. The king, in a loud voice, invoked the ancient vows of loyalty of the Red Branch Knights, who now fell back.

Eogan, an ally of Conor, led a platoon of warriors forward, somewhat tentatively. The sons of Fergus fought them off. For a while, owing to a general air of uncertainty, the fighting ceased. In the lull, Conor sent over a delegation offering huge gifts of land to Fergus's sons. Those immature young men were thus lured into breaking their father's bond.

This gave Eogan the opportunity he needed and he and his men attacked again. This time he hit Naoise with a spear which broke his back – the crack of his spine could be heard across the wide ground. As Naoise lay there dying, in full view of the crowds, his brothers were disarmed and then run down, from one end of the sward to the other and back again until at last they were slaughtered like pigs. As the last blow fell on the reddening neck of Ainle, and as he gave his last cry, hooves thundered up the crest – Fergus and his men. Conor wheeled and rode back into the palace dragging Deirdre with him; Fergus, seeing the bodies, screamed revenge and declared war upon Conor. There and then he killed Conor's son, and, as the prophecy at the house of Phelim MacDall had foretold, Ulstermen died in hundreds because of the child who cried out from her mother's womb. Fergus, though he fought magnificently, found himself eventually outnumbered and had to flee. He took three thousand men with him and made for the west where King Ailill and Queen Maeve welcomed and honoured a man of such prowess.

Deirdre's capture brought little good to King Conor MacNessa and Ulster, no joy and certainly no marital love. She simply hung her head and kept it low, a tear perpetually lighting her eye. Her old nurse Lavarcham died of shame, and now she, still a great beauty, came to acquire the name by which she would always be called – Deirdre of the Sorrows. She had never spoken to her gloating royal captor since the moment Conor had dragged her weeping away from the blood-sodden corpse of Naoise. Through the halls of the palace at Emhain Macha she chanted her lament for the Sons of Usna.

> The lions of the hill are gone,
> And I am left alone – alone –
> Dig the grave both wide and deep,
> For I am sick and fain would sleep!

> The falcons of the wood are flown,
> And I am left alone – alone –
> Dig the grave both deep and wide,
> And let us slumber side-by-side.
>
> The dragons of the rock are sleeping,
> Sleep that wakes not for our weeping:
> Dig the grave and make it ready
> Lay me on my true love's body.

She lived for a year and a day after her beloved husband's death until the morning when Conor, finally angered beyond endurance that his prize had so turned to dust, asked Deirdre what in life she most hated. She answered 'You – and that animal, Eogan, the one who killed Naoise.'

Straightaway, Conor, to pay her off for her bitter and aloof attitude to him, ordered his charioteer to drive Deirdre immediately to the house of Eogan. But *en route*, with a scream as loud and as eerie as the one with which she had first called from the womb, Deirdre flung herself from the speeding chariot and died instantly when her head struck a rock.

On the spot where she fell, the ground opened like an embrace to receive her. From this natural grave grew a great yew tree. Out across the wide countryside it spread until the twigs and limbs vigorously clasped those of another huge tree – the one that grew out of the grave of Naoise near the ramparts of Emhain Macha. To this day they have never been parted.

THE LOVE STORY OF DIARMAID AND GRAINNE

inn MacCool, the founder and leader of the Fianna, had grown surprisingly old; widowed, there were times when he looked as decrepit as a mortal. However, his wisdom remained sharp and profound and he must at least have felt young because he declared that he intended to take a bride again. After deliberation, consultation and much personal examination of many lovely women, he chose Grainne, the beautiful daughter of Cormac MacAirt, the High King at Tara. On the face of it he had made a good match, the wedding of a god to royalty, consistent with the demands of society, a great hero-hunter and warrior marrying the daughter of a king, knowledge breeding with beauty. He might have been better advised – in Grainne there resided a strain of restlessness that manifested itself on the very night of the wedding-feast.

While all the warriors, Finn's colleagues and his sons and lieutenants, sat around the table, Grainne, in two minds about Finn as a husband – but given no choice – asked her father's Druid why Finn had chosen her for his ageing self: surely she would have been better suited to one of his brilliant sons, such as Oisin? The Druid pointed out that once it had become known that Finn had fancied her, none of the Fianna would dare cross him, especially in such volatile matters as love and desire.

Grainne, more than a little longingly, continued – and quite openly – to scrutinise the men at table. She particularly admired one, a tall, strong young man with blue-black curling hair worn quite full at the back, and a healthy outdoor complexion, yet who managed to convey some of the studiousness of a man of thought. Grainne's eyes kept being particularly drawn to an unusual mark in the centre of his forehead; she had the impression that it somehow had a special, irresistible aura which she found exciting, daring. She mentioned this to the Druid – who, though he raised an eyebrow and said, 'Careful' – then told her how the young man, Diarmaid, got this 'love-spot'.

'He went out hunting one day with three of the Fianna, Conan, Oscar and Goll MacMorna, and they hunted all day. As night fell on the hillside, they came to a hut in which there lived an old man who had for company a girl, a wether and a cat. The warriors asked for shelter and were made welcome. Just as they sat down to dine, the sheep jumped on the table and began to prance about, up and down, kicking the plates and the goblets, an unmannerly display which annoyed the warriors and interfered with their digestion. One by one, each in turn, the four Fianna tried to pull the wether off the board, but, each time, the animal not only shook them off but trampled them and then baah-ed a long laugh at them. Most embarrassing! Finally the old man, giving the young warriors a look of contempt, told the cat to remove the sheep. The cat rose on its hind legs, collared the wether with one paw, led it quietly from the table and chained it up in its stall over in the corner of the hut – at which point the four champions got up from the floor and left the hut at the shame of it all.'

The Druid conveyed all this information to Grainne in a low voice, his face turned towards her lest anybody should hear – she, meanwhile, did not have enough discretion to stop staring at Diarmaid. The Druid continued with his story.

'As the warriors went out through the door into the darkness, the old man of the hut rose from his chair. He followed them and called them back, asking had they not understood that they had been involved with magic? He began to interpret for them what had just taken place, what it signified. The sheep they had been fighting represented the world itself, the force of Life, and the cat the contrary power, the power of Death, of Darkness. He then prevailed upon the four warriors to stay the night and led them to a large and beautiful room not evident from the outside shape or size of the hut, where four couches resplendent with furs and rich tapestries had been prepared for guests.

'The four men settled down for the night – at which point the girl who had been at table came into the room where, as she indicated, she also intended to sleep. She went to a fifth couch, the most prominent in the room, and provocatively got ready for sleep. Within the hour, one after another, the warriors rose and propositioned her. One after another she rejected them, and to their bewilderment said to each one, "No. I did belong to you once, but never again."

'Diarmaid, far and away the most handsome, took his turn last of all, and sat in all his power and strength beside her great couch. But where before she had been brazen with Goll, haughty with Oscar or mocking with Conan, now she wept a little and said, "Oh, Diarmaid, I cannot accept your love either, for once you were mine too, but no more, no more."

'Diarmaid said, "I don't understand. What do you mean – that I was once yours but I'm not any more?"

'She relented a little, saying, "Look, I am Youth. That is why I cannot have you again. But don't be so distressed. I will compensate you wonderfully." And she raised her fingers and put that mark you see on his forehead saying, "Any woman anywhere, ever, who sees this love mark will be unable to resist loving you or wanting you." Diarmaid went back to his own bed not sure whether this was a good or a bad thing that had just happened to him.'

And that was the end of tale the Druid told Grainne about the man whom she now clearly wanted – instead of her betrothed, Finn MacCool.

All the while Grainne had never taken her eyes off Diarmaid. When the Druid turned away to talk to someone else, she called over her most intimate handmaiden, and gave her instructions to prepare a sweet drink according to a secret recipe, which only they knew, for a sleeping-draught. It took a little while to prepare, especially in the abundance Grainne asked for, but eventually the servant brought it in and passed it round the table, offering it as Grainne's special contribution to the wedding-feast. Her father, the king, drank it; so did her betrothed, Finn.

All the guests and musicians and servants fell asleep, except five warriors to whom she had deliberately not given the drink – Finn's son Oisin, Oisin's son Oscar, then Goll MacMorna, Caoilte Mac-Ronan and finally Diarmaid himself. Grainne rose from among the slumped bodies, made her way to where they sat in the centre of the hall and formally requested each to be her lover. Each in turn, looking from one to the other, hesitated, then refused. They all knew full well that whoever accepted her would have one day to face Finn.

Grainne knew anyway that each man would refuse her – which is why she waited to approach Diarmaid last of all. By now completely unable to resist the love-mark on his forehead, she invoked, as she stood before him, the magical bonds that had long been the right of all their society, and which nobody, human or god, could resist.

'I am putting you under a bond,' said Grainne standing above him where he sat, 'that will oblige you to take me out of Tara tonight and carry me away with you.'

He replied, indicating his companions with a troubled gesture, 'Lady, this is a distressing bond, an evil bond – and you have obliged me to it in front of everybody here.'

Grainne said, 'Diarmaid, I have been in love with you ever since I saw you at the sporting matches here. I watched you from my window.'

He said, 'That's not my fault.'

She pressed on. 'Now I expect you, like a warrior and gentleman, to respond to my bond and take me from here.'

Diarmaid, who felt the trap closing on him, stalled. 'I can't. Finn has the key of the gate and nobody is free to leave without his knowledge.'

'There is a wicket-gate you can get to from my room.'

'It would not be fit,' said Diarmaid, 'for any warrior to sneak out through a woman's bedroom and then a wicket-gate. That would be a demeaning ploy.'

'Then, be a warrior as you wish. Any man of the Fianna can leap these ramparts, we are told. So do it – you can use your spear as a vaulting-pole.' She stalked away with her lady-in-waiting to prepare for the elopement she knew would now take place.

Diarmaid, in some desperation, appealed to the other warriors for help. They shifted, restless and disturbed, but ultimately they refused, because, as they saw it, he had no choice – Grainne's bonds had decided his immediate destiny. He told them of his dilemma: he loved Finn, did not want to steal his wife, did not want to leave the company of the Fianna where he belonged and where he was loved. In tears he left them where they sat at the feast, with everybody around still fast asleep, mouths open, heads thrown back or deep in their forearms down on the table amid the debris of the meal.

As they watched him go, Caoilte MacRonan, the fleetest of foot, Goll MacMorna the stoutest in battle, Oisin and Oscar, Finn's son and grandson, all turned sadly to each other speculating that they might never again encounter Diarmaid except at the end of a spear.

Out at the gate Diarmaid tried one last time. He implored Grainne to return, people were still asleep, he argued, this brief sojourn would not be detected, she had an honour and a duty to observe her betrothal to the great Finn. She dismissed his plea saying she had made her choice, she had thrown the net of her bond, and would now never be parted from Diarmaid except by death. She quenched every argument he put forward and he had no choice but to act on her wishes. They stole a chariot from the castle compound, released a pair of horses from the stable and, standing up in the chariot, his arm round her shoulder, cloaks flying in the wind, they raced out into the moonlit night.

The sky lightened with the dawn, and, with the crowing of the cocks on the ramparts, the musty, snoring banqueting-hall slowly shook itself. The Druid, first to wake, knew at a glance what had happened – should he wake Finn to tell him? Finn decided the matter by waking next. He did not need to be told – he looked around, then roared. That yell, mighty enough to wake everybody else, amounted to the only luxury Finn permitted his rage. Cold thereafter and in an ever-increasing fury, he began a meticulous plotting of the pursuit which, he told the Fianna, would last winter and summer, day and night, until such time as he had the lovers in captivity.

'They are to have no sleep, no comfort, no rest. Do not even allow them to finish any meal they have started.' Finn's voice rose higher. 'Every bush and cave, every hill, river-bank and tree-shade is to be searched through and through. Every rock will be climbed to have its hollow inspected, every oak tree shaken lest they hide in its leaves.'

All the hounds were called out, all the warriors fully armed and after a noontime meal – and raw meat to whet the dogs' appetites – the band of pursuers set off from Tara.

The lovers' head start had taken them far into the countryside. Diarmaid tried diligently to find a way out of the bonds Grainne had thrown over him. All such efforts failed. He then tried some damage limitation; he thought to mollify Finn by indicating that he had not, as yet, made love to Grainne. This he did by leaving messages in the form of symbols at each site they visited – a piece of bread unbroken, an intact salmon, a wine vessel full to the brim and clearly not touched, a broad piece of white linen unsoiled. Furthermore, he fully intended to keep the relationship on this celibate level but Grainne, as usual, had other thoughts. As they forded a river, the chariot wheels splashed her and she taunted him, 'Look, the water has more courage than you, the water is prepared to touch me even if you're not.' Diarmaid gave in.

They travelled hectically, barely ahead of their pursuers. Wherever they stopped to cook their food they could not stay to eat it, and wherever they stopped to eat they did not stay the night, and wherever they lay down for the night they did not remain until the morning.

The lovers sought out Angus, Diarmaid's foster-father, who cloaked them with his magical powers. One night, though, they almost got trapped. Finn, driving his warriors ever more furiously, came to the high palisade which Diarmaid had erected in a wood. To make escape as easy as possible he had inserted seven doors – at each, when Diarmaid awoke, stood one of Finn's guards.

While Angus hid Grainne under his cloak and, like a bird, flew her out over the fence and away, unseen, across the fields, Diarmaid approached the first door. He found it barred by the strong Goll MacMorna, for whom no man was a match. Diarmaid moved on. At the second door stood the fleet-footed Caoilte MacRonan, from whom Diarmaid knew he could not escape. At the third stood the father and son, Oisin and Oscar, and so on – each door insuperably blocked. And at the seventh door there stood old Finn himself.

'Who stands there?' Diarmaid called out, though he knew full well.

'Finn MacCool, your mortal enemy.'

'Then this is the door through which I choose to pass!' cried Diarmaid.

'Try it,' replied Finn, angling his spear.

Diarmaid, however, took his two spears, made them into a vaulting platform, sailed over the high fence and landed far beyond Finn and the other warriors, so far that he had a tremendous start. They failed to catch him and, in a distant wood, where he had arranged to meet Angus and Grainne, they enjoyed wild boar and honey cooked over a fire of heather branches. In celebration they all drank deeply, slept the night invisible under the protection of Angus's magic and woke at dawn much refreshed.

Angus said, 'I have to go now; I leave you with my prayers and my advice. If you want to escape Finn and the Fianna you must never flee to an island that has only one landing-stage, never enter a cave that has only one mouth, never hide in a tree that has only one trunk.'

With this advice always foremost in their minds, Diarmaid and Grainne travelled the length and breadth of Ireland for many seasons afterwards. They slept beneath the dolmens, those huge stone monuments which, to this day, will be pointed out as 'one of the beds of Diarmaid and Grainne'; they carved out heather couches in the hollows of the rocks; they wrapped themselves in bracken within the clearings of the woods; they lay in the cracked-earth, dried-up shallows of ox-bow lakes, hidden in the tall reeds with only the snipe and waterfowl to observe them. They ate berries and sweet plants and roots and nuts which Grainne plucked, and venison and trout and wildfowl killed by Diarmaid; they drank morning dew from the long stalks of grasses and plants and water from mountain streams that chilled the teeth and from springs in secret places in the corners of woods. And all the time Finn pursued. Sometimes he got so close they could see his band of warriors on a distant hill, their shields gleaming in the sunlight, as the lovers hid in the ferns and brambles, and the hounds bayed.

Sixteen years this pursuit lasted, sixteen long years while the spring came and blew its fresh winds to dry the damp woodlands, while the summer shone and burnt the corn to gold, while the autumn came and turned the ferns brown and dropped the fat hazel nuts into the pools, while the winter came and covered the earth with hard frost to break the clay and kill the old weeds.

During these years Diarmaid and Grainne had many adventures: they clashed with ogres and hid in hostile woods; they ran down mountains and swam in deep pools; they talked with old men or old women living in huts deep in the woods – people who gave them advice; they received cures from wizards, warm clothing from farmers' wives. Deer who ran with them helped them keep up their pace; birds flew alongside entertaining them, lightening their troubled minds; wild animals did not attack them, as if by arrangement; and time and again they hid in the rushes as the hounds of Finn came hurtling past; so closely did the party often pass by, they could see the sweaty frowns on the foreheads of their pursuers. Sixteen years of this, sixteen years – the lovers never caught, Finn never relenting.

Eventually Angus intervened and so did Grainne's father, the High King. These diplomatic men led Diarmaid and Finn towards peace of a kind. Finn agreed to call off the pursuit, Diarmaid agreed not to flaunt his beautiful wife. He returned to Tara, where his relieved former companions, who had never relished pursuing him, embraced him and gave the pair a discreet dinner. Then, from the High King's own hands, Diarmaid received the title to his ancestral lands where he and Grainne lived in love and splendour for many years, procreating many children, farming flocks and herds, mining gold and silver.

Grainne, though, remained unsatisfied, as if the business felt unfinished. Her provocative nature required more than a practical solution. At her bidding, therefore, her father, the High King, gave Finn another of his daughters, and to honour this betrothal a year-long feast began at Tara. As the year drew to an end, Diarmaid, asleep in bed with Grainne by his side, awoke at the cry of a hound. Grainne hushed him, told him it was nothing but a faery dream. Again the hound bayed, again Diarmaid jumped. Three times in all it occurred, and Diarmaid saw in it a sign that he should rise and go where the baying of the hound led him. In the light of dawn it drew him to the west where, on the magic table mountain of Ben Bulben in Sligo, the Fianna had gathered to hunt a wild boar.

Now during Diarmaid's young childhood his mother, the queen, had borne another son, fathered by her husband's steward. Never reconciled to this infidelity, the father one day caught this child, Diarmaid's half-brother, and, in a rage, dashed him fiercely to the ground. The child did not die but, in bad magic, turned into a boar with no ears and no tail: a large, wild and magical animal. This creature dedicated his whole life to the eventual killing of his half-sibling Diarmaid, upon whom he blamed his own violent fate. On the other hand, as protection, the Druids had placed on Diarmaid a magic bond that prevented him from ever hunting boar. Yet here was Diarmaid joining a hunt with his spear and his own dogs – Grainne must have interfered with the bond in some way. Worse still, this particular boar, roused from its bed in a cave-mouth by the hounds of the Fianna, was the deadly half-brother.

From the side of Ben Bulben, Finn watched every step of Diarmaid's approach. Whatever the diplomatic niceties, Finn had never stopped hating Diarmaid for, as he saw it, abducting Grainne. Now he provoked Diarmaid. First he taunted him with the Druids' bond, how it had made Diarmaid afraid of hunting boar. Then he said that the hunt had taken a very dangerous turn, and that therefore Diarmaid should not get involved, this being work for real hunters. Incensed, Diarmaid made ready to hunt.

The boar roared from cover. From his sling Diarmaid let fly with a marble stone straight to the middle of the boar's brow. Though a perfect shot, and, in any other hunt, a killer, the animal still came pounding on. Diarmaid next unslipped his best hound, but the dog fled in the opposite direction. Diarmaid unslung his famous spear and standing firm, legs apart, arms raised in the classical manner of the Fianna, he threw the spear. It bounced off the hide of the boar who now impaled Diarmaid's other arm on his tusks.

The boar's momentum carried Diarmaid backwards, bouncing along the hard stony ground. Diarmaid managed to swing himself up on the boar's back and draw his sword. As the boar dragged him down again, shaking him loose and then tusking the warrior's stomach until his bowels burst open, Diarmaid drove the sword deep into the boar's throat. The enchanted animal, without ears or tail since the dreaded spell cast on the unfortunate infant, regained its human form as Diarmaid's half-brother and died.

The Fianna gathered around, standing above Diarmaid trying to shade him from the hot sun. They looked to Finn, as they always did when a member of the Fianna suffered grave wounds. Many years ago, when he tasted the Salmon of Knowledge, Finn had been given the gift of saving life; this he accomplished by drawing water in his hands from a spring well. But would he do it for Diarmaid?

Finn bent down. In a low voice so that nobody else could hear he sneered. 'Good to see you reduced to this, Diarmaid. A pity all the women of Ireland couldn't have a look at you. Where's your great beauty now? You're ageing by the second. There's blood oozing from your famous love mark. Look at you – handsome one.'

Diarmaid replied by reciting to Finn a list of all the favours Finn owed him – for excellent days in the old times hunting out on the mountains, for battles fought and won, for backs protected when hostile tribes attacked the Fianna, for the saving of his life when Finn suffered treachery at a banquet. It reduced Finn to silence.

Diarmaid then said, 'Finn, you alone can save me. Your gift – of saving life, the water, in your own hands, from a spring well.'

Finn grinned a dry grin, that only Diarmaid could see. He said aloud, 'Alas, there are no spring wells near here.'

The Fianna and Diarmaid corrected him, pointed to a spring well nine yards away. Finn shrugged and strolled over to it reluctantly, cupped his hands and filled them. On the way back, as he neared where Diarmaid lay on the ground, he thought of Grainne. He stumbled and the water spilled.

To a man the Fianna yelled, reminding Finn of how loyally Diarmaid had served him in the old days. Finn went back to the well, cupped his hands again and returned. Again he thought of the many years of envy and pursuit, again his hands opened and the water slopped through. On the third trip he managed to bring the water unspilt to the very spot where Diarmaid lay, even though a little had already begun to trickle through his hands. Too late: Diarmaid died as Finn bent down towards his face.

The heartbroken Fianna recaptured Diarmaid's hound and leashed him. They laid the dead warrior on their shields, wrapped in their cloaks, and they marched him back to the palace singing their renowned funeral chant. Grainne heard the dirge as it floated towards her on the wind. She walked out beyond the castle walls to meet them, greeted the corpse with wild howls and fainted. Oisin revived her, handed her the leash of Diarmaid's hound and they paraded the gashed body into the great hall. Angus, Diarmaid's magical foster-father, already waited there, and, as the body was borne in, he and his followers raised three terrible shouts. The women of the court came forward to wash the corpse with sweetened water and wrap it in linen but Angus's soldiers, unimpeded in their magic, strapped Diarmaid to a gold bier of their own and carried him away out across the skies to the west. Grainne then mourned in seclusion for many years.

Finn came to see Grainne when custom deemed her to have finished grieving. This time he formally claimed her for his own, calling upon all the stature at his command. She spurned him, reminding him of his failure to give Diarmaid the saving drink of water. He persisted, this time abandoning the formality and using all his gifts of sweetness and magic, until at last she gave in.

She dressed in her finest robes of purple, red brocade and white linen bordered with saffron and Finn took her back to his home. At their arrival, the warriors of the Fianna set up a mocking chant – as far as they were concerned Grainne still belonged to their dead comrade Diarmaid. Nevertheless, after a haranguing from Finn, an entreaty from Grainne – 'Diarmaid would want you to treat me well' – and a conference among themselves, they accepted the couple.

As a last word on the subject they murmured a warning to Finn.

'Keep Grainne locked up safely out of sight in case she bewitches any more men.'

And he did.

OISIN AND THE LAND OF YOUTH

estwards over the sea there lay a realm of glory. The exact geographical position has never been determined – somewhere in the direction of the Azores perhaps, a skyline so bewitchingly clear on occasion that men set sail futilely to find this eternal place. Some called it Atlantis, the lost city which every seven years had permission from Manannan MacLir, the god of the sea, to raise its gilded towers above the waves; some called it Hy-Brasil, the Isle of the Blest, and when Spanish sailors pursued this Isle as it lay ahead, always ahead, the land they eventually reached, they named Brazil.

Tir na n-Og, the Land of the Young, was as sweet as Elysium, as vivid as Nirvana, as desirable as Valhalla, as green and sunny as Eden. All souls aimed to gain this eternal heaven and every time one of the Atlantic waves, the 'white horses', folded over on to the shore of the Land of the Young, another spirit received permission to enter.

In Ireland, Finn MacCool had a beloved son, Oisin, whose name meant 'young deer', or 'little fawn'. To join the Fianna, Finn's élite hunter-warrior band, a young man had to run like the wind – Oisin ran fastest of all. All had to leap a spar set at the height of their foreheads – Oisin leaped highest of all. All had to run silently through a wood, without touching a leaf or rustling a twig – Oisin had the lightest step of all, lighter than starlight. All had to possess the gift of poetry: Oisin wrote the finest verses of all.

One morning the Fianna's hunt took them to the shores of Loch Lene in the mountains of Kerry, a long lake where heather and lavender grew among the mottled white rocks at the waterside. Mist lingered as the big hounds put up a stag and followed him into the edge of the thick woods. The fastnesses of the mountains rang to their shouts and the ringing of spear upon shield. There they lost him; later they saw the stag again, high above them, out on a spur of rock. As they rode back in ones and twos along the lakeshore to congregate and discuss the next chase, Finn, who had an extraordinary gift of hearing, turned in his saddle and said, 'Listen? A horse with silver shoes?'

Galloping towards them, on the surface of the rippling lake, came a woman rider of great skill, and, indeed, her white horse did have silver shoes. She sat very high, a small woman, a slight frame, leaning a little forward and holding the leather reins in both hands; the horse, though a huge creature, did not seem one jot too large for her.

All the Fianna turned to behold this stranger. They marvelled at her magic, riding over water, and then quickly admired her skill, commenting among themselves on the surefootedness of her horse, and her excellent handling of the animal as she left the water and then as smoothly rode across this uneven ground. When she drew close to them she spoke to the horse who immediately slowed down to a canter, then to a trot, then to a smart walk.

Her clothing brought a flash of bright colour to the drab lakeside. She wore a silk mantle of dark red, lit with stars of bright, red gold, the borders of her cloak embroidered with gem-studded flowers and honey-bees. A small white crown sat forward on her high mane of deep red hair, a golden plume nodded on her horse's head above the bridle. Her cloak had been gathered up for horse-riding, revealing small black boots of shiny leather, fastened along her calf with crossed thongs. Her small face with sallow skin and dark eyes did not seem like those of an Irishwoman. A large white bird, soaring high above, seemed to follow this rider from a distance.

She reined in and with a deep bow of her head acknowledged Finn with all the respect due to his stature. He, puzzled but courteous, returned her greeting with a big outgoing gesture of his hand, and said,

'Welcome madam, to this wild place; although we do not belong in this locality, and our homes are far away, may we offer you our hospitality?'

She thanked him but declined with such grace that it seemed as if she had accepted:

'I have heard of your fame, of your speed in pursuit of the stag, of your two mighty hounds, Bran and Sceolaing. I have heard of your great powers of thought, and your wisdom tooth, and your power to know so much that is happening in the world.'

Finn said, 'What do you want of me? Ask and I must do what I can, though I must know your name and your origins, so that my wisdom may never assist an evil purpose.'

The horsewoman replied, 'My name is Niav Cinn-Oir, Niav of the Golden Hair, and I have ridden to meet you because I want something from you.'

'Speak and I shall give it to you if I possess it, and, if not, I shall get it for you.'

'You have it but you do not possess it. It is yours but you cannot get it,' replied the rider with the Golden Hair.

'Am I to solve your riddle, or do your countrymen always speak in such fashion?'

'No. To the contrary. I wished to show courtesy to your people's love of word games, though what I say is also true. I want, not you, but your son, Oisin.'

Finn turned to look at his son who sat a little behind, his eyes fixed upon this extraordinary young woman. He looked back at the stranger, saw that she seemed quite calm, and asked her, 'Where have you come from?'

She sat forward on her horse, and with a look that took in all the members of the Fianna, began to speak in verse.

> Beyond all dreams my land delights
> Fairer than any eyes have seen,
> All year round, the fruits hang bright
> As the flowers bloom in the meadows green.
>
> Wild honey drips from the forest's trees,
> We have endless stocks of mead and wine.
> No illness comes from across the seas,
> Nor death, nor pain, nor sad decline.
>
> No boredom comes to feast or chase,
> The music plays as the champions sport,
> The light and splendours all increase
> Each day in the golden Land of Youth.

She chanted the rhymes, in a powerful and commanding singsong voice, never taking her eyes off Oisin's face, fixing his green eyes with her look of peace and power. She had caused a trance of sorts to fall among the Fianna and had worked some magic with the air about them; the lakeside fell still, not a sound was heard, not the lapping of water, not the shake of a horse's head, or a whinny, not the rattle of a bridle, not a hound's cough.

She stopped her chanting, and addressing Oisin directly said, 'In the Land of the Young, Tir na n-Og, my father's kingdom, you shall have horses that can run faster than the wind and hounds that can outrun the horses. My father will give you a hundred warriors and huntsmen, each one a chieftain, to do your bidding. I will give you a hundred maidens to sing you to sleep in my arms. You will carry a sword that will always save your life against enemy or wild beast. You will wear a slim gold crown to show your sovereignty over my land and myself. The Land of the Young shall be your kingdom and I shall be your loving queen.'

She turned to Finn, who had never been rendered speechless before, and said with a sad note on her voice, 'For seven years and seven days I have been searching for your son, the young deer. I first saw him when my father and I rode over this land. Your son ran like the deer through the meadows of the morning, a warrior and huntsman through and through. We watched him carefully from a little distance, we were invisible in your land. I fell in love with him, with his strong limbs and singing voice, and only now, having ridden here many times to see him, has my father given me permission to become visible, and ask you for Oisin.'

Finn said, 'Your riddle was correct, Princess of the Young; he is mine but he is not mine to give. He is my son but I do not possess him.'

'And how am I to marry him?'

'You must ask him.'

She turned to Oisin. 'Will you come with me to my father's country?'

He, who had not yet spoken a word, said, 'Lady, I will, and until the world ends.'

He manoeuvred his horse to where her white charger stood, climbed across behind her and put his arms around her waist. She clasped a hand over his joined hands, with her other hand shook the leather thongs which reined her horse; the bell in the horse's golden plume tinkled as they turned away and galloped down the lakeshore in the direction of the woods. Light followed them as the morning mist cleared; the hounds by Finn's side whined and growled and shivered; Oisin's riderless horse moaned and shook his bridle as the two young people, without a backward glance, rode across the lake water, in a flurry of spray and out of sight. The beam of light disappeared and the morning damp returned.

The lake was connected to the sea by means of a long wide river, which, for part of the way, flowed steeply downhill between drooping willows and thickets of beech. As the woods grew thicker, the sunlight occasionally shafted through the trees and lit a glade a little way in from the bank. The horse galloped like the wind, even Oisin had to gasp in wonder at the power of the animal and its surefootedness. Swans and wildfowl flew out of the way as the horse raced downstream, leaping over a high weir and landing softly on the waters below. They passed by some people, a man, two children and an elderly woman, in a large coracle being rowed downriver, hugging the bank. The people did not look up; they showed no sign of having seen the riders. Oisin, Niav and their horse had now become invisible.

Past a gathering of huts they rode, where smoke rose from the thatch. The children, throwing leaves on the water, playing some game or other, stopped for a moment in wonder, and ducks quacked busily and left the river in a flurry – only the young and the creatures of the natural world could see and hear the horse bound for the Land of Youth.

The river broadened, the banks on either side grew less wooded; wide cornfields, heavy with yellow grain, came into view. Soon, cliffs appeared on either side, earthen ramparts to begin with, then rockier, sprinkled with white flowers, and in the air the smell of sea; on a headland to their left a great stone fort with sentries standing on the walls, looking out over the waves to the west. Where the river flowed into the sea a small boat rocked on the merging currents, and ahead of them spread the ocean.

The sun shone down, much hotter. As Oisin looked back at the receding hills, a sea-mist enclosed them as if in a pocket – except overhead, where the sun shone straight through. In this mist he could just sense the black-blue spray kicked up by the silver horseshoes; Niav sat absolutely rigid, leaning forward, still clasping firmly Oisin's hands joined round her waist.

In the sea-mist things occurred or appeared, suddenly, and without warning, and then they disappeared again. A deer pursued by a swift-running black bear sped by: Oisin half-turned as if he might hunt both – a tap on the back of his hand from Niav reclaimed his attention. To their left appeared a large castle keep, with a high tower, from which long pennants fluttered. A riding-party passed slowly by; on the leading horse sat a girl, very stately, very correct, upright, looking ahead in a regal fashion. She wore a deep saffron robe of satin and in her hand she held a large golden apple, as a queen might hold an orb; behind her, at a respectful distance, rode two young men and an older, white-haired one. One of the men, the furthest forward, had a gold sword on his hip, and a short white cloak; the other a silver sword and a short black cloak – the older man, tall and wise-looking, bringing up the rear, held a casket before him, resting on the pommel of his saddle. They too rode on the water, all on chestnut horses, except the woman – she sat astride a black horse. Another deer appeared, this time pursued by a hound with one red ear, the other white. As if she sensed that Oisin was about to enquire into the meaning of these apparitions, Niav called out, 'Do not ask. Prepare yourself for the Land of Youth.'

She raised a hand, the mist cleared and directly ahead of him he saw the beaches of a country, white sands sloping up to high brown dunes, so high he could not see what lay beyond them. On the beach a party of horsemen waited, and as Niav and Oisin rode from the surf on to the sand, the riders drew in alongside wordlessly with tranquil, settled faces which never stopped smiling. All wore white and gold, some many jewels, others none at all, save a ring or a great brooch. Their leader bore on his left arm a small oval shield made of gold and bronze, with inlaid glass and gems, which caught the sunlight and flashed slivers of reflected light along the sloping sands.

As they rode up the slope, the land revealed itself. In the distance a huge bright castle, more broad than tall, rose immediately in front of a hill of the most vivid green grass. It seemed to have only two levels, no high towers – a vast circular building, a fort of the type they had seen on the headland as they entered the ocean. Silk banners of seven colours flowed down the sides of these vast walls. Oisin realised that these colours, billowing down in long fat streamers from the roof to the ground, came from the rainbow.

Set in the centre of the castle, which was reached by a long ceremonial avenue with flowering trees, stood a huge wooden door with twin gold panels which, like the shield of the riding-party leader, caught the sunlight. A large crowd had drawn up in front of the building and the people strolled or sat on the ground without hurry or care. The riding-party stopped on the crest of a small hill. Niav turned to Oisin and said, 'Those are the people who will become your subjects once your foot touches that green sward in front of my father's castle. This will be the country over which you will rule. The crops do not fail, the rains fall only when asked for, the land is always luscious and fruitful and pleasant. You may make of it what you will.'

Oisin asked, 'Are there no conditions?'

Niav replied, 'Yes. Once your foot touches that sward you can never go back to old times. You will cease to age, and those years will never catch up with you as long as you are in the Land of Eternal Youth, Tir na n-Og. But should you ever leave, either with or without my blessing, I would be no longer empowered to hold you under the Guardianship of Youth. Then all the years of the country you have just left – and remember you have no knowledge of how many will have passed – will fall upon your shoulders like trees in a forest landslide.'

He shivered, and she went on, 'Now, though, look at your land, this kingdom that will be yours. Cast your eyes upon it and then tell me if you have ever seen a more beautiful country.'

To his left stretched a cherry orchard. As far as the eye could see, weighed down with fat, red-black cherries, rows and rows of trees radiated, in neatly kept avenues. Among them, in an air of contentment and with much laughter, pickers worked in pairs or family groups, placing the cherries in large baskets on the ground into which they had folded layers of white linen cloths. On the other side of the roadway, a similar harvesting took place in a peach orchard. To Oisin's right hand an orchard of oranges gleamed in the sunlight, and across from it a vast orchard of lemons. All these orchards stretched as far and wide as the avenues of cherry trees.

Oisin asked Niav, 'How many such orchards are there in this country?'

'As many as you will need. And the fruits never die, nor suffer disease, and, when plucked, are immediately replaced on the bough.'

Then, pointing to the east, he asked, 'What lies over there, beyond those hills?'

Niav replied, 'The farms of the country, where the people live.'

'What do they farm?'

'Dreams.'

'What lies over there, beyond those mountains?' – pointing to the west, to a range of purple peaks, where rivers tumbled down.

'That is the Land of Silence, where people may go to contemplate the wonder of existence.'

'Who goes to the Land of Silence?'

'Anyone may go who has agreed that silence has an importance, even though such agreement does not in any way take from the gaiety and love of the rest of the kingdom.'

'What happens in the Land of Silence? What is it like there?'

'Nothing happens; all is still and sweet, people may sit with their eyes downcast and if they do they will see that the surface of the earth is inlaid with brightness and shade, with colour and darkness. Their lives may flow before them and they may contemplate the world in a peaceful way. Their thoughts will not be intruded upon and their souls will be cherished by all in a way which reflects the silence they have chosen. If they choose to look up, they will find that the air is full of colour and pattern, pleasing to the eye and stimulating to the mind.'

Oisin asked, 'How long may one stay in the Land of Silence?'

Niav replied, 'There is no time here, you must understand that, no sense of time – at all. When you wish it to be day, with the sharpness and early warmth and clear light of morning, then it is morning for you. When you desire the hot stillness of late afternoon, when small creatures rustle in the undergrowth, then so it becomes. When you long for the life of the night, the velvet of the dark and the silver of the stars, then the night falls. Each person in this land has his or her own time and no other. And it is like that for everyone.'

'How big is this Land of the Young?'

'As big as you wish it to be. Bigger than the ocean, as small as a forest clearing. Bigger than the sky, as contained as the home of ants beneath a stone.'

As they drew near the great castle, striped tents had been arranged on the lawn; bears danced, musicians played short bulging pipes; friendly bright birds, each the height of a youth, stalked among the people. The sound of trumpets, sweet and thrilling, filled the air, and Oisin said to Niav, 'We have arrived during a festival.'

'No. They have gathered to greet you, their new prince.' The smiling riding-party, under orders from the fine young warrior with the bright shield, fell behind, taking up a position behind Niav's horse, so that she led the way down a small hill on to the ceremonial avenue. As they rode, children came forward and cast flowers beneath their feet, and the silver shoes of the horse made no noise upon the ground. Everyone smiled; the children, the young men in their bright colours, the young women in their fluttering silks, the old people.

They crossed a long glittering drawbridge of solid silver, over water on which floated black and white swans. Under an archway they went, beneath the billowing rainbow banners, between the

white walls which, when looked at closely, had been made of a stone
dotted with gleaming nuggets of schist. They came into a courtyard
where, on a horse, sat an old man to whom Niav bore a striking
resemblance. She greeted him with great love and respect.

'Father, I have come back with my prize – with Oisin the deer.'

The king nodded. 'Straightaway we must introduce him,' he said,
then rode out of the courtyard, through the gate they had just
entered, over the silver drawbridge, and reined in on a height
overlooking the festivities. Trumpets sounded and the people came
forward, standing back a little, all smiling. They stood on the grass
and the king dismounted. He turned to the people and said, 'Today,
you have gained a new prince. My beloved daughter, Niav Cinn-Oir,
has come back from across the oceans with the great hunter, the
mighty warrior-poet she has desired. As soon as he puts his feet on
this sward he will become the Lord of the Land of the Young.' As
if to complete the young poet's disconnection from Ireland and that
world over there, he did not mention Oisin's name.

Niav, still in the saddle of her great white horse, turned to Oisin,
looked him straight in the eye, and said, 'As soon as your feet touch
that sward you will become ruler of this land. You will hunt and
you will sport and you shall have chieftains as your warriors, and
your verses will be applauded as if they were music – but all of these
things may only be carried on in this country.'

Oisin tossed his head. 'I gave you my word that I would come
here. I am a warrior of the Fianna. I will become the Lord of the
Land of the Young and you will become my wife, but I will always
be Oisin, the poet and warrior and hunter who rode the hills
and the lakeshores and the great plains with my father and our
companions. Nothing can ever change that.' Before Niav could say
another word he dismounted, leaping lightly to the ground.

As his feet touched the grass, the onlookers saw how he changed.
His complexion darkened a little; now he had the same kind of skin
as Niav. The furrow in his brow disappeared; he grew younger, his
hair lightened and became abundant, curling as they watched. His
broad shoulders widened even further, he gained in stature and a
light seemed to emanate from him.

He had been wearing hunting clothes, a tunic of a rough weave,
a short wool cloak over it and strong leather sandals cross-thonged
almost up to the knee. All of these changed too. The tunic became
a vivid blue made of strong silk, with damask patterns; the cloak a
light wool of bright saffron; the clip he had used to hold his cloak
at the neck a brooch of bronze and gold, with an emerald in the

centre; his sandals shoes of kid leather, inlaid with panels of gold at the toes and heels.

The crowd, growing larger all the time, began to cheer. The king embraced the young warrior, who then turned to help Niav from her horse. She, for the first time since Oisin had met her, began to smile. They kissed and stood alongside the king acknowledging the applause. A child, an expert tumbler, careened across the grass in front of them, straightened up, bowed, and ran off. The trumpeters blew and the king told the people to prepare a great feast.

Niav and Oisin walked back together over the sward, over the silver drawbridge, into the castle. The young man who had led the riding-party came over to them, still bearing his shield.

He said to Oisin, 'I am to be your officer. I am to take care that all your wishes are met, that all your demands are fulfilled. When you have rested we will go to the stables, down by the river, and choose your horse; then the armoury where they have finished the forging of your sword and the pointing of your spear; then the wardrobe which one hundred women have sewn for you; then the instrument of your musical desire – whatever you choose, the strings will be of the finest gold, woven as fine as the threads of a spider's web, each one as strong as the edge of your sword.'

The couple walked into the vast hall of the castle where great myriad rugs of brightly coloured plaid had been thrown on the stone floors. As they reached the great staircase, Niav said, 'After our wedding today, my father the king will go to the Land of Silence. For some time he has wanted to go there, but his duties towards his subjects have not allowed him to go. You and I will reign in his absence – and now we marry.'

At the top of the stairs they parted. Servants waited to take Oisin along a stone corridor to large chambers. He was shown into a great room in which a bath steamed. All withdrew except one old and smiling woman with an exceptional face, who poured more hot water into the stone bath when Oisin gestured.

He asked her, 'Why does everybody in the Land of the Young smile all the time?'

She replied, her smile growing sweeter, 'Why not?'

Then he asked her, 'If this is the Land of Eternal Youth, why are there old people here?'

She replied, 'We were much older when we came here, and since that day we have never aged.'

'And the young people, and the children – have they remained the same age?'

She replied, 'They are what we will become. They were once old, but they grew young, and they grow younger, so that the very youngest has the wisdom of an old person and the intelligence of a child.'

Oisin dressed in a long white robe of soft wool, with a red and grey mantle draped over it, white and gold slippers, and went to the window. He could see for miles – the wide regions of orchards whose fruit-pickers now made their ways to the castle for the wedding; a corner of the farms beyond the hills that had earlier concealed them from his view; the light changing on the purple mountains which hid the Land of Silence. But even though the journey from the shore to the castle had seemed to him a short one, he could get no glimpse of the sea across which he had ridden to the Land of Eternal Youth, nor could he see the roadway leading from it. It was as if they had been erased.

The years did not pass in the Land of Youth, nor did time impinge. And even though his adventures grew ever more enthralling, something inside Oisin remained unsatisfied. Not that the spell of the place wore off – he marvelled every day at some new enchantment, some new thrill, some even more remarkable facility. Niav proved lovelier and lovelier, the people of the kingdom more loyal and supportive than he could have described had he been seeking an ideal. Yet his dissatisfaction grew and with it came an increasing sense of the element he thought never to know again – time.

When Niav, observing his increasing pensiveness, approached the matter directly, Oisin admitted to her that he missed his companions and his family. Niav, relenting, and against her will, lent him her white horse to revisit Ireland one last time. She cautioned him most particularly that he must not dismount, that if his foot ever touched the earth there he could never return to the Land of Youth.

Oisin set off. He galloped over the waves, but saw none of the strange sights they had encountered on their way to the Land of Youth. He made his landfall a few miles up the coast from the point where they had left Ireland and he made for the woods and lakelands where he knew the Fianna hunted habitually. No sign could he find of them, and his search grew more diligent and anxious. Things had changed. The people tilling the soil, walking along the pathways, had grown smaller and, stopping to watch him ride by, they seemed to consider him a curiosity.

When he failed to find any trace of their hunting and eventually made for the ancestral home of the Fianna, he found the ramparts overgrown with rich green grass. In anguish he called out the beloved names, 'Finn', 'Oscar', and the dogs, 'Bran', 'Sceolaing', but neither answering shout nor bark came back.

Distressed, he turned his horse's head towards the east to try and find Ben Edair, the hill where they hunted and rested so often in the sunshine. As he raced along the shore he saw some men by a cliff moving large stones. He reined in but could barely understand their language – they had similar difficulty with him. Then they realised he was trying to tell them who he was – Oisin, the son of Finn. Astonished, they told him the Fianna had died long ago in ancient battles, that they only dwelt now in legends – new regimes had come into force.

Shocked, Oisin reined his horse hard away and the girth broke in mid-stride depositing him on the sands of the beach. On hitting the ground he began immediately to change, and by the time the workmen reached him his clothing had turned to dust, his hair to white powder, his eyes reddened and misted over. All his centuries in the Land of Youth accumulated there and then – Oisin the young deer became a man of several hundred years.

They called Patrick, who at that time walked the land preaching of the new god. Patrick managed to take down some of Oisin's stories of the old days, and then received him into the new religion, at which point the warrior-poet of the Fianna died.

Thus ended, sadly and with little dignity, the ancient regime of the Celts.

PART TWO

The Cattle Raid of Cooley, from the Gaelic *Tain Bo Cuailgne*,
part of the Ulster Cycle, is the longest continuous Celtic
legend of the Irish. Created in the oral tradition – *Tain*, a
raid, *Bo*, a cow – it dates linguistically to the late seventh/
early eighth century, though it belongs to earlier times:
some suppose the events to have taken place in or around the
century of Christ's birth. It has always attracted translation,
from the earliest versions which appear in twelfth- and
fourteenth-century manuscripts, to the outstanding 1969
text by the poet Thomas Kinsella. In essence it began as a
long Homer-type tale of early Ireland, handed down – like
the rest of the Ulster Cycle – via the learned bards and
storytellers and taken onwards into literature by the
Christian monks who, storytellers also, enjoyed embellishing
(even, as we have seen with Oisin and others, adding the
new dimension of Christianity).

The story merits description as an Iron Age political and
adventure novel, describing the wars and machinations
between two powerful provinces of Ireland, Ulster and
Connacht. The bull at the centre of the conflict, the
all-powerful *Donn Cuailgne*, the Brown Bull of Cooley
coveted by Queen Maeve, may be seen as a metaphor for
power and virility, or as a desirable practical possession in an
economy where the begetting and ownership of cattle
constituted wealth and political strength. Tension runs high
throughout the racy and proud narrative; the storytellers
employed the machinery of film-makers – sound, fury,
colour, costume, incident – as great deeds take place
involving racing chariots, multiple decapitation, vast wounds
and incomparable heroism.

The *Tain* falls into four clear parts – the mustering of the
armies and their early marches; the boyhood of Cuchulainn; the
battles which raged between Cuchulainn, Ulster's lone
defender, and the armies of the west and the final conflicts
as the hitherto spell-cursed Ulstermen recover their strength
in time to come to Cuchulainn's rescue.

Some embellishments of my own have surely crept in; in the
first place I inherited the story orally – Cuchulainn was as
much a childhood hero as any Wild West cowboy – and
therefore I feel sure I have taken further liberties with the
descending written versions of seven centuries.

THE CATTLE RAID
OF COOLEY

In their marriage bed, in the western province of Connacht, King Ailill and Queen Maeve lay chatting – but when those two, competitive to the hilt, got down to pillow-talk it always had more to do with riches or power than with love. This time they began for the umpteenth time to compare their possessions. 'I have more than you have': 'No, you haven't, I have more than you have' – to listen to them squabbling you would swear you were eavesdropping on a couple of children swanking with their toys.

This time they even got up from their couch of luxurious furs and animal hides, took out all their lists, and ran a complete inventory of everything each owned, whether magnificently valuable or humbly domestic, whether jewel or utensil, brooch or jug. Then they counted their clothes, silks, brocades, linens, wools and cottons – Maeve had a slight edge over her husband in this department. He, however, won back that advantage – and more – when it came to what they raised on their farms.

Here the trouble began in earnest. Each had beautiful animals whose fineness they measured as keenly as if selling them at market prices; they measured the height of their stallions, the girth of their rams, the weight of their boars and found that hand for hand, inch for inch, pound for pound, they did not differ in the overall total by as much as the weight or breadth of a sparrow's feather – until they came to the cattle.

As they counted and measured Maeve began to get vexed, began to exhibit a certain irritation, which finally burst forth in anger. Ailill, you see, had in his herds a wonderful bull, mighty and wide and enormously potent, and Maeve had nothing remotely like it. Ailill's benign and satisfied air as he looked at the animal really got on her nerves, and a steward rubbed the salt further into her wounded pride by telling her something she had wished to forget. The animal had actually been calved in Maeve's own herd in these very fields, but, shaking his head at the thought of being owned by a woman, he had gone unstoppably over to Ailill's herds, mowing down fences on the way, and had stayed there ever since. The bull even shook his big head at her now, as she looked at him envying her husband.

The animal had the name Finnbennach, meaning 'of the white horns', a beast wonderful enough to be known throughout Ireland, and at this thought Maeve's depression deepened seriously. Not only did Ailill irrevocably outstrip her in wealth and possessions, he did so with a bull that she herself had once owned.

She wheedled him a little; surely the bull could be trained to come back to her herds? Ailill doubted it. Surely he would want her, his loving wife and queen, to be the proudest woman in all the land, which she nearly was anyway on account of being married to him, a noble king, and owning the bull would clinch it? Ailill thanked her for the compliment but seriously doubted that the bull would stay, and anyway what would his own cows do without their powerful companion? Maeve tried a few more twists and turns and got nowhere; there was no question of her regaining this bull.

She sent for her most senior courtier, the shrewd and knowledgeable Mac Roth and asked him did he know where she might obtain a better creature, or at least an equal. 'Somewhere? Anywhere?' she asked.

Mac Roth told her of a bull over to the north-east, in Cooley, in the southern half of the province of Ulster – 'a great, full beast called *Donn Cualigne*, the Dark One of Cooley.'

By telling her Mac Roth gave himself a job. Maeve dispatched him at the head of a delegation to the man in Cooley who owned this dark brown bull. She gave Mac Roth wide powers of negotiation; he could offer up as far as fifty prime heifers in return for a year's loan of the bull. As a big sweetener he could throw in a tranche of land from one of Maeve's plains, that is, if the owner wished to accompany the bull – and if he did he could have a superb chariot worth twenty-one female slaves. To clinch it, Mac Roth had the liberty to offer Maeve's favours, a place for the bull's owner in her lively bed. And if all this failed he could take the matter into his own hands, as long as he returned with the bull. Mac Roth set out, dressed as if he were himself a king, and with him went his heralds and diplomats. They reached the Cooley peninsula after two days of hard riding.

The owner of the Brown Bull greeted them with enthusiasm, accepted their offer of heifers, land, slaves and favours with delight, and he treated Maeve's delegation to Ulster's finest hospitality: drink and goodwill poured like a tide over the night, and they ate excellent food and talked great talk.

This part, the talk, undid them. Such circumstances are always dangerous, especially if the tongues loosen among the lower ranks. In this case, a couple of the messengers in Maeve's delegation made some unfortunate remarks within earshot of the host's ostlers – to the effect that anyway if the owner had not given the bull as easily as he did, and indeed he had been treated generously in the bargain, more generously than an Ulsterman perhaps deserved, they would have taken the big beast home to Connacht by force. Not, in the circumstances, the wisest or most courteous thing to say: the owner's own servants took the details of this overheard conversation straight to their master. When the new day dawned, and Maeve's men came to collect the bull from its stall and fetch it back to the west, they received a curt refusal and a sharp encouragement to leave. Only the laws of hospitality, the owner told them, had prevented him from slaughtering them in their sleep, and they could get out now and damnation take their boastful provocations.

Extracting his group with some dignity, Mac Roth had no option but to go home empty-handed and report all to Maeve. She cut through his excuses and in a rage plunged Connacht headlong into a hectic campaign; the Brown Bull of Cooley must be captured. By convincing her husband Ailill that any insult to her also insulted him, she thereby secured his help and therefore guaranteed herself not only the support of every chieftain in the province but made sure also of a massive army. Warriors from the hills and plains of the west began to gather in the royal forecourt, the spirit of war smouldered and burst into flame as the Connachtmen mustered to march on Cooley and rustle the bull. The influence which Maeve and Ailill wielded had also attracted support from far outside their own kingdom, and from the south and south-west, from the east and south-east, several regiments, donated by kings in Munster and Leinster, marched to their call.

The principal western warrior, Fergus, late of Ulster whence he had fled in rage at the treacherous murders of his colleagues, led the armies alongside Maeve and Ailill. Maeve, seething all the time, rode up and down, back and forth along her ranks, supervising, checking for laggards and drinkers and those who needed discipline. She singled out men who showed energy and battle zeal, she marked down the soldiers who seemed likely to perform well when it came to battle, and she checked for traitors, for those who had come in from outside who might well undermine her efforts at a crucial future moment.

Her anger unbalanced her judgment. On a whim she decided that one particular regiment, the men from north Leinster, three thousand superbly trained soldiers, brilliant individually as well as collectively, must not be included any longer in the campaign. Her complaint sounded unhinged; she said their efficiency so outshone her own armies of the west that her soldiers would lose face, and the Leinstermen would get all the credit for success. She pointed out that they had already shown up her own soldiers: the Leinstermen had already roofed their camp and had begun to cook while her men were still finding a decent place to pitch camp, and then, while her men were still eating, the Leinstermen had long finished, and had begun to relax and listen to the music of the harpers. She raged at this, and could not be persuaded that this boded magnificently well for any battles ahead.

Ailill tried to point out all this to her.

Maeve said, 'No. Out with them. Send them home.'

'But we'll insult the man who sent them.'

'No. Out. They are not to come with us.'

'Well if we can't send them back, let them stay here, so?'

'For what?' said Maeve, 'and have them take over our province in our absence? Are you mad?' Ailill looked at Fergus and they knew they would have to try and humour her – nobody could speak to Maeve in this mood.

'So, what do you suggest?' said Ailill. 'You won't let them join us and you won't let them stay back?'

'Kill them.'

'What?'

'Kill them.'

Fergus spoke, on behalf, he said, of the Ulstermen who had been exiled and who had now enlisted with Maeve and Ailill.

'These Leinstermen are our allies. I went specifically to their king and asked for them. I'm not having this nonsense, we have a war to fight. If you want to kill them you will have to kill us first.'

Ferocious negotiation broke out, it even came down to a counting of heads. Fergus and Maeve went at each other verbally as if they vould have each other's throats – they sounded like two warriors at a fight, each besting the other psychologically before taking up arms. Eventually Ailill intervened, and his suggestion appeased both sides.

'Disperse the Leinstermen throughout the whole army,' Ailill said, ticking off the reasons on his fingers. 'Each one is a fine individual soldier in his own right. We will not have to insult their king by sending them home. We will still have the use of them. And we can tell them that the idea is that they should strengthen the army generally. They will be flattered.'

This solution both preserved Maeve's pride in her own soldiers and retained the valuable resource of the Leinstermen. They now scattered among all the troops of the huge army, bolstering the weaker regiments and, rather than putting Maeve's soldiers to shame any more, setting examples by their inspirational efficiency. In the morning everyone struck camp and marched north-east.

First they crossed a wide bogland where the advance party and their hounds stirred a herd of nearly two hundred wild deer, which they naturally hunted. After a short and brilliant chase, with the deer widely outnumbered, they slaughtered them all and added the carcasses to the supply train. (Interestingly the Leinstermen dominated the chase, killing all but five.) Fording the broad river now called the Shannon, they broke for food at Trego, north of Lough Ree.

Over the evening meal, one of the seers in the retinue chanted a prophecy, which predicted a savage and destructive conflict ahead of Maeve in her search for the Brown Bull. The augurer said that the herd in which the Brown Bull of Cooley dwelt would be guarded by one man, a fearful warrior, worth a whole army in himself, who would generate huge carnage. The soothsayer cried that he saw the crows drinking the blood of Maeve's soldiers. This prophecy, when it spread among the thousands of troops, greatly disturbed them. Maeve addressed them and managed to calm them down sufficiently to press on with their advance, and after a hard day's march they made their next camp at Granard.

Fergus knew from the soothsayer what kind of trouble might lie ahead. Always hoping for a negotiated settlement, and for the sake of his old loyalties, he sent messengers to Ulster chivalrously warning them of the great army approaching their border. No response came – the Ulstermen lay under a great curse which had rendered them useless.

This had come about when a man called Crunnagh boasted at a fair that his fine and remarkable wife could outrun the king's swiftest chariot. He was made to bring his wife there to prove his boast. She, heavily pregnant, begged release from this obligation, even appealing to the women of Ulster in their own role as mothers, but they still made her race the chariot. She outran it and then gave birth to twins, but in her labour she screamed a curse that all the men of Ulster for the next nine generations would be reduced to the strength of a woman in childbirth. She exempted only the youngest boys, their mothers – and the warrior Cuchulainn, whose wild and invincible figure Fergus had recognised from the campfire fortune-telling.

Thus, the armies of the west marched on a province that had no defences. The woman's curse had debilitated the Ulstermen to such a degree that they could only walk slowly, not quite upright, or lie around dopily. No wonder Fergus's messengers brought back no formal response. However, by word of mouth Fergus's warning reached Cuchulainn. He had been playing a board game with his father and now he set out for Crossakeel to keep a watch on the entrance to Ulster through which he expected the armies of the west to march. Before he left, he took a wooden ring, the kind used for spancelling cattle or goats to prevent them straying, cut a message into it in the Ogham symbols, and left it on a standing stone, as warriors did when laying down a challenge.

The armies of the west marched steadily onwards. Fergus had persuaded Maeve, through the reasonable Ailill, to let him lead. He did not march due north-east as he should have done: instead he made a detour to the south. This curious strategy ran counter to the military interests of the armies he led, though in keeping with the honour of the warrior. He hoped, in fairness, that such a delay would still give his former countrymen in Ulster, whatever their disabilities, time to muster some kind of army. Maeve, always watchful, challenged him.

'Fergus, where are you leading us? We seem to be straying, zig-zagging. King Ailill is beginning to have doubts about whose side you're on. Is there some reason you're so hesitant? Old loyalties? Old friendships?'

Fergus answered, 'Sorry to disappoint you, Maeve, but this is neither treachery nor trickery. The reason I am taking this round-about route is because I do not want us to run into the man who guards the Plain of Muirhevna.' Maeve subsided.

Soon the leading warriors discovered the spancel-ring which Cuchulainn had left on the standing stone. They also found the traces where his horses had been grazing – they had not eaten just the grass, they had gnawed down to the red clay. When the rest of the army arrived Fergus dismounted and turned the spancel-ring over and over in his hands. In Ogham Cuchulainn had written,

'Unless you have among you a man skilled enough to fashion a hoop like this out of a single piece of wood, using only one hand, then come no farther. I lay this challenge down to each man in your armies, except my old friend Fergus.'

Fergus handed the spancel-ring to the Druids and asked them for an interpretation of the message's meaning – with special reference as to who put it there, and whether his troops could safely advance beyond the place where the ring had been left. The Druids replied in a chant.

'This ring was made by a true champion. This man alone will single-handedly stop you. And the rules of war say that we must not go beyond this point unless or until we can produce a man to answer the challenge of the ring.'

Fergus brought this judgment to Maeve and Ailill. If they attempted to ignore the challenge, he said, the rage of the man who left it there would find them out wherever they were. Unless they could bring forward a man equal to the challenge one of them would be killed before morning. Ailill, a better negotiator, a more expedient individual than Maeve, suggested that they take a different route, one which would not lead them past the place where the challenge had been thrown down. They turned back, diverted through a forest and camped that night not far from Tara.

Snow fell, right up to the hubs of the chariot wheels. In places the snow drifted to waist height, no chance of lighting a fire to cook. Still hungry, the army had to shift onwards. A short distance back from where he had left the ring with the inscribed challenge, Cuchulainn had spent the night with a woman. When he arose he regretted his dalliance; his incaution had let the enemy soldiers slip away. From the footprints in the snow he tried to assess the size of the army. The marks taught him a lot – with his second sight he could tell, for instance, that they had dispersed the Leinstermen throughout the entire force, helpful information which enabled him to judge how he should pitch an attack: otherwise he might have aimed himself at the crack Leinstermen first.

By now, though, he hungered for some action, some flavour of war and he set off to catch the enemy on a flank. Searching for a chariot obstacle at a ford near their army, he hacked off the large fork of a tree and stuck it in the water. Then he yelled abuse to draw attention to himself. In answer to the ploy, two chariots, obviously uninformed as to his identity or prowess, broke off and thundered towards him, a warrior and a charioteer in each one. With the cleanest of sword-strokes Cuchulainn swiped off their heads, caught them as they fell and in a single movement stuck them one at a time on the points of the forked tree in the stream.

When the blood-smeared horses and empty chariots returned to their armies, the waiting soldiers believed that a huge troop had massed to defend the ford and accordingly sent word along the ranks to Fergus. Instead, as a reconnaissance party reported back, only the track of a single chariot had been left on the other side – and they found another Ogham message on the fork of the tree where the four heads had been impaled. Fergus, Maeve and Ailill then rode to the ford to learn that the dead men had been among their best soldiers. How could they have been killed so easily? Fergus, on foot in the water, and searching for clues, reckoned that the tree-fork had been severed with a single sword-stroke and then embedded in the river-bed by someone who had thrown it with great force from the back of a chariot.

He was proved right by the message in Ogham, which contained another challenge; unless one of their men could do the same with a tree-fork of equivalent size, their armies could not, according to the rules of war practised among all trained champions and heroes and agreed by all kings and Druids, pass the point. Ailill then asked Fergus for the identity – and an assessment – of the man who had accomplished such huge deeds. Fergus began by reminding them of the seer's forecast back in Trego – the Brown Bull of Cooley would be guarded by one man, a fearful warrior, worth a whole army in himself, who would generate huge carnage. The crows would drink the blood of Maeve's soldiers.

'This signifies only one man,' said Fergus. 'There is only one warrior who would come to the border alone, accompanied by only one charioteer, only one man who would be capable of such bravery and strength. That man is Cuchulainn – "the equal of an entire army", as the seers said.'

'Tell us about him,' said Ailill, and Fergus began to tell the story of the greatest Ulster warrior, the Hound of Cualann.

'When he was five he came to Ulster, to the great fort of Emhain Macha, to study the use of arms. At the age of seven he was educated in the arts of war, and a year later he bore arms. Now, he is aged seventeen. You will find no lion more fierce, no hammer as hard, no hand more swift. For youth and energy and eloquence and intelligence and terror, no one can match him. For strength or discipline or bravery, or intellect, no one can equal him. For creating havoc, slaughtering enemies, gaining victory, no one can excel him. He is potent, fearless, turbulent and independent beyond any man. He is alert, furious, accomplished and devastating beyond any champion. He is wise, articulate, dependable and rigid more than any man who has ever walked these river-banks. His feats in battle defy the imagination.'

Maeve said, 'Ach! Let us not get carried away by his reputation. First of all he is only one man. Secondly, he is only seventeen, still a youth, he hasn't yet done the real deeds of manhood. Thirdly, he can be wounded, can't he, he can be killed, can't he?'

'Whatever you do, don't misread him,' said Fergus. 'Years ago, before his teens, he had already begun to defeat and outwit warriors three times his age – it became a thing among the men to try and defeat him and they all failed.' And under further promptings from Ailill Fergus began to tell stories of Cuchulainn's famous boyhood.

'When he was almost five he persuaded his mother to let him leave the family home on the Plain of Muirhevna, and seek a place in the troop of a hundred and fifty boys training to be warriors in the palace of Emhain Macha. He wanted no company on the long journey north and he took the boredom out of his travels by taking with him a boy-sized javelin made of gold and silver, and a silver hurling-stick with a golden ball. First, he would strike the ball with the hurley and drive it far, then throw the hurley after the ball, hitting it in mid-air and driving it still further. Next he would throw the javelin after the hurling-stick, its point would spike the end of the hurling-stick handle, drive it forward further until it hit the ball again and then he would run forward and catch all three before they hit the ground – and repeat the action all over again.

'When he arrived at Emhain Macha, the boys in training there were out playing on the sportsfields, and our boy joined in. Since he did not know their rules he thereby made himself into an intruder. They yelled at him to clear off out of their way: he ignored them. Then they stopped their game to deal with this intruder and came at him, all hundred and fifty of them throwing their javelins in a hail. He defended himself against each spear, blocking them until his shield looked like a porcupine, all the javelins sticking out of it. Then they withdrew a little, regrouped, and from a distance pounded their heavy hurling-balls in his direction. He either took each one on his chest or whacked them out of the way with his hurling-stick; their hurling-sticks he either dodged, or caught and broke across his knee.

'They then formed a solid wedge, all hundred and fifty of them and came at him, intending to kill him. Now, to this day, when Cuchulainn becomes fired up to enter battle, a spasm shakes him and transforms him. It was a gift in childhood from the goddess of war. His hair seems to stand up and catch fire, each individual strand separating and shooting sparks into the air. One eye closes almost shut, the other opens impossibly wide and rolls around in its socket, and he bares his teeth and his lips in a wide smear of fury. This he did in front of the hundred and fifty boys, and then launched himself at them. He cracked heads and limbs, their moans echoed off the mountainsides. Those whom he did not level to the ground scattered, and ran as fast as they could for shelter. He chased one group and caught nine of them as they ran to the king for protection.

'I was sitting there myself, playing a board game with the king, when up they came, screaming their heads off and ran around behind us, terrified, in tears, no way for young warriors to behave. The lad came in after them with the speed and force of a chariot and rushed around the table trying to get at them. The king grabbed this wild boy by the arm and said, "Eh, eh, eh? What's this about? Take it easy, youngster, who are you anyway?" He told the boy not to handle the other boys in such a rough fashion, and sat him down and asked him to explain himself.

'Cuchulainn complained that it was the other way round, that it was they who had handled him roughly. He then introduced himself to the king – he was, in fact, the king's nephew. The king, after much questioning, realised the boy's exceptional quality and straightaway made him the protector of all the other boys. This calmed matters down, and those injured boys whom the young Cuchulainn had attacked out in the field were slowly helped to recovery by their parents and friends. But it took ages – some of them had very severe injuries, as if the lad who attacked them didn't know his own strength.'

Noticing the impressed silence among his listeners, Fergus drew breath. 'I'll tell you another story. Cuchulainn complained of sleeplessness at Emhain Macha – he couldn't sleep unless his head and feet rested at the same levels. The king, always testing the lad, ordered one block of stone for a pillow, and another to put under the boy's feet. This worked fine and he slept soundly. Then one morning some man at the court went in to wake the boy earlier than usual, and Cuchulainn, annoyed at this, hit him so hard he drove the front of the man's forehead back into his brains. From that day on it was well-known at the court that you never wakened him, but always allowed him to wake up by himself.

'On another occasion, he was playing in the sportsfield, himself against the other hundred and fifty boys – a not untypical contest, and naturally he always won. On this one occasion, though, he laid out a third of them, then for some strange reason, for it was not his habit, he ran – and he hid under the king's bed. The whole province came out to try and dislodge him from there, including myself,' said Fergus. 'I was there, and the king, too. We heaved and pulled, but he held us down, the bed and thirty warriors hanging on to it. This now is the man we are up against – you have no idea of how strong he is.'

Fergus continued to regale Ailill and Maeve and the other wide-eyed listeners with detailed accounts of Cuchulainn's deeds. 'Once upon a time the Ulstermen, fed up with relying so much on one man, went to battle without Cuchulainn – he was asleep when they left. They were hammered, and the king and his son suffered terrible injuries. All around them on the battlefield lay piles of their dead warriors-in-arms. Even though it came from a great distance away, the agonised moaning from the battlefield woke Cuchulainn. That's another thing about him – his senses and faculties are much more acute than anyone else's. In the process of waking up so suddenly he cracked his two blocks of stone, the one under his head and the one under his feet. I met him at the gate of the battlefield as I was coming back in shreds with my wounds, and he asked me where the king was. I told him I didn't know, and off he went into the pitch-black night looking for the king, and all the while he kept crying out the king's name.

'He found the king, in a trench, half-buried under a mound of dead bodies, and Cuchulainn with strength greater than six men pulled him out. He lit a fire to warm the king, who said he would be fully revived if only he could eat a cooked pig. Cuchulainn went out and met in the woods a man with the savagery of a lion. This man was cooking a succulent-looking pig on a fire, with his weapons at the ready in case anyone tried to get the pig from him. He put up a brave enough fight but he had no idea who or what he was up against. Cuchulainn cut off his head first and then grabbed the pig. The king ate it, revived fully and they headed back for the palace.'

Since there were plenty among the exiled Ulstermen in the armies of the west eager to tell other tales about the valiant boyhood of Cuchulainn, Fergus stopped. He looked at Maeve and Ailill, indicated the scene where they stood, at the ford where the four men in the pair of chariots had been killed and their heads impaled upon the tree-fork and said, 'Is it any wonder that a boy who accomplished all of those great feats should in manhood so easily defeat a couple of warriors and their chariots?'

Then up spoke Conall Cearnach, another of the exiled Ulstermen. He had fostered Cuchulainn, and now he told them the extraordinary story of how Cuchulainn got his name.

'Cualann, the Great Smith of Ulster, had planned a feast to entertain the king. He asked the king not to bring too many in his entourage, because he didn't own a place large enough, nor did he have sufficient wealth to feast a great number of courtiers. So the king brought only his most distinguished warriors, fifty chariots, a short procession, instead of the usual two hundred or so. Along the way they stopped by the sportsfield and there he saw Cuchulainn playing a game of hurling, single-handed as usual, against the hundred and fifty other boys, and, as usual, beating them. His eye was so good that when they played a game requiring them to drive the hurling-ball into a hole he was defending he stopped every one of their shots – yet when his turn came to hit the ball against them, he scored goal after goal after goal. At wrestling he wiped out the lot of them; the number they needed in order to throw him couldn't get near enough to him to do so. Finally, with the king and the fifty chariots of people looking on, they played a game called 'Stripping', in which each side is supposed to remove all the other's clothing. In minutes he stripped them completely, went through them like a high wind, and they couldn't even get off his cloak.'

Conall went on, 'The king was astonished and he wondered aloud whether, when they all grew up into men, the same gap in superiority might separate Cuchulainn from the rest? A Druid, overhearing, assured the king that this would indeed be the case, and the king therefore invited Cuchulainn to join his company of champions on their way to Cualann's feast, indeed to ride in the king's own chariot. The boy rather gruffly said he hadn't yet finished playing, said he would follow them later. The king smiled and indulged the young fellow's impertinence and lack of manners.

'When they got to Cualann's, the smith made a specific point of asking the king whether anyone else was to join them, and the king, in the pleasure of the welcome, forgot about Cuchulainn. Cualann asked the question because in order to guard his place he had a savage dog, so ferocious he had to be tied down with three chains and three heavy and heavily armed men hanging on each chain. When the king's entourage was safely installed, Cualann then instructed the minders to release the guard dog.

'The boy ran up shortly afterwards, just as the meal began, heading for the gates of the smithy, waving to the royal party. To their consternation, the hound made for him. Young Cuchulainn paid no attention, merely went on with the last strokes of his usual travelling game, throwing the hurling-stick after the ball and then the javelin. The hound sprang just as Cuchulainn caught all three items falling from the sky. The boy clutched the mastiff with one hand by the throat and with the other hand by the spine, and dashed it against a pillar with such force that the hound's eyes splashed out of their sockets. To finish it off Cuchulainn then rammed the ball down the hound's throat, and it subsided, gurgling, to death. The king's party saw all this, rushed out to meet the boy and raised him on their shoulders.

'The smith soberly welcomed the boy too, but said he was bereft without his hound. Who would now guard his property? Cuchulainn said that he would rear for the smith a dog of the same family, and that until that dog was fully grown he himself would guard Cualann's property. The Druid who was present said that Cuchulainn should be called "The Hound of Cualann, Cu Chulainn".'

Conall Cearnach, pointing towards the ford and addressing his remarks to Maeve and Ailill, concluded his story with the observation, 'Therefore is it any wonder that the six-year-old boy who killed the hound of Cualann, could put those heads on the spikes over there when aged seventeen.'

They went on assessing this extraordinary man who they now knew had begun to confront them. In story after story they described his amazing, unequalled physical and intellectual prowess. While still a child he destroyed several members of an alien family who had killed many of his own Ulstermen. He once brought down a dozen birds with the throw of a single stone. When, after fighting, he returned to his own quarters in the king's palace, the only way they could quell his thirst for more fighting was by sending naked women to shame him into hiding his face, and then by cooling him off in huge tubs of cold water – the water, it was said, actually boiled with the heat of his fury. And this was the warrior, now a fully grown man, who stood between the forces of Maeve and Ulster: even Maeve, not a woman given to introspection or self-doubt, wondered whether she could have considered all the possible consequences of her desire to possess the Brown Bull of Cooley.

Time to move on. Contemplating the stories of Cuchulainn, the armies of the west marched again, and soon ran into trouble from the very man himself. In trying to cross the plain ahead they found that

Cuchulainn had blocked their path with a huge felled oak – and another warning, carved into the bark this time, again in Ogham. This method of blocking an army's path had a particular significance. Under the ancient rules of war their regiments could not cross such a fallen tree until one of their champions had jumped it in his chariot. They had no choice but to try. (As usual, under arrangements which prevented old colleagues and friends fighting each other – and since this blockage formed part of the conflict – Fergus had been exempted.)

The Connachtmen, riding one by one in their chariots, began to attempt the felled oak. So hugely did it bulk across the stream that many died in the effort. Away from all this, a scout, spying Cuchulainn having his morning wash in the river, attempted an ambush. But the reflection in the water gave the scout away: Cuchulainn saw the man coming up behind him, grabbed him by the hair, whipped him over his shoulder and held him under the current until he drowned.

How it must have looked: these advancing armies constantly thwarted and held at bay by this one young man who always ranged ahead of them side to side across the terrain. And how frustrating for those still somewhat incredulous of Cuchulainn's reputation – yet at every encounter they paid dearly. With ease he slaughtered every soldier, every champion he met, one or several at a time, it never seemed to matter. And behind, raging at the impotence of her troops, rode the furious Maeve, taunting them, screaming abuse.

They had no choice but to endure the insults: the Hound of Cualann proved both incomparable and outrageous. In one of his sallies towards their lines Cuchulainn encountered a man – watched by his master – making a new shaft for a chariot and gave him a helping hand, whittling and shaping the timber. The charioteer, discovering Cuchulainn's identity, trembled for his life. Instead, Cuchulainn turned and beheaded his master Orlam, the son, as it happened, of Maeve and Ailill, and made the charioteer take the head back and show it to Maeve. Furthermore, at the precise moment when the charioteer stood to attention before Maeve and Ailill, Cuchulainn, from far off, split the man's head open with a long slingshot.

On another occasion, three arrogant brothers came against him, assisted by three skilled charioteers. They intended revenge for the killing of Maeve's and Ailill's son: six to one, and great fighters too, but he carved them all the same. The fight, though effortless to him, irritated Cuchulainn because it broke the rules of fairness, so he swore an oath that whenever thereafter he could actually see Maeve and Ailill, near or afar, he would let fly at them with his sling. An opportunity soon arose and with his first shot he killed the pet squirrel sitting on Maeve's warm neck, with his second he decapitated the pet bird on Ailill's shoulder. Thereafter, every time one of Ailill's or Maeve's immediate entourage raised his head to see where Cuchulainn stood, a slingshot split his brains – in one morning he bagged four.

Day in, day out, Cuchulainn cut through the host of the west like a deadly reaper. A man beheaded at a ford, several others shattered in the open plain, dozens with their brains split open: King Ailill feared that the armies of the west would end up at a third of their strength. Elsewhere, so intensively did Cuchulainn concentrate his sling attacks that Queen Maeve had to travel hidden under a phalanx of shields lest Cuchulainn's missiles penetrate her skull.

Over at Cooley the Brown Bull, in his stall, began to sniff the distant carnage. In this anticipation he received encouragement from a source never far from such trouble – the war goddess, the many-shaped Morrigan. Sometimes a bird, sometimes a beast, sometimes a wind, sometimes a woman, she now perched, as a black raven, on the bull's shoulder and, goading him, cried death and slaughter in his interests. The bull took off on the rampage. Head down he levelled all before him, his horns tearing a deep furrow in the earth. Everyone ran for their lives.

Maeve, Ailill and their forces first encountered the Brown Bull in a deep glen. Believing him trapped, they tried first to surround him, but he gored their herdsman to death. Then, with his retinue of fifty gorgeous heifers, he trampled Maeve's camp, killing fifty soldiers, before disappearing across the country.

About this time, too, an intrigue began between Maeve and Fergus. From her point of view such a relationship could prove ideal; she needed Fergus entirely on her side in the forthcoming conflicts, and he had to make sure that he could trust her, or at least compromise her into doing what he wanted. Besides, to put it more carnally, he was a big fellow and she a voluptuous woman.

In camp not much passed unnoticed. The suspicious Ailill asked his own charioteer to spy on his wife and her warrior. The man found them lying together and stole Fergus's sword, replacing it with a wooden one that had a more or less identical hilt. Ailill relaxed, the devil you know being better than the devil you don't, and pointed out to himself that Maeve needed to keep her hero sweet. None the less, the incident stirred some little rancour in Ailill – he even taunted Maeve and Fergus as they sat playing a board game – but never took it any further with either of them.

Out in the plain Cuchulainn, true to form, tore onwards, attacking the fringes of the western armies and preventing them from forming into battle lines – as Fergus said, 'shaking the forests, calling up rivers to drown his enemies'. The morale in the camp sank ever lower, and finally Ailill's son Maine said he would take him on. Useless – Cuchulainn killed Maine and also destroyed his personal guard of thirty soldiers. Immediately afterwards, just for sport, he eliminated thirty-two more warriors, and things had grown so serious that some of the generals from the west decided to try and negotiate with the young invincible. By now of course, everybody had been asking for weeks why the great Fergus had not challenged Cuchulainn. Time and again, Fergus and the Druids pointed out that as old comrades-in-arms they could only fight by agreement, which had not been forthcoming from Cuchulainn. Now, at the scene of Ailill's son's death, they reached an arrangement, suggested to Fergus by Cuchulainn himself, that instead of their armies rampaging after him and losing men in droves, he should fight selected western warriors in single combat every morning at this very ford.

While these negotiations went on, another young man, a foster-son of Ailill and Maeve stood staring at Cuchulainn.

'What are you looking at?' asked Cuchulainn.

'You,' said the foster-son, 'and there's not a lot to see.'

'If it had not been for the fact that you came with Fergus and are therefore protected by his honour,' said Cuchulainn, 'your guts would by now be writhing on the ground there, food for the pigeons.'

'Tomorrow,' said the younger one, 'I'll be the first to take you on in your single combats, and I'll be the last, because I'll finish you off.' And with a toss of his foolish young head away he went in his chariot.

He turned, though, and came back, impatient to get at Cuchulainn – who with his sword first of all literally cut the ground from under him, so that the young officer fell on his face. Cuchulainn cut his clothes off him at the armpits, then gave him another chance to quit by shaving his hair with a few deft strokes. When the young man still would not go away Cuchulainn split him from his forehead to his waist in two even sections. At that moment Fergus returned, angry that their deal appeared to have been broken. However, he accepted the word of both Cuchulainn and the dead man's charioteer that Maeve's and Ailill's foster-son had asked for trouble, and Fergus could do nothing but tow the body behind his chariot back to Maeve's camp.

On the following morning they held an early meeting to find a warrior willing to face Cuchulainn in the first of the single combat bouts. When no-one came forward a bribe was offered: the eventual chosen man had a fearsome reputation, especially as a spearsman, and sure enough he brought with him nine spears made of the hard wood of the holly tree; to harden them even further he had charred the tip of each. When these spears found their target – and this man had an unerring aim – they proved fatal. Cuchulainn, engaged in catching birds on the wing, one of his favourite sports, ignored the spears which, owing to his ducking and dodging after the birds, all missed him. When the last spear drove a flock of the birds away, Cuchulainn ran after them, giving his advancing opponent the mistaken impression that Cuchulainn had run away from him.

Maeve and her people watching from a hill began to cheer at what they took for Cuchulainn's cowardice. Foolish people. Cuchulainn turned round and shouted at them to send an armed man into combat next time, that he regarded that day's warrior as unarmed.

'You can't call a holly spear a serious weapon,' he yelled.

The westerners' backs were well and truly put up, but the negotiators made a fresh appointment with Cuchulainn for the following morning.

During the night Cuchulainn wrapped his great red cloak around himself – in the process he gathered up in it a large standing stone. In the dawn light they met to choose spears. When combat began, Maeve's chosen soldier for that day hurled his spear first, but it broke on the standing stone in Cuchulainn's cloak. Cuchulainn, in his turn, buried his spear in the head of his opponent, who begged leave to go back and show his twenty-four sons this amazing wound. When he returned Cuchulainn jumped on the rim of the man's shield and with one blow cut his opponent into four equal parts.

Directly after this Maeve's men, who had never ceased searching, once again found the Brown Bull and with a hundred men hanging from it with ropes and nets took it into custody. Just as they had stowed the animal safely away, Cuchulainn drove by and, as a matter of course, killed the leader of their platoon, and shortly afterwards, several more of their most prominent warriors who had ventured forth from the camp. Knowing nothing of the Bull or its capture, he then took up a position to defend his own homeland, the Plain of Muirhevna.

Maeve and her troop camped just south of Muirhevna, at Faughart. Here, the herdsman from the Brown Bull's home at Cooley, captured when the westerners took the bull, tried to make a break for it. The unfortunate man was given an ironic death – by hammering on their shields the westerners drove after him the whole herd that had once been his care and his pride. The frightened animals, stampeding through a narrow gap, crushed the man to death as he turned and tried to stop them.

Not that this solved any of Maeve's problems; she still had the greatest difficulty in finding warriors to fight in single combat at the ford. One came forward, called Cur, the son of Daly. Cur, not fully aware of Cuchulainn's prowess or reputation, took offence at being asked to fight a boy of seventeen. When finally persuaded that this youngster had slaughtered all before him, Cur languidly warned them that they should all prepare to march early since the job would not take him too long.

In the morning Cuchulainn got to the ford first. Like all champions he had a low boredom threshold, and he passed the time in practising his many feats with javelin and sword, and improving his already phenomenal adroitness and speed: he could, for instance, stand on the point of a flying spear. In his preoccupation he failed to notice that Cur had begun to attack. Someone, probably Fergus, who acted as overseer at these encounters, called out a warning. Cuchulainn turned: he held only an apple in his hand but he threw it with such force that it drove a hole into the front of Cur's forehead and went out the other side. For several days thereafter, it proved almost impossible for the westerners to get anyone down to the ford in the mornings. Though they press-ganged and dragooned many powerful and valiant men, Cuchulainn shattered them all.

One morning the westerners did manage to put up a champion about whom Cuchulainn felt briefly apprehensive – an old friend, highly trained, expert in single combat. They met the night before to discuss their respective positions and Cuchulainn suggested, unsuccessfully, that his opponent remember their friendship and renounce his allegiance to Maeve. As Cuchulainn left in a fury at this dishonouring of the rules, a sharp stake lying on the ground penetrated his foot, travelled up inside the tendons of his leg and emerged at his knee. Cuchulainn plucked it upwards and threw it at his erstwhile friend, whose head it pierced. Exit yet another of Maeve's heroes.

Day in, day out, the warriors from the west went mournfully to the ford. Day in, day out, broken and sundered bodies were carried back to their camp long before noon. Out of them all, only one man lived to tell the tale, a champion whom Cuchulainn, in a fit of impatience, seized by the throat and rattled until the unfortunate man's bowels ruptured and split, leaving him an invalid for the rest of his life. Otherwise no matter what sort of fighter the westerners sent against the seventeen-year-old he proved immeasurably superior. And the only thing they could hurl at him during all of these jousts was the gibe that he had no beard.

One day by way of diversion Cuchulainn saw a grand young woman gaily dressed, picking her steps towards him. Although always attracted to a good-looking girl, he felt suspicious. She chatted to him, and first said that she was a king's daughter bearing gifts of treasure and cattle. He made it clear to her that the demands of combat reduced his capacity to pay her due attention. Irked at this rejection she threatened him: at his most hectic moments, she said, she would turn herself into an eel and trip him in the water. Or she would turn herself into a wolf and stampede the beasts in his path. Or she would turn herself into a red heifer and lead the cattle to trample him in the waters. Cuchulainn hated this kind of nonsense, especially from women, and he told her to clear off. She, departing, warned that she would return.

In the camp of Ailill and Maeve, morale had sunk almost beyond recovery. Now prepared to use any ploy, Maeve delegated a hand-picked and specially trained team to ambush Cuchulainn at night when deep in his sleep: this, incidentally, broke all the rules of war. Cuchulainn, however, always woke in time. On each of the first three nights he killed seven of them, eight on the fourth night and ten on each of the fifth, sixth and seventh nights, a total of fifty-nine men in one week. He did not even breathe heavily as he dispatched them.

And in case he got rusty through lack of practice, by day he slew two brothers at the ford, the second having come to avenge the first. During that particular skirmish an eel tried to trip Cuchulainn, followed by a wolf that stampeded the cattle at him, followed by a heifer that led the cattle against him. He stamped on the eel's body, shattered the wolf's eye with a sling, fractured the heifer's legs under her. Then he remembered the woman of whom he had been suspicious, the one who told him she was a king's daughter. No princess did those things. The Morrigan, the goddess of war, had returned. There was a reason for her re-appearance. She always arrived when war looked as if it might have to give way to peace – and by now anyone could see that the forces of the west had little to relish.

In fact, Ailill and Maeve decided they had no option but to sue for peace. Cuchulainn said he would listen, but only after the next day's combat – in which they tried to cheat him. Instead of the agreed single combat, six brothers went out together, justifying this ruse by saying they had all come from the same womb, therefore they counted as one. They were returned – dead. Maeve, by now both furious and anxious, tried further trickery. She set up a meeting at which she intended to have Cuchulainn jumped by her best remaining men.

His charioteer warned him: Maeve had won no prizes for trust-worthiness. She, trying to heighten the impression of safety for Cuchulainn, arranged for the meeting to take place in the company of her women only, and in accordance with custom she had therefore asked him to go unarmed; he, however, brought a sword, at his shrewd charioteer's insistence.

As well that he did. Fourteen of Maeve's men hid in wait for him and burst out of their hiding-place right in front of his face. Cuchulainn's reflexes and skill dazzled them. So rapidly did he turn and twist that their heavy throwing-spears never even grazed him, and he duly killed all fourteen. This blatant treachery infuriated him beyond endurance. He burst out of Maeve's tent. At Faughart he attacked the main army, killing eight men on the fringes of the encampment: he slaughtered them brutally and with greater swift-ness than even he had previously exhibited.

Given this new demonstration of Cuchulainn's prowess, and the encouragement of Maeve's treachery, which, according to her, of course, had almost succeeded, the westerners abandoned all thought of fighting according to the rules they had made. On the following morning, instead of one-to-one they sent out five combatants, coming at him in a wave. Not that it mattered – he hammered them all.

Fergus, though, overruled in the arguments, felt shabby that such crookedness had taken over. Since the results showed no improvement he managed to persuade the westerners that single combat should be resumed. It still made no difference; Cuchulainn won, and com-prehensively, every time. Again Maeve's duplicity rose up in parallel with her frustration, and this time instead of one man or five, or ten, she sent a hundred to the ford. These, too, Cuchulainn devas-tated, each and every one. In some cases he hit them so hard that their blood-spattered heads bounced off the far bank of the river.

Never had an army been at such a loss. No matter who they flung against him, no matter what kind of warrior, a Leinsterman, a hard Munsterman, a brilliant Connachtman, he could not be defeated. Stratagems had also failed, so had rule-breaking. Would a bribe keep him at bay? Ailill and Maeve offered him – and Cuchulainn accepted – their daughter. And they could not do even that without trickery. They knew that honour would not permit Cuchulainn to doubt the word of a king, so they dressed the camp idiot to look, from the distance, like a king in order to seal the betrothal and thus keep

Cuchulainn under some kind of control. He simply took out his sling and drilled a hole in the idiot's head, then turned him and the girl into two standing stones. That just about finished any attempt by Maeve or Ailill to reach a truce.

Throughout this extraordinary campaign, the men of Ulster remained stricken under their curse, each man as pained and immobilised as a woman in labour. Logically it seemed therefore that weight of numbers must eventually defeat Cuchulainn, as long as he had no army to back him up. Maeve and Ailill sent messengers out to all their allies and asked them, in the name of old allegiances and military debts, to lend them every force at their command. With all warriors from all kingdoms thus deployed, they pointed out, no threat existed to anyone's lands or property. Thus, armies came from all the corners of the country (except, obviously, Ulster) and camped in a huge spread all across the Plain of Muirhevna. Maeve and Ailill briefed them and despite Fergus's protests made it plain that all must march together until Cuchulainn disappeared beneath the weight of their bodies.

The sight of this vast host filled Cuchulainn with a rage he had never known before. He let forth a battle cry that had in it all the worst vibrations of every imaginable demon. A hundred armed soldiers died of fright when they heard it. Then he went down to the ford and stood there in the stream, legs apart, ready to take on all comers. At an order from Maeve the troops poured into the narrow defile leading to the ford and came at him, wave after wave.

Consequently Cuchulainn now had to fight all the time, not just the morning's single combat, or the occasional cheated engagement, or the random ambush. From the end of that summer to the beginning of the spring he defended Ulster with unremitting power. He hardly slept – he grabbed an occasional snooze while standing propped up by his spear, before being awakened again by the call to battle as army after army flung themselves against him. Outnumbered, frequently wounded, he held his ground. He hacked and slaughtered and carved and cut; he decapitated and dismembered the men of Ireland who came at him like a huge red tide, and he paused only to allow them to remove the bodies that piled so high in front of him they had to climb over them to get at him.

Relief arrived: his father, Lugh, came from the OtherWorld, gloriously decked out in brilliantly coloured clothes, carrying powerful weapons and invisible to all except Cuchulainn. He stood magical guard while Cuchulainn slept for three days and three nights, and during that period he washed and oiled all of Cuchulainn's wounds so that when the young man woke up he had been completely restored.

Other help came too – a troop of boys from Ulster, free by virtue of their age from the accursed weakness pangs. The western armies, however, destroyed them, even though the boys killed an opponent each before they expired. One escaped, and when he went to try and kill Ailill, he died at the hands of Ailill's protectors.

When Cuchulainn awoke, his father Lugh refused to stay in case he took any of the credit for the great deeds about to come. He had given his son the protection of the OtherWorld and the young man now prepared to do battle on a grand scale. His charioteer, wearing his most special uniform, got ready the chariot of the sickles. This meant that the horses wore armour from which spikes protruded at every angle. The body of the vehicle had itself been fitted with hooks, points, blades and piercing needles so that as a unit the entire rig would tear a swathe through any opposition.

Cuchulainn then dressed for battle in his traditional twenty-seven layers of waxed cowhide on which he laid a layer of weapon-proof horsehide. He armed himself with eight swords, eight short spears, eight javelins, eight darts and eight shields covered overall with a blood-red shield, large enough to carry a boar within its scoop, sharp enough on the rim to cut a single hair in two. Then he raised his crested helmet, so great that his war cries, when they echoed inside it, sounded like a hundred warrior-demons. He also carried his magical cloak, a gift from the Land of Promise – by spreading it wide he became invisible to his enemies.

Now, fully geared, the mood for battle inundated him, his entire body and person distended and he changed into a wild and weird monster. Inside his skin his frame twisted completely around. The sinews on his neck became bulging knots of rope. His eyes took off on journeys of their own, one inward, the other outward. His mouth opened huge and red, gaping back to his throat's edge and his jaws gnashed together in bites that would kill a beast. He trembled violently, from the soles of his feet to the highest strand of his hair. A red mist, like a fog of vaporised blood, rose off him and each strand of his hair became an electrified, impaling spike. As he stood upright, ready to climb into his chariot, a column of thick, dark red blood spouted high in the air from the centre of his crown. Whatever combat and powerful rampaging had gone before, the Hound of Cualann had now set himself to war.

And war he gave them. Two fleet and elegant horses drew his chariot faster than deer or swooping bird, and in his first attack upon the massed armies Cuchulainn killed five hundred opponents. Avenging the Ulster boy-soldiers who had died in his honour, he drove around the perimeter of the massed armies making vicious raids into their midst and slaughtering in a way that had never been seen before in Ireland. Nobody could have withstood that man and they fell six deep, corpses piled high upon each other. They could not keep count of how many died on the Plain of Muirhevna in that rout – the figure has never been calculated. It did include, though, a hundred and thirty kings, scores of animals, even women and children. Of the survivors almost every single man had some permanent scar or maim. Cuchulainn, in his glorious armour, received not a scratch, nor did his charioteer or horses.

Next morning the conqueror surveyed the ruins. For this moment of triumph he had dressed for beauty, not for war. Word spread and the women, always loving a winner, foregathered to see him in his red silk, carrying a red shield and holding in his hands the heads of several slain enemies. Even Maeve, although she still feared his deadly sling, came out from under her permanent shelter of shields to see this wonder. The men tried to tell her that she would never conquer this man they saw now, and he would continue his slaughter until the men of Ulster had overcome their curse and then, when they joined him, all other forces would be wiped out or routed.

In all of this Fergus, as ever, remained true to his own sense of honour. He had endured much. Ailill taunted him with being an Ulsterman and therefore suspect, perhaps even a sympathiser with Cuchulainn. Maeve pressed him to go out there and fight his old friend, promising him the earth if he did so. Fergus drew on the dignity he had been taught as a young warrior and continually implored the westerners to behave likewise, to reduce these hugely unfair odds which were getting them nowhere, and to reinstate the principle of single combat at the ford. As for his role in the affair, he reminded them that he was Cuchulainn's foster-father.

In a new development, an emissary arrived from Ulster, Diarmaid, the son of King Conor MacNessa himself. He suggested that the hostilities be suspended and to settle the matter that Maeve and Ailill bring Ailill's bull from the west to fight the Brown Bull of Cooley. Maeve disagreed and in a skirmish one of her men killed Diarmaid. This proved another mistake. Nobody had stopped to enquire whether, if Diarmaid had been fit enough to ride so far south, the Ulstermen might now be recovering. As indeed they were and were marching in force to help Cuchulainn.

Single combat now returned, albeit briefly. Another hero had a go, a man called Lynch, also from the west, but no friend of Maeve and Ailill whose borders he constantly raided. To get back into their good books, he decided that he would try and bring them the head of Cuchulainn. Always a foolhardy man, he felt further encouraged by these stories: how this beardless Ulsterman had held all Ireland at bay from the end of summer to the beginning of spring, who killed a hundred people every night and who had proven unbeatable at the ford by day, who had piled up corpses the height of the earthen ramparts of many palaces. Lynch had twelve soldiers in his platoon and even though they all played dirty and attacked in unison Cuchulainn beheaded them all with one wide sweeping blow and set their heads on separate stones sitting on the ground.

The following morning Maeve pulled yet another deceitful stunt. She sent out twenty-nine men of a single family to fight Cuchulainn. When Fergus argued that this totally broke the rules Maeve disagreed, using the argument someone had used before, that they all belonged to, and had sprung from, the same flesh, blood and bone. Fergus now felt sure – and the thought saddened him – that Cuchulainn would die, since the members of that family always carried poison in their weapons.

And they nearly got him. First they threw their spears and all twenty-nine stuck in Cuchulainn's shield. He drew his sword to cut away the spears, so that he could fight unencumbered and as he did so they all attacked at once, knocked him to the ground and then jumped on him. Fergus had sent an observer to ensure fair play. This man now jumped out of his chariot and cut off the right hands of the twenty-nine attackers. But if this development had been reported back to Maeve, it would have jeopardised the lives of all Fergus's troops, so Cuchulainn, to protect his protectors, then finished the job by killing the twenty-nine poisoners.

Maeve, naturally, could have called the whole thing off and gone back to the west. A more sensible, less proud woman would have done exactly that a long time before, but humility and commonsense had not emerged as prizewinning qualities in her character. She had come to capture the Brown Bull and in the course of this her pride and her forces had been insulted by the blond stripling, but she was not going to go home defeated by one man. She questioned everybody, seeking ideas, looking for ways that would tie Cuchulainn down psychologically as well as physically. If anyone could defeat him – and Fergus was ruled out – it had to be somebody who knew Cuchulainn supremely well. And that is how she reached the decision that, honour or no honour, one more single combat would have to take place and that she would be represented this time by Cuchulainn's own beloved foster-brother, Ferdia.

A perfect choice, all agreed, over-ruling Fergus, and they began to calculate Ferdia's qualities. He knew all of Cuchulainn's tricks and could equal him at feats-of-arms. He knew how Cuchulainn thought, how he responded, how to anticipate him. He had the same sleight-of-hand with weapons, whether spears or swords or razor-sharp shields. The only advantage Cuchulainn might possess lay in his magic flying spear, the *gae bolga* – but Ferdia had a covering of horn all round his body and perhaps it could deflect the famous weapon which Cuchulainn fired from the point of his foot. Now they only had to convince Ferdia of the value of their case.

It proved a problem. Ferdia would not even travel to meet Maeve, sent her equerries home without him. She, the crafty woman, knew that a quality other than persuasion might work. Like all warriors, Ferdia feared ridicule. She therefore assaulted him with the most bitter satirists and ballad-makers and left him with no choice but to come and see her. When he arrived she changed tack and sweet-talked him outrageously, let him smell the perfume of her bosom, primed her daughter to feed him and give him three times as many kisses as he took drinks from their best goblets. They set him up thoroughly and when the mood had grown mellow, Maeve took to the kind of persuasion she had found so effective in the past, the promise of gifts wine, land, a chariot and harness, her most valuable brooch, her virgin daughter, her own mature delights. Ferdia, much though he appreciated the offer, he said, would forego any possessions rather than fight his own dear foster-brother. In Maeve's hands, however, he wilted, especially at her next ploy.

In an aside to her courtiers she commented upon the truth of a remark Cuchulainn had made. Ferdia's curiosity stirred, and Maeve passed on the alleged remark – that Cuchulainn would not find it remarkable to defeat Ferdia at the ford. Ferdia fell for it and promised to travel to the ford first thing in the morning to fight Cuchulainn.

Triumphantly Maeve sang great promises to him: forests to give him timber, rings for his fingers, her daughter in marriage, the support of her loyal chieftains and as a token a wide round brooch inlaid with pearls to catch the light and inspire him in the period before the battle.

That other fine warrior Fergus, ever more disillusioned with Maeve's notion of bargaining, left the negotiations depressed. He called out his charioteer and drove to find Cuchulainn. The foster-brother connection between Cuchulainn and Ferdia upset Fergus on account of his own relationship as Cuchulainn's foster-father. Cuchulainn reflected disenchantment at the news Fergus brought, not, as he said, because he feared Ferdia, but because he loved him.

Back in Maeve's camp Ferdia could not sleep. He had too many imponderables facing him, because part of the bargain included a pledge to Maeve that if he did not fight Cuchulainn then he would have to fight six of her best warriors – not that she had too many left by now. He roused his charioteer and told him to get ready for a meeting with Cuchulainn. On the way out of the camp he stopped to bid Maeve and Ailill farewell. Maeve gave her opinion to Ailill, still in bed, that Ferdia would not return except feet first.

When Ferdia and his charioteer reached the ford they could see no sign of Cuchulainn; wishfully thinking, they wondered whether Cuchulainn had fled rather than face his equally competent foster-brother. The charioteer, a genuine admirer of heroic prowess, reminded Ferdia of past events where Cuchulainn had been Ferdia's saviour and that therefore he should not so easily slander the man now. Ferdia, disgruntled, chose to rest a little, or try to – in the event he could hardly close his eyes, much less take a refreshing sleep.

Cuchulainn, from the other direction, approached the ford with his veteran charioteer, a grizzled man called Laeg. Ferdia's charioteer heard them coming, then saw and described them, mighty and forthright, hound and hawk in attendance, and Cuchulainn without a bother on him, hammering forward like a clap of thunder. Ferdia asked his charioteer to cease this excessive praise of Cuchulainn and went forward to greet his foster-brother.

Cuchulainn turned away his greeting, declaring his suspicion of Ferdia. He went further and rebuked Ferdia for having accepted the challenge, for having fallen prey to Maeve's goadings and ruses. The old relationship between the men had clearly turned sour as a result of this challenge and they began to square up to each other, with the recognised preliminaries of name-calling and taunts. Their threats of what each intended to do to the other would have made armies flee in terror, with Cuchulainn hurling one of the final insults by telling his foster-brother how much he was going to miss him when Ferdia died. The choice of weapons he gave to Ferdia.

Then began one of the most memorable battles since the first light of time. First they chose shields with razor-sharp rims, accompanied by darts, and straight short swords and they fought for hours throwing with exquisite grace and accuracy. But so clear and even were their skills, their experience, their training, that neither scored a hit on the other, their defence proving as remarkable as their attack.

For their next choice of weapons they wielded long, smooth spears with flaxen grips on the handles, and to defend they chose the two toughest shields. This time the greatest skills were proved in the throwing rather than the fending, and by day's end they had each suffered several wide wounds. Giving their weapons to their charioteers for cleaning and maintenance, they embraced each other. Then they made camp in the same enclosure and lay on beds not far from each other, and when Cuchulainn's doctors had finished dressing his wounds he sent them over to Ferdia, and when Ferdia's servants had finished giving him good food and sweet drink he sent them to Cuchulainn. Some unfair imbalances existed in the separate entourages – all of Ireland seemed to service Ferdia's camp, whereas Cuchulainn only had a few neighbours to minister to him.

Next morning they chose their big stabbing-spears, hoping, as Cuchulainn said, to bring matters that much nearer to an end. They chose their biggest shields too. Not that they were much good: each punched in the other's shield holes large enough for birds to fly through. Lunging and sallying, the horses often rearing and snorting in fright, the charioteers emerged dazed and deafened with the flashing sparks from the weapons and the noise of the clanging shields. Again the day ended even, all square, and the fighters embraced and went to camp.

That night the medicines, for the first time, proved useless. Magic had to be called down to try and stop the blood flowing from their massive cuts and wounds. When Cuchulainn's magicians had finished with him he once again sent them over to Ferdia and on the way they again passed Ferdia's messengers bringing the very best meat and drink to Cuchulainn.

As dawn broke both men met in the dim light to fight again at the ford. Laeg, Cuchulainn's charioteer, thought he observed a change in Ferdia's demeanour, as if he had fallen into shadow, as if a light in Ferdia had been quenched. Cuchulainn regretted this apparent dimming, this diminishing of his dear foster-brother and said so. If his charioteer was right, they both knew from that moment that Ferdia was doomed. Ferdia, after an initial protest, acknowledged that his spirits had lowered, that he felt doom-laden and together they sat and mourned.

They rose to fight and as weapons they chose the heaviest hacking-swords. At first slash they cut off each other lumps of flesh big as a baby's head. The fight rocked back and forth, advantage switching sides again and again and finally they came to rest at the end of the day weary and despondent. This night they did not embrace, nor did they camp near each other. Something had definitely changed, the mood between them had grown apprehensive and final.

Early next day Ferdia got up and went to the ford long before Cuchulainn, feeling that this day would prove crucial. He sensed that Cuchulainn might, for the first time, use the *gae bolga*, and Ferdia dressed in anticipation. He put on his most effective battledress, seven layers of silk, leather and stone covered by an apron of beaten iron and on his head an impregnable helmet encrusted with jewels and crystals. As weapons, one in each hand, he carried his fiercest spear and his hardest sword, and to his back he strapped the widest shield he owned, the one with the huge centre boss and the fifty knobs round the perimeter, each knob the size of a wild boar's head. Thus dressed, and much hailed and admired by Maeve, Ailill and their men, Ferdia, while waiting for Cuchulainn, practised his great leaps in the air.

In this mood Cuchulainn found him and observed to his charioteer Laeg how thoroughly Ferdia seemed to have prepared. Asking Laeg for encouragement, not just at that moment but all day, Cuchulainn then dressed for battle, no less gloriously than Ferdia, and proceeded to accomplish even more dazzling feats. When the moment came to choose weapons Cuchulainn, within his rights, suggested they fight in the waters of the ford itself. Ferdia then knew himself to be doomed – nobody had ever survived in water-combat against Cuchulainn.

Such a fight had never been seen before, nor would ever again. They rocked and screamed and clawed and clashed. They tore at each other, leaped over each other's heads seeking advantage. From the high bank of the river Cuchulainn jumped on Ferdia's shield in an effort to get his great sword on to the crown of Ferdia's skull. With a kick Ferdia routed him as he would a child. Laeg, from the chariot, taunted Cuchulainn:

'I wouldn't give much for your reputation if you go on fighting like a baby or a cub or a little sprite,' he shouted, by way of encouragement.

Cuchulainn, thus goaded, again gave a mighty jump, faster almost than the eye could see, and landed straddling Ferdia's shield, but again Ferdia shook him off and sent him spinning into the water. The rage of Cuchulainn swelled and he expanded with it, to the proportions of a giant. He tore into Ferdia with such ferocity that the crowds lining the banks of the ford winced and drew back. With their faces an inch or two apart, the two warriors slugged it out. They split their shields from crown to crotch; they bent their spears from point to haft. The noises of metal upon metal screeched like wild devils and their battle raged so fiercely that they bent the river off course and sent people and horses and cattle fleeing over the countryside.

Ferdia got an opportunity, a momentary drop in Cuchulainn's guard, and through the gap Ferdia thrust his sword straight and deep into Cuchulainn's chest. The blood tumbled forth. Cuchulainn, in fear for the first time in his life, called to Laeg to bring him the *gae bolga*. Laeg slipped it into the water and it travelled downstream with the current. Cuchulainn bent down, picked up the short spear and let fly with it as he had been trained from the point of his right foot.

It penetrated Ferdia's outer apron of hammered iron and his inner coat of stone and his innermost shirt of silk. The armour split into three parts and the spear went into Ferdia's body and coursed through every vein and organ leaving a spike in each cranny. He dropped his weapons and looked sadly at Cuchulainn, knowing that the end had been declared. Cuchulainn dropped his weapons in the reddening water and ran over to his foster-brother. He gathered Ferdia in his arms and carried him from the river, but not towards Ferdia's camp. He laid the dying man on his own bank of the ford and lay beside him, trying to ease Ferdia's last moments. Overcome, Cuchulainn fainted.

As he did, the men on the far side wondered whether their opportunity had come to attack Cuchulainn. He heard their mutterings but took no notice; instead he began a great lament for Ferdia. He wept over the body, described Ferdia's great deeds and character and fine qualities. In the mighty praise-singing which a great warrior's death always demanded, he cursed the day that Maeve persuaded Ferdia to go to what would inevitably bring him death.

Cuchulainn ordered Laeg to strip Ferdia and take the *gae bolga* out of him – the sight of the bleeding body occasioned more and greater grief and wailing. Finally Laeg dragged Cuchulainn away and they left the ford, with the body of Ferdia lying on the ground, all life gone. (To this day the ford where he died bears his name, Ardee, *Ath Fhirdia*, 'the Ford of Ferdia', *ath* being the most ancient word for 'ford'.)

Cuchulainn had been badly wounded. As he left Ardee friends came and took him in hand. They bathed his body in several rivers, each with a different healing quality. In the distance to the south, the armies gathered, still immensely wary of this extraordinary man. Mac Roth, ever the diplomat and scout, rode out from the westerners' camp to try and assess what Maeve's next move should be.

While he returned a chariot followed him, occupied by a silver-haired warrior waving a silver spike. This champion, an Ulsterman called Cethern, son of Fintan, did a Cuchulainn-like deed – he attacked the western armies in their camps and inflicted great damage, even though he himself suffered serious wounds in the engagement. He retreated and went to Cuchulainn's camp, where he hoped his wounds might receive the best of attention.

Regrettably, though, Cethern, a contrary and suspicious man, routed every one of the healers sent to see him, killing several because they diagnosed that his wounds would cost him his life. Eventually one told him that he could either live out his life carefully waiting for death, or that he could get himself together, organise enough strength within a period of three days and take on the enemies who had given him his wounds. The cuts had been so specific that the healer could recognise who gave them – one came from Maeve herself, one from Fergus's son, and Ailill's foster-sons had had a go at him, as had others.

Cethern needed bone-marrow to heal him. Cuchulainn went out and slaughtered several beasts to find the right type and for a day and a half Cethern lay in a bath of it. Then he found he had no ribs, so Cuchulainn fixed him up with the ribs from a chariot. Cethern found that he had no weapons and at that moment his wife appeared in his chariot bringing his weapons. Happily armed he set off against the forces of the west.

In terror of his arrival they tried to deceive him by putting Ailill's crown on top of a standing stone. Cethern drove his sword through it before discovering his mistake, and the ruse so enraged him that he insisted that one of the westerners put on the crown – and Cethern cut him open. He then went on the rampage and only when several regiments fell on him together did he die.

By now the Ulstermen had fully recovered from all their enchantments. When they tackled Maeve's massed armies, the final confrontations proved full of incident. Some Ulster regiments did huge slaughtering and lived to tell the tales. Others fell prey to Maeve's duping. At Teltown a hundred and fifty Ulster charioteers killed four hundred and fifty of Maeve's troops before they themselves died. Another day the men from the west had to hide beneath their shields: the sky above them filled with clashing stones as two conflicting warriors hurled rocks at each other over a great distance before eventually agreeing to stop.

While all these great events went on, the earthly father of Cuchulainn, the distinguished Sualdam (Lugh was Cuchulainn's magical father from the OtherWorld) knew nothing of it. When eventually he heard that his son, much harassed and attacked, both in single combat and in unfair play, had been wounded in every part of his body, that his left hand alone, in which Cuchulainn held his shield, had fifty cuts, he rushed to see his son – much to Cuchulainn's dismay. If the men of the west killed his father he, Cuchulainn, might not have enough strength left for revenge.

Sualdam, distressed at his son's condition, travelled to the palace of King Conor MacNessa at Emhain Macha and cried out to the men of Ulster all the details of the depredations to which his son had been exposed in the matter of the Brown Bull of Cooley. So vehemently did he apply himself to this task that he tripped on his shield and the razor-edge beheaded him. But when the head was brought to Conor's table it still shouted the same warnings.

Against his Druids' advice the king of Ulster raised further armies, vowing to rout Maeve in battle. He sent his son into every corner of Ulster to rally every chieftain and champion. From all the glens and hillsides and green fields they should come and join him in his struggle against Maeve and Ailill. Mustering forces proved no problem – they had only waited to be asked, and so a great host gathered at Emhain Macha.

South this new force headed to assist the earlier warriors, and the armies of Maeve and Ailill waited for them. Mac Roth the scout rode out to see how great a host came towards them and therefore what preparations should be made. He reported back that he had seen no soldiers but that he had seen the wild beasts and the birds leave the woods, that he had seen thick fogs fill the glens with red sparks gleaming within, and that thunder had rolled and lightning had flashed, and a great wind had lifted him vertically out of his saddle and dropped him back again.

The interpretation of these visions was provided by Fergus: the animals fled the trees because the feet of the marching men of Ulster shook the foundations of the woods; their fighting breath had condensed into a thick fog; the sparks of fire came from the battle ardour in the men's eyes and the thunder, lightning and great wind presaged great fury from their roused anger.

Mac Roth, after a further scouting mission, reported on the remarkable calibre of the men who seemed to be leading the Ulster armies, fair and graceful, yellow-haired heroes, grave and wilful all at once, or dark and brooding men of muscle, or grey-haired men with deadly yellow eyes, or sallow, haughty men, or pleasant, loved men, all carrying wonderful weapons – beautiful jewelled shields and five-pointed spears and golden swords. All in all he described companies of soldiers both beautiful to behold and potentially deadly in battle.

Fergus, still in Maeve's camp, knew all of these heroes personally from his days with the Red Branch Knights. He had trained with them, had intimate knowledge of their prowess and skill. He pointed out that the men whom Mac Roth had already described would by themselves most likely defeat Maeve and Ailill – and their greatest warriors had yet to come, and he advised the people from the west to seek a treaty.

King Conor and King Ailill met to discuss a truce. They had chosen camps with wide spaces between them and now they agreed to hold their peace until sunrise. They had reckoned without the Morrigan, the war goddess, who flitted between the tents and provoked them to blood. Ailill, to stimulate and encourage his soldiers, called forth in hailing tones all the soldiers who had survived the earliest onslaughts of Cuchulainn. Peace, clearly, had not seriously entered his considerations.

When the battle began Cuchulainn, still recovering from his great wounds at Ferdia's hands, kept track of the action by getting reports from the charioteers. Then as he saw the kings of the west advancing with their golden crowns gleaming in the morning light, he urged his charioteer to awaken the Ulstermen. They rushed from their tents, according to their custom naked, except for the gold torcs gleaming round their necks, and the last battle began in earnest. Cuchulainn had a good view and grieved that he remained too ill to fight.

At last Fergus had yielded to the taunts of Maeve and Ailill and took a major part – Ailill returned to him the sword which the charioteer had stolen while Fergus and Maeve slept together. Fergus went berserk – he had scores to settle. On his first attack he carved a swathe in the line of battle and killed a hundred of those Ulstermen who could, he felt, have prevented the deaths of his dear friends, Deirdre and the Sons of Usna, whose protection he had been tricked into betraying several years before when they came back from Scotland. Next he confronted the king himself, Conor MacNessa, who called him only fit company for a cur, and as Fergus raised his sword to penetrate Conor's mighty shield, two hands grabbed him from behind and pinned him. A friend had intervened and with wisdom and tenderness advised that anger should not be permitted to interfere with the potential alliances of the future. Then Fergus was persuaded to direct his blows elsewhere and he cut the tips off three hills.

Cuchulainn heard the great noise which this caused and, while wondering what mighty warrior made such a din, felt the old battle-fever rising in him. He prevailed upon his servants and physicians to let him loose, killed the two treacherous fake healers Maeve had sent to keep his wounds open, girded himself and his chariot and went after Fergus. In an old agreement Fergus had promised always to give way to Cuchulainn and he kept his word. Cuchulainn cleared the battle-field by noon, wrecking his own chariot in the process.

Maeve's army retreated, a phalanx of shields protecting their rear flank. Cuchulainn caught up with her as she attended to women's business in the place that they call the Poisoned Glen, ever since Maeve's blood fouled it. While she squatted there she asked Cuchulainn for mercy and he granted it – as he said, he did not kill women.

All remaining warriors now stood down and the armies dispersed. Maeve still had in her camp the Brown Bull of Cooley and on the way home from the battle they met, near Rathcroghan, the other bull, Ailill's one, called Finnbennach. The Brown Bull planted a hoof on Finnbennach's head and Fergus had a job to get him to remove it. Then the bulls began to fight, all day and all night, and they shook the mountains. In the morning the Brown Bull trotted towards them and on his horns hung all that was left of Finnbennach.

All across the country that day the Brown Bull rambled, trying to find his way home. At various stages he dropped some of the entrails of Finnbennach or the organs and to this day the places where he dropped them bear the names of the pieces of a bull. Then, back in the Plain of Muirhevna he dropped dead, and that brought to an end the greatest of all the Celtic sagas.

The west of Ireland made peace with the Ulstermen and persuaded Cuchulainn to leave them alone, a peace that was to last at least seven years, and full of shouts and celebration the Ulstermen returned to their province in glory.

PART THREE

The stories known as *The Mabinogion* form one of the latest
and most colourful strands in the legends of the Celts. Lady
Charlotte Guest brought the term into general literary usage
when, in 1849, she made a translation from two Welsh
manuscripts, the early fourteenth-century White Book of
Rhydderch and the late fourteenth- early fifteenth-century
Red Book of Hergest.

The direct meaning of the word *Mabinogion* has continually
provoked argument; it appears to derive from *mab*, meaning
'young', and in some cases, as in the word *mabinogi*, applied
to an apprentice bard. Lady Guest added a suffix to create
a plural and made it mean 'a collection of stories for children'.
This seems a misconceived definition: it is much more likely
that the original tales either had a function as the curriculum
for those sitting bardship examinations, or were given their
mab root because they tell of young men's adventures.

Similarly, the exact cultural origins of the stories are
surrounded by confusion, though Lady Guest's summary
remains effective and incontrovertible: 'We have throughout
Europe, at an early period, a great body of literature, known
as mediaeval Romance, which amidst much that is wholly of
Teutonic origin and character, includes certain well-marked
traces of an older Celtic nucleus.'

In the strictest terms, though, the full title *Mabinogion* should
only apply to the first four stories in Lady Guest's edition, and not
the entire eleven she translated: I have followed her sequence,
though I have only included nine tales altogether (not caring
as much, in storytelling terms, for the two I left out).

However late these legends come in the development of Celtic
civilisation – by the thirteenth century the Celts' apogee
had long passed – they have the hallmarks of their ancestors
in the oral tradition. Whereas the events of the early stories
occur among the ancient Celts, as witnessed in the
relationships between the Welsh and the Irish, the later stories
possess the colour, pageantry and chivalry associated with
Saxon and Norman courts, a factor confirmed by the
appearance of Arthur.

Story means everything in *The Mabinogion*. The tales possess
pace, imagery and action. The characters and incidents
reinforce the peacock display, the intellectual games, the stylish
valour, the famous Celtic flaunting that made them such a
bright, if nomadic colour on the map of early Europe.

THE LORD OF DYFED

ne dawn, Pwyll of Dyfed, lord of seven hundred families, went hunting. In the mists he rode with his hounds to where the forest might yield up the richest chase. The hounds, snuffling and moaning in great anticipation, went into the thick woods first, with Pwyll hard after them, blowing his hunting horn to try and bring them to heel. The other riders in his hunt lost Pwyll and the dogs in the mist which suddenly thickened, swirling around them like a cold grey cloak – soon he could no longer even hear their hunting horns. Pwyll, though, then heard a new sound, the baying of a different pack, from way ahead of him, as if a separate party had descended upon the forest from the opposite direction. In fact the sounds seemed to be approaching so directly that unless the mist cleared Pwyll wondered whether he and his hounds might collide with the other hunt.

Pwyll heeled his dogs and, with the mist lifting, rode down towards a wide, level clearing. As he emerged from under some low-hanging branches he saw the other pack race into the clearing towards him, and in full pursuit of a stag. The animal had obviously run a long way and, exhausted, had begun to stagger. The other hounds, with no huntsman visible, closed on the creature and brought it down. Pwyll had whipped-in his own hounds hard behind him, but he noticed that uncharacteristically they seemed anxious, too easy to control especially when faced with a kill. His attention focused on their rivals and it struck him that never had he seen such a breed or complexion. They had bright white coats, shining white like snow and even more peculiarly bright scarlet ears, the colour of blood; nowhere had Pwyll ever seen such markings on a single hound, let alone an entire pack. For a moment he appraised this phenomenon and then with horn and whip routed the rival pack so that his own hounds could blood their appetites on the dying stag.

Pwyll rode ceaselessly in a circle around this scene, supervising and controlling. As the dogs' muzzles grizzled and dripped on the fresh venison, squabbles breaking out, Pwyll cracking his whip to break up their fights, a huntsman rode at top speed into the clearing, spurring his horse out from under the overhanging hazels. Dressed in grey, on a grey horse with a brown leather saddle, he saluted Pwyll saying, 'I do not know who you are, whether you're king or commoner, and therefore I have no intention of offering you more than a cursory greeting.' This fell only a little short of insolence, because Pwyll, a remarkable looking man, had the presence, bearing and costume of an aristocrat and, besides, his fame and face were known widely.

He could not let this pass. 'Perhaps it is the case that you do not have sufficient rank to greet me as an equal?'

'Not a matter of rank,' said the stranger.

'Then a matter of what?'

'A matter of bad manners.'

'How so?' asked Pwyll.

'Never,' said the stranger, 'have I come across a man so rude as to drive away a rival hunting pack – who had in any case got there first – so as to give his own hounds bait from the rivals' kill. I feel dishonour towards you. Lucky for you that I don't consider such matters serious enough to warrant revenge.'

Pwyll replied, 'Stranger, if I have offended you I have therefore broken my own code. I saw no huntsman.'

'But you did hear one?'

'Yes, I grant you that.'

'So you should have stayed your hounds? And you should certainly not have driven mine away?'

'Goodness. You are aggrieved.'

'Well, wouldn't you be?' asked the stranger.

'All right,' said Pwyll. 'I apologise and not only that, I will redress my ill-mannered deed so comprehensively that I bet I will actually win your friendship.'

'And how do you propose to do that?' asked the stranger, hoisting an eyebrow.

'In a manner entirely appropriate to your rank, provided I can be allowed to know what that is. I don't even know who you are.'

'I am a king, the crowned leader of my people.' At which Pwyll bowed.

The stranger went on, 'My name – and you probably know it – is Arawn, the king of Annwyvn.'

'At your service indeed,' said Pwyll. 'I am honoured to meet you. But with your great rank, hadn't you better therefore give me some clues as to how I might now set about earning your friendship?'

Thinking for a moment, the man in grey said, 'I am troubled by a neighbour who torments me along our joint borders. They call him Havgan; he's a confounded nuisance – and dangerous. Eliminate him and you will be my friend.'

'My pleasure,' replied Pwyll, 'but give me some pointers.'

The stranger there and then drew up a plan, so swiftly and easily that when you think about it he must have been figuring it out long before he met Pwyll.

First, he would establish without delay, he declared, a deep and acknowledged bond of friendship between his kingdom and Dyfed. Second, he would then invite the Lord of Dyfed into his own country; and so that the people of Annwyvn would assume they were still dealing with their own king, Pwyll would magically assume his, Arawn's, shape. And straightaway Pwyll would have a beautiful woman, the queen of Annwyvn, for his nightly bed. Third, after a year and a day of this arrangement Arawn and Pwyll would meet again in this very same woodland clearing. Their meeting would have great significance and, he hoped, joy, because the previous day Arawn was due to fight his great enemy Havgan – but now Pwyll would be standing in for him and, presumably, defeating him.

All very neat, and then Pwyll raised the question of how he would recognise Havgan when the moment came.

'Easy,' said Arawn, 'he will be the one waiting for you in the ford exactly one year from now. This is how you fight him. Hold your hand until you have chosen the spot and the moment. Then strike him only one telling blow, mark you, one blow and no more, which you know he cannot survive. He will know it too, and will then beg you to bring his life to a merciful end. Do not. He possesses magic whereby the more often you strike him the fitter he rises next day. But he cannot survive a lone, killing blow.'

'Fair enough,' said Pwyll, 'but there is one outstanding matter. Who will look after my kingdom in my absence?'

'That's easy. We will simply reverse roles – just as you go to my kingdom looking exactly like me, likewise I will go to your kingdom looking exactly like you. Not even your closest courtier will know.'

As gentlemen, they shook hands. Arawn wheeled his horse beckoning Pwyll to follow him and they rode to a nearby promontory at the edge of the woods. In the distance lay the land and palaces of the kingdom of Annwyvn, and very prosperous they looked.

The men parted. Pwyll rode along the edge of the escarpment and down to the borders of Annwyvn. The first people he encountered, in the fields and lanes, bowed, greeting him as their king Arawn – it took only a moment or two to get used to it. When he reached 'his' castle, the servants, with much deference, took his horse, and attended as he changed from hunting clothes to court dress, brocade and cloth-of-gold. Nobody for a moment suspected that he was other than Arawn; and in his disguise Pwyll kept making private observations to himself that this court seemed infinitely finer and richer than any he had seen, including his own, that his own servants back at Dyfed could do with a lesson or two in respect from this lot. His comparisons continued when he saw the superbly drilled soldiers march by in orderly ranks.

Then, awaiting him, the queen – exquisite. She, Arawn's wife of course, sat beside him, and he found her a quite extraordinarily compatible and agreeable woman, gracious and well-bred, with stunning looks which seemed not to have affected her disposition, except in a very benign way. They sat down, which signalled a beginning to a most enjoyable feast. When it ended Pwyll and the queen went to bed, but to her chagrin her 'husband' turned his back, and after a prolonged – and, to her, rather sullen – silence, Pwyll fell asleep.

Next morning, he had risen long before her and when they met in the corridors of the court he effortlessly resumed his affectionate cordiality of the previous day. Still she had no clue that her husband's identity had changed and that night again, despite their obvious daytime delight in each other's company, cold relations between them returned, imposed entirely by Pwyll. Nor did that coolness relax one whit during the year which Pwyll spent in the strange and pleasant kingdom of Annwyvn, a marvellous year – hunting and talking and companionship and good food and music.

At the end of it Pwyll set out to keep his appointment at the ford with the enemy, Havgan. Every man of distinction went along to give their leader moral support. A herald, on horseback in midstream, blew a horn, then proclaimed the fight in terms of a battle for superiority and that the kings alone would do the fighting. The two men, Havgan, and Pwyll, disguised as Arawn, met on either side of the herald, who then withdrew, allowing the combatants to touch swords. They then squared off to tear into each other.

With Pwyll's first blow, aimed right at the boss of the shield, the very heart of his defence, Havgan's armour split open and he found himself pitchforked backwards off his horse. He lay in the water and with his magic saw through his opponent's disguise, recognising him as Pwyll. As Arawn had predicted, Havgan asked Pwyll to kill him. Pwyll refused and Havgan indicated to his followers that he now expected to die.

Anticipating their leader's death, they gathered to discuss future allegiances, and soon made their submissions to Pwyll. On receiving Havgan's kingdom to add to Annwyvn, Pwyll's task of gaining the friendship of the stranger he had offended in the woods was handsomely complete.

The following morning he set out to keep his appointment with Arawn, the appointed year and a day after they had first met at the hunt. Arawn exuded the greatest possible warmth and expressed the fullest possible congratulations. Pwyll briefed him fully on the year's extraordinary surrogacy and its culmination – Havgan's death and the annexation of Havgan's kingdom. When Arawn, still declaring his appreciation, restored Pwyll's shape, the Lord of Dyfed set off for home. So did Arawn, overjoyed to see Annwyvn, his subjects and his beloved queen again. She, of course, had never known that he had absented himself for a year and a day.

The secret soon came out, though, because that night Arawn displayed ardour. The queen, accustomed for over a year to daytime warmth and night-time aloofness from her 'husband', reflected astonishment at what she took for the suddenness of this change. When she expressed her surprise, Arawn, appreciating Pwyll's honourableness, revealed the whole story to his queen. She, likewise, was touched and impressed; with the full advantage available to him Pwyll had never once transgressed the sanctity of Arawn's marriage.

When he returned to Dyfed, Pwyll asked his courtiers how they judged 'his' past year's rule. They told him that he had excelled himself, that never before had he ruled with such wisdom and sensitivity; his judgments had never seemed more profound and sound, his largesse never so noticeable. All matters of commerce and politics, of militia and patronage, had improved; laws had strengthened and proven more just, neighbourliness had increased and grown more bountiful; in short an exemplary year, 'something', one old courtier ventured, 'of an *annus mirabilis*.'

Pwyll smiled and decided to tell them the story of the year's events. To his relief they did not frown and wonder whether they might prefer Arawn permanently; instead they chose to praise him for his choice in friends.

The outcome of the hunting encounter, that is, Pwyll's vow to win Arawn's friendship, thus made a major contribution to the countries of Dyfed and Annwyvn. Gifts travelled back and forth, horses and hounds and falcons and weapons, with both overlords eager to declare outright political love. The alliance between Arawn's and Pwyll's kingdoms grew and grew, and Pwyll even received an honorary title from the kingdom of Annwyvn. And whenever the two allies met they never failed to recount, in increasingly colourful detail, that morning long ago when the white hounds with red ears pulled down a stag in the woods.

Many years later, with the relationship stabilised as a steady and mutually fruitful alliance, Pwyll held a session of his court in Arberth. The business of the court had ended for the day and the feasting had begun. After the first course Pwyll took his customary walk in the fresh air. Followed by his retinue, with some of whom he chatted, enquiring of their prosperity, their sons, their view of the kingdom and the proceedings of the court, he walked towards the grassy hill which overlooked the lands of the court.

As he climbed, one of his most loyal men in that locality came up and said, 'My lord, there is a tradition that to anyone born of royal blood who sits on that hill one of two things will happen. Either they will be assaulted and perhaps receive many cuts and bad wounds, or will have revealed to them something marvellous.'

Pwyll replied, 'I'll take my chances. Who's going to damage me with you as my host? See if we discover wonders.'

No violence occurred. Instead, while they sat on the grass, a woman appeared on the dusty road that wound beneath them. Her white horse gleamed and jingled with gold harness-pieces and she wore rich golden brocade. None of the retinue had ever seen her before, so Pwyll dispatched a messenger, who could not catch up with her. Though she appeared to travel at a normal pace, the more he hurried the more she increased the gap between them, and yet never seemed to move faster. The courtier came back, out of breath. Then Pwyll sent a horseman after her, and he, even by riding the horse flat out, the best horse in the court too, could not catch up with her either. In fact, she simply opened up a bigger and bigger gap between them, though never increasing her pace. The horseman also returned crestfallen.

Pwyll mused all night on how he should interpret this phenomenon. Next afternoon at the same time, having instructed the
courtiers to have the fastest horse in the land standing by, he again
walked to the hill. Sure enough the woman in the brocade appeared
on her pale horse and before she drew level Pwyll sent the rider to
intercept her. But even as he moved towards her she again opened
up a gap entirely disproportionate to the speed at which she seemed
to be travelling. Pwyll's man slowed his horse down to a walk in
the hope that by pursuing her in her own idiom, so to speak, by
playing her at her own game, he might gain some ground. That
ploy also failed. He changed tactics, drove his horse flat out, but
again, with no sign of increased speed, she opened up an even larger
gap between herself and her pursuer. The exhausted horseman
returned to the hilltop where Pwyll sat with pursed lips.

Next day they repeated the process. By now the word had spread
through the court and a great crowd walked slowly behind Pwyll to
the hill. This time, Pwyll's own horse had been saddled. As the
woman rode into view, Pwyll raced after her but he could only get
within earshot. He called out, 'Woman! In the name of the man you
love – wait.'

She halted, raising the riding-veil from her face.

'Who are you? Where do you come from? What is your business
in these parts?' Pwyll launched a stream of questions at the mysterious
rider who, it transpired, possessed exquisite looks. She responded
to him openly and warmly, saying she had business to transact in
these parts.

'May I be so bold as to ask the nature of your business?' Pwyll
asked, with his most perfect good manners.

'Yes. My priority was to meet you, my lord.' While Pwyll barely
had enough composure to conceal his astonishment she introduced
herself. 'Rhiannon.'

'A melodious name,' said Pwyll.

According to custom, she recited her lineage and her family.

'But your business with me?' Pwyll inquired, having listened
patiently through the formalities.

She told him her story – that she had loved him from afar and for
many a long day, but, alas, fruitlessly. Her family had pledged her
to marry 'suitably' a man whom she hated. Only one thing could
save her from this living grave.

'And what might that be?' asked Pwyll, already captivated by this
glorious and mature girl with the mellifluous voice.

'My lord, that you requite my love.'

He dismounted, knelt on one knee, and hand on heart assured her that he would choose no other woman in the world. To seal their bargain they agreed to meet at her father's court in exactly one year – she obliged Pwyll to this solemn promise. He rode away to spend the most thoughtful year he had ever known.

On the appointed night Pwyll assembled ninety-nine of his most favoured courtiers around him, and in their most ornate robes the party rode out to meet Rhiannon at her father's court. Preparations had long been in progress for the visit of this great leader from Dyfed, and they received a mighty welcome, banners and trumpets, while proceeding ceremonially up the hall to sit in the most honoured places. Pwyll was placed between Rhiannon and her father; the feast began with music which gave way to laughter and a buzz of fine talk.

Just as the servants cleared away the remains of the first course, with Rhiannon ceremonially pouring the wine for the next, a tall young man with auburn hair and a princely, though sullen, appearance walked through the door. He had a natural power and dignity and he strode up between the long tables to where Pwyll sat. Bowing to Rhiannon's father though refusing to sit down, he addressed Pwyll.

'I have come, Lord of Dyfed, Head of Annwyvn, to ask a favour.'

'I am here to grant it,' replied Pwyll, gracious as ever, but he uttered it before he had seen the alarm on Rhiannon's face as she stood, wine jug in hand, a little way behind the young man.

The young man's favour, it transpired, took the form of an entreaty. He begged Pwyll that instead of sleeping with Rhiannon he should hand her over to him. Pwyll was dumbstruck – he had given his word, and therefore, it seemed, was about to fall into the trap of his own generosity. Too late did he perceive what had happened; the anguished Rhiannon came round the table and told him this was the man whom her family was forcing her to marry.

'Do something,' she hissed at Pwyll.

'I can't,' he said, 'I am bound by the laws of hospitality and now I am caught, it seems, by my own word of honour.'

In reply Rhiannon whispered a ruse. Pwyll would formally give her to the man; in return she would hand Pwyll a small bag to keep by his side. She would then formally set a date for the man to sleep with her – one year thence. When that night arrived, though, Pwyll and his ninety-nine followers must be armed and ready, scattered in hiding throughout the orchard just outside the window.

Rhiannon gave Pwyll his instructions for that occasion. He must disguise himself thoroughly as a decrepit old beggar and shuffle into the hall. No host may turn away an alms-seeker, and when queried by Rhiannon's betrothed, Pwyll, the beggar, should demand food for the little bag she had just now given him. But all the food in the seven kingdoms could not fill the magic bag, and to pacify the host's growing impatience Pwyll should then say that the bag would never be replete until a true and great nobleman stepped into it, carefully pressing down all the food within. The man, keen both to prove his pedigree and rid himself of this ungainly beggar, would certainly rise at Rhiannon's prompting, and step in the bag – at which point Pwyll should draw the strings tight. With the man safely trapped, Pwyll should then summon his men by his hunting-horn.

Agreeing this plot in hurried whispers, the pair turned to the young nobleman who, hands on hips, said, 'I'm waiting for an answer, Lord of Dyfed.'

Rhiannon cut in. 'The Lord of Dyfed will keep his word, but at the moment he is our guest in this house and must not be insulted.' With a show of formal deference she agreed to sleep with the young man exactly one year from then. The man strode away and the feast continued, though somewhat subdued.

On the appointed night Pwyll with his ninety-nine associates, not in regalia now, but fully armed and ordered, rode hard across the country to the court of Rhiannon's father. In due course the rival came, languid in his conquest, and received a rich welcome. Pwyll, hiding his men under the apple trees, waited until the feast was under way, then entered the court dressed as a limping beggar with filthy clothes and ragged boots. In accordance with tradition no servant or sentry barred him, nor did anyone turn him back as he walked up the hall to the top table where the rival sat between Rhiannon and her father.

'Yes?' snapped the young man, though it was not his place to do so.

'Food for my bag.' Pwyll held it out. The lordly young rival, again outstepping himself, snapped his fingers.

The servants worked and worked, heaving joints and loaves and fruit all ferried energetically from the kitchen – but the bag showed no signs of filling. The guests clamoured round to watch.

'Old man,' said Pwyll's rival, 'is that wretched bag ever going to fill up?'

'Only when a man of truly noble birth and good heart and honour stands in it,' replied Pwyll, 'and presses the food down inside and instructs the bag to be satisfied.'

'Make way,' said the rival, egged on by Rhiannon. 'I will stand in it happily,' and rose to the task. Pwyll held open the neck and assisted the man, who, shoving away the helping hand, stepped inside up to his waist. Then he fell in head-over-heels when, with a violent jerk, Pwyll up-ended the bag. Pwyll then drew the strings tight and tearing off his disguise blew a long loud blast on his horn. His ninety-nine armed men rode at full speed into the hall and rounded up all of the rival's supporters.

Pwyll had hung the bag with the haughty rival in it high up on a beam and as each of Pwyll's men rode or ran by the bulging, shaking bag, they belted it joyously with a club or the flat edge of a sword, crying out, 'What's in the bag?'

Back, always, came the jovial reply from Pwyll, 'A badger.' This impromptu game became known throughout the farms of Dyfed as 'Badger-in-the-Bag'.

During a lull in the noise and laughter, the man in the bag spoke up.

'My lord, I have had too proud a birth to deserve a death in a bag.'

Since it was not clear to whom he had addressed his remarks, Pwyll or the host, Rhiannon's father, they had to let him out, and he tumbled on to the floor, bruised and torn, his pride askew as his clothing.

Rhiannon instructed her father and Pwyll that the man should be made to give an oath.

'Swear never to seek vengeance,' said Rhiannon, 'and to assist my Lord of Dyfed, Head of Annwyvn, in the giving of gifts to all who seek favour.' This effectively reduced him, temporarily at least, to the rank of Pwyll's courtier, and he was allowed to slip quietly out of the hall and have his wounds bathed and his dress adjusted. When he came back he sat in a discreet place three-quarters of the way down the table.

For the next seven days great feasting and bestowing of patronage took place. Pwyll could now be seen in all his authority and lordly stature, revealed as a generous and good man. He spent some time building a relationship with Rhiannon's father who could not be other than impressed with this nobleman and when the feast ended the two men had reached an understanding that the overjoyed Rhiannon should return to Dyfed as Pwyll's wife.

They left on a lovely sunny morning, sent off with many blessings, laden with gifts; the courtiers came out of the castle gates to shower them with petals and stood a long time waving after them. And when Pwyll rode down into Dyfed and presented Rhiannon to his own people, they had the warmest possible greeting for her. They loved her from the beginning; the old people had tears in their eyes, the young were enchanted by her beauty and dress. Every person who came up to her, who met her, gave Rhiannon some kind of gift, a bird or a jewel or a cloth or a flower. After a tremendously festive wedding, she and her beloved Pwyll settled down to an immensely happy rulership over Dyfed.

A cloud gathered over them, though. After three years Rhiannon had borne no children. Guaranteed, safe succession remained the principal source of any kingdom's stability and Pwyll's chieftains sought a secret meeting. They reflected their concern; the harsher ones among them, with old experience of instability in other realms, even urged him to find another wife who would bear him children. Pwyll, though hurt on Rhiannon's behalf, comprehended the validity of their concern and asked for a year's grace, since he and Rhiannon had not been married very long. And if, after that year, she still seemed barren he would abide by their counsel, though it would break his heart.

Happily, Rhiannon bore a son within the year – at Arberth where she and Pwyll had first met as she rode by on her white horse. Six midwives, the best available, were appointed by the court to care for the mother and baby. On the night after the boy was born all the women, including, though more understandably, Rhiannon, fell asleep. When they woke the baby had disappeared.

The nurses feared execution for their negligence, so they conceived a plan to save their own skins and throw the blame on their royal mistress. The greyhound at the court chambers had just given birth to a litter, and the midwives killed the pups, smearing Rhiannon's face with the blood. When she awoke they told her she had slaughtered her own child in her sleep.

Apart from her anguish over the missing baby, Rhiannon immediately perceived both their ploy and the desperate danger in which it placed her. She pleaded, implored, quite left the shores of her own dignity, and even promised them succour and safe passage out of Dyfed if they told the truth. The midwives stuck to their story, and managed to convince the court when it convened to consider the tragedy.

Pwyll used all his considerable authority to defend his wife. He saved her from the death penalty, refused to banish her, but finally had to agree to punishment. The court sentenced her to sit for seven years outside the walls telling the sad story of her baby son's death to all who arrived or departed. Into the bargain she had to offer to carry – on her back – any visitor, rich or poor, thin or fat, heavy or light, climbing the hill to the court. The birth, disappearance, trial and sentence took several months and Rhiannon served out her first year in all the changing weathers. Not a visitor entered or left that court without hearing her wailing confession.

During all this time, it so happened that the Lord of Gwent, a great man called Tiernan, also had a problem which was coming now to a head. He owned a truly wonderful mare which foaled every first of May – but every year the colt, like Rhiannon's baby, disappeared. Tiernan had lost several foals this way and at the end of his tether he told his wife that he was absolutely determined to hold on to this year's foal.

Came the night of May's Eve, the great magical feast of Beltaine. By a silken halter Tiernan led the mare indoors, and sat down to watch. On the stroke of midnight the mare dropped the foal, a lovely roan colt, and at the same moment in a great whoosh of noise a giant curved claw reached through the high window, grabbed the wet staggering foal by its little curly mane and began to haul it up through the air and out of the great hall. Tiernan drew his broadsword and hacked off the giant claw-arm at the elbow and foal, forearm and claw fell back on the stone floor. A huge scream rang out through the night followed by a crashing noise, and Tiernan raced down the stone hallway to the great door and out into the night. He could see nothing – only the darkness and the stars, with the noise fast receding.

When he turned back, in the doorway he saw an infant, a small boy, wrapped in swaddling-clothes of white damask, a cheerful child, smiling at him. Tiernan picked the boy up, carried him into the bedroom where his wife – long childless, always yearning for a son – sat awaiting the outcome of the foaling. As they recovered from their astonishment they agreed that the child had obviously been nobly born – but of whom? Nothing for it but to raise him, and so he grew with them, extraordinarily strong and bright. When he reached the age of six, by which time he had begun to prove useful in the stableyard, they gave the lad, as a gift, the colt foaled on the night they found him.

In due course, Tiernan, an intelligent man, inevitably came to hear, from a traveller to Dyfed, of Rhiannon and her 'dead' son. The more he looked the more it seemed to him now that the boy he was rearing bore a strong resemblance to Pwyll, the Lord of Dyfed, in whose entourage Tiernan had once held a position, and whose goodwill he had retained. With sadness, though with truth and an interest in seeing justice done, he told his wife. Much though they loved the child they agreed that he, a prince after all, and heir to Dyfed, should be returned to Pwyll and Rhiannon – thereby also releasing Rhiannon from her unjust and awful punishment.

Tiernan, accompanied by the boy, now growing up a fine youth, rode to Pwyll's court. At the gate they observed Rhiannon who called to them, 'I will carry any of you who wishes on my back up to the court. That is my punishment – I killed my son with my own hands.' Tiernan refused her offer, so did the boy.

Pwyll received his former courtier Tiernan with great delight. Feasting and music took place, but with an awkward difference, because Rhiannon, at Tiernan's request, sat with them. After the serving of the first course, Tiernan asked Pwyll for permission to address the banquet. He rose and told the whole story – of the mare and the foal and the giant arm and claw and the depositing of the damask-swaddled, smiling baby. He turned to Rhiannon and told her of his conviction that she had suffered great injustice.

'Look at the boy whom I have brought here as my son. Touch him, feel his hair, look in his eyes, watch him smile, and then tell me if that is not your lost boy, the son of the Lord of Dyfed!'

A hush fell over the hall; somewhere a woman sobbed.

'If this were true,' said Rhiannon, 'then my care would be eased from me.'

She rose and with all eyes watching went hesitantly towards the boy. She put out a hand gingerly. The hand trembled as she laid it on the forehead and the fair hair of the boy who, not quite able to understand what was happening, had bravely risen to greet her. She sent a hand slowly over his yellow hair, afraid, it seemed, to touch it. She looked in his eyes. Then she took his fine smiling face gently between her hands, as if he were still a baby and suddenly hugged his head to her bosom, bursting out in sobs.

'Every woman everywhere knows her own child,' she wept.

Pwyll, overcome, did not know whom to embrace, Rhiannon, or the boy, or Tiernan, now in tears himself.

As one person the hall rose and cheered and wept simultaneously. They banged goblets and tables and clanged swords against shields. When the applause died down they discussed whether the boy should continue with the name his adoptive parents had given him, Gowrie, which meant 'darling one of the golden hair'. One of the elders pointed out that Rhiannon had used the word 'pryderi', that is to say 'care', and they agreed on this as the most fitting name, Pryderi son of Pwyll.

Tiernan then spoke in his turn.

'I want the boy to remember the woman who loves him deeply and who reared him. She will now be heartbroken at losing him.'

Pwyll promised that thenceforth he and his son would support and protect Tiernan and his wife. He appointed them foster-parents to Pryderi so that they might always have a say in the boy's life and decisions, and that he could have access to their love. Tiernan prepared to return to his own land, taking a loving farewell of the golden-haired boy. Pwyll and Rhiannon pressed upon him gifts of horses, hounds, jewels, cloths, but out of dignity and duty Tiernan would accept nothing whatsoever.

In his new life, Pryderi son of Pwyll received the most careful and thoughtful upbringing and not a day passed in which his parents did not rejoice in his beauty, intelligence and all-round skill and prowess.

Long years after, when his father Pwyll died, Pryderi had grown to such stature that he effortlessly took over all the seven kingdoms of Dyfed, and the protectorate he enjoyed over the lands and king-dom of Annwyvn. He conquered further territories and grew ever more loved and respected.

In due course he took a splendid wife and continued in the same tradition of wisdom and authority as his distinguished parents.

BRANWEN, THE DAUGHTER OF LLYR

he crowned king, Bran, son of the great Llyr, sat by the rocky shore at Harlech, accompanied by his court and retinue. As they talked a fleet of thirteen ships appeared in orderly formation over the horizon, from the direction of southern Ireland.

'Alert the household guard,' said Bran, 'find out who these mariners are.'

The strange fleet drew nearer, sailing beautifully before the westerly wind, the brilliant, embroidered insignia on satin pennants becoming plainer. The flagship detached itself and came forward, bearing high above the prow a shield – the sign of peace. It put down longboats which, also making signs of peace, rowed ashore to a point directly beneath the rock on which Bran sat.

He welcomed the boatmen with a blessing and asked whence, and from whom, they came. The fleet, they said, belonged to the powerful Irish lord, Mattholoch, who had come to good purpose – to seek the hand in marriage of Bran's beautiful sister, Branwen of the snowy bosom. The marriage, explained the envoy, seemed suitable and logical – the daughter of Llyr, sister of Bran, would have a husband worthy of her family, and the two countries would thereby form a powerful alliance. Bran sent back an invitation to Mattholoch to discuss the matter and the envoy's longboat, pushing out from the rocks, returned to the flagship. In the afternoon Mattholoch came ashore, a fine and dignified man, and Bran gave him the greatest hospitality: far into the night they feasted and talked. True to the

rule of their kingdoms they discussed no business until all entertainment had been enjoyed.

Next morning Bran's Council met and took a decision that a
marriage between Branwen and Mattholoch implied many benefits.
Both sides met again and began to make the formal arrangements –
that the Irish would sail round the coast to Aberffraw, site of the
wedding, Bran leading his people overland; that the feast would be
arranged so that Bran sat with his full brother Manawyddan (he also
had two half-brothers) on one side and Mattholoch on the other,
with Branwen placed next to Mattholoch so that he might talk to
her, get to know his new bride. All of this would take place inside
specially erected tents, since no house had ever comfortably accom-
modated the huge Bran, and on the night of the feasting Mattholoch
and Branwen would sleep together. All began to take place as agreed.
Ireland and the Island of the Mighty, Britain, seemed about to form
an alliance – a consideration which, as much as Branwen's famous
beauty, had encouraged Mattholoch to seek this marriage.

Next morning, sleepy-eyed, the administrators of both parties met
to discuss the facilities needed by the mighty retinue accompanying
Mattholoch, in particular the quarters for the horses, so numerous
that they had to be stabled far and wide. All of these great transactions, however, had taken place without the knowledge of Bran's
half-brother, Evnissien, a notoriously quarrelsome man, who had
been away about his own business. When he returned, riding past
these great corrals of horses, he asked who owned them. The reply
enraged him – that the King of Ireland had been honoured with such
extravagant hospitality and above all that Branwen had been given
away without his own permission.

In his rage, and because he couldn't fight all the soldiers, he
maimed the Irish horses awfully, cutting their lips back to their
gums, their ears down to their skulls, their eyelids to the eyeballs,
their tails back to their rumps. The unfortunate animals, screaming
in agony, presented a hideous appearance. Into the bargain, they
now had no sale value owing to their injuries, and had to be put
down *en masse* – which meant that Evnissien in his violent mischief,
as well as insulting a visiting king, had also vandalised a major
portion of the Irishman's assets.

The Irish courtiers persuaded their king to see this as a calculated
insult.

'But,' Mattholoch puzzled, 'if they wanted to insult me, why
would they have given me Branwen at all? It isn't consistent.'

'We don't know their ways,' said his courtiers, 'but their actions are plain enough,' and they persuaded Mattholoch to head for the fleet riding at anchor in the bay and sail home.

Court intelligence brought this news to Bran who, surprised and upset, sent messengers after them. The envoys, who knew nothing of the horses' maiming, listened in enraged astonishment to what Mattholoch had to say. They tried to assure him that Bran, had he known of this appalling deed, would be even angrier. Which was indeed the case, though Bran shrewdly put politics first.

'We can't let him go away from here in such dudgeon,' he declared. 'It's not so much that we need their friendship – it's more that we don't need Mattholoch and Ireland as enemies.'

He now sent two of his most experienced courtiers – his brother Manawyddan being one of them – to prevail upon Mattholoch one more time.

'Tell him this,' instructed Bran. 'For every horse disfigured I will give him a better horse; I will further pay him an honour-bound fine consisting a stick of solid silver, tall as himself and a finger's thickness, and to go with it a gold plate the circumference of his own face. Then tell him of my family dilemma – that if anyone else had done this they would now be roasting on a fire, but since the maiming has been carried out by my half-brother I can't easily have him executed. Most of all, have him come to a meeting with me so that face to face I can offer him a humble apology and whatever peace terms he wants.'

The Irish, in conference, understood that the moral advantage had now switched, and that if they did not accept the huge generosity offered them by Bran they would lose face. Mattholoch graciously thanked Bran's messengers, accepted the offers and returned to the greensward where all the tents were now being rearranged to create the equivalent of a great hall. Bran had arranged a feast to cement the reparation and he sat beside Mattholoch and paid him deference. He found his Irish guest listless, though, and wondered why.

'Is the compensation I offer you too small? If so, I will increase my offer with a special gift. Tomorrow I will begin to pay you the replacement horses and as well as that – I have a magic cauldron. If one of your men is killed in battle, throw him into this cauldron. The following morning he will climb out over the rim of the cauldron, restored fully, ready to fight again. I should say, though, that there is a drawback – any man thus renewed will have lost the gift of speech.'

Mattholoch thanked Bran profusely for this great gift. Next day Bran kept his word about the horses, and handed over to Mattholoch as many good stallions and colts as he could lay his hands upon.

That night at dinner Mattholoch asked Bran where he had found the magic cauldron. Bran told him the story. An Irishman had given it to him, an Irishman with dirty yellow hair, who had escaped from an iron prison in Ireland, a jail which had been turned into a red-hot furnace.

Mattholoch said he had known this man and his dreadful wife in Ireland, that in fact he had met them while the man emerged from a lake with the cauldron on his back. He told the story.

This Irishman's wife, twice his size, four times as awful, eight times as grotesque, climbed up out of the lake after him. The man told Mattholoch that the wife would soon conceive – at the end of a month and a fortnight – and give birth to a fully grown, fully armed, fully trained warrior. In consideration of this Mattholoch took them into his palace and gave them shelter. But in little over a year they had become unendurably offensive; they grumbled odiously, they complained incessantly, they stank, they molested his people, even the courtiers – the woman made unbelievably gross advances to the men – and delegation after delegation asked Mattholoch to expel them.

But the two offenders refused to quit, so the court council decided to imprison them in a specially built iron house made by all the blacksmiths of Ireland. Upon completion of the building the courtiers would lay on a feast for the man and his wife, and during it the couple and their awful family were to be locked in. The blacksmiths would then heap the building high with coals and light it like a forge furnace.

All went according to plan. Inside, the churl and his churlish wife began to make merry and wild, and outside the blacksmiths went to work on their bellows. They pumped and pumped until the house became hotter than hot. As the metal walls reddened, the truth began to dawn on the people inside. When the house began to change from red to white-hot, the churl hurled his huge bulk against the wall, bursting it open and running with his wife into the open air.

After that the horrid couple fled Ireland, which is how they came into Bran's kingdom; he sheltered them gladly while they repaid him by breeding regiments of fully armed soldiers.

Bran and Mattholoch exchanged many similar tales all through that night; when tired of talking they listened to the musicians who played session after session until dawn broke and nobody had a wink of sleep. With much joyous leavetaking and renewals of their firm alliance, Mattholoch thanked Bran for his hospitality and for turning bad to good. In the royal fleet of thirteen ships with their satin pennants, Mattholoch, Branwen by his side, set sail from Menai for Ireland. The Irish people loved their queen at first sight and piled the castle yard high with gifts. In due course Branwen bore a son and the realm throve under their care.

After a couple of years though, when all the excitement of Mattholoch's marriage and heir had died down, his leading counsellors began to reflect upon the insult which lay beneath the maiming of the horses. They confronted Mattholoch with it and continued to pester him, saying he had exacted no revenge upon the Welsh, that he had not responded like a man, much less a king. They obliged Mattholoch to take it out on his wife Branwen and made him expel her from his favours and his court. He relegated her, his queen, the mother of his son, to the kitchen. Daily she had to endure the indignities of being bullied by the head cook and the slurs of the kitchen boys who boxed her ears. As an added precaution Mattholoch then took his counsellors' advice: his navy intercepted all ships going to Wales from Ireland while impounding all in the opposite direction, so that Branwen's family should never hear of her downfall.

This state of affairs obtained for three years. In the kitchens, Branwen, to take her mind off her humiliation, had made a pet of a starling. It perched on the rim of her mixing bowl and listened as she taught it words, and how to carry out small errands for her. One day she fastened a letter to the underside of the bird's wing and dispatched it to Wales. By good fortune the bird landed in Caernarvon during one of Bran's legislative assemblies, coming down like an arrow from the sky and perching on his shoulder, exhausted. A courtier noticed the letter under its wing, perceived that the bird had been a domestic pet, guessed that it had been taught to carry messages and retrieved Branwen's note. As Bran read it his emotions swung between sadness and fury.

He decided upon a war of revenge, sending messengers to all his domains and chieftains: when their king called with such urgency they knew they must down tools and bear arms. From the one hundred and fifty-four districts of his kingdom Bran convoked his fellow-countrymen and told them of the vile injustice done to his sister, the royal princess Branwen, daughter of the great Llyr. Troops and mariners from all over Wales augmented the royal guard and, leaving behind seven chosen men, led by Caradoc, to run the affairs of the kingdom, Bran led his armies down to the shore heading for Ireland.

He struck out ahead, wading through the waters, carrying on his back the harpers and lutanists so as to keep the strings of their instruments dry. Behind him sailed his huge fleet of great ships.

On a long shoreline, Mattholoch's swineherds looked out to sea and saw an extraordinary sight – an entire landscape, it seemed, moving towards Ireland. There was a forest, a mountain, a high escarpment with a pair of lakes on either side. They ran and told their king of this amazing sight and he, unable to divine what it meant, sent them to ask Branwen, since it seemed to be heading from the direction of her native land. She suggested that her brother might have sent a fleet to rescue her, that the forest illusion had been created by the masts of the ships, the lakes created by the eyes on either side of the high ridge of her brother's nose, and he, Bran, the mountain that moved through the water, since no ship had ever yet been built large enough to contain him.

After a rushed conference the Irish retreated across the river Shannon, on the bottom of which they laid a huge stone to prevent ships from coming upriver. Just before Bran and his troops got to the river bank they found that the Irish had destroyed the bridge. At that moment Bran, surveying the military difficulties of getting his armies across to engage the Irish, said:

'The man who would lead his people must first become a bridge,' and he prostrated himself so that his huge body reached from bank to bank, permitting his troops to march across.

Mattholoch's men, seeing that the Welsh armies had advanced successfully, tried to pre-empt Bran's attack by making extravagant gestures of friendship. They told Bran that Mattholoch had given up the kingship of Ireland in favour of the son whom Branwen had borne, and that the boy was to be invested that very night in front of Bran as a reparation for the indignities Branwen had been made to suffer.

Though Bran seemed pleased, he asked for a further gesture and after lengthy consultations the Irish offered to build him a house, since he had never found a house large enough to accommodate him. After deliberating, Bran accepted the offer, largely on the anxious promptings of his sister Branwen who feared tremendous carnage.

The Irish built the house – huge, impregnable, noble enough to honour and flatter Bran's kingship with enough room for the armies of both nations. But Mattholoch's supporters laid a trap in it for the

Welsh: from a peg on every pillar they hung a large bag and in each bag they concealed a warrior instructed to spring out during the first feast and kill the nearest Welshman; in all, hundreds of bags hung from the pillars which supported the great roof.

The Irish, though, reckoned without the quarrelsome Evnissien who, arriving to inspect the house, walked along the colonnades looking at the bags.

'What's in them?' he asked an Irish equerry standing by.

'Flour,' said the man, 'oatmeal for making cakes.'

'Oh yeah?' said Evnissien, and pinched one bag so hard that his fingers pulped straight through the skullbone and brain of the man inside.

'And in this one?' he mocked.

'Flour,' said the next Irishman, 'wholemeal,' and so on until Evnissien had crushed the head of every man in every bag.

Directly after this the investiture began. The boy-king charmed every observer and participant, a sweet boy, greeted with tenderness by his relatives from Wales.

Evnissien complained loudly that the son of Branwen had greeted everyone else in the hall except him. Bran directed the boy to salute his uncle, but Evnissien picked the little prince up by the heels and before anyone could interfere swung him headfirst into the huge fire. Branwen, crazed, tried to snatch the child from the flames but Bran stopped her, knowing she would get killed. In the fighting that broke out Bran continued to protect Branwen, putting his shield around her shoulder. He escorted her safely from the house, avoiding a battle the likes of which had never been seen in either Ireland or Wales. Hacking and hewing and gouging and grunting, they tore each other apart. The Welshmen had the best of it until the Irish called up their secret weapon – the regenerative cauldron Bran had given as an appeasement to Mattholoch.

With it the Irish renewed their soldiery – even the two hundred men from the bags reappeared, as good as new except for the gift of speech. Silently they began to fight and Evnissien saw that he had once again brought great trouble upon his countrymen. He decided upon a last heroic act. He hid himself among the dead bodies of the Irishmen piled up waiting to be thrown into the cauldron. When the cauldron attendants came along they picked him up too and slung him into it. Evnissien stretched his great body in four different directions so fiercely that he shattered the cauldron, and himself with it. As a result, amid huge losses on both sides, the Welshmen won. Only seven of Bran's men escaped alive. A magic dart, though, had wounded the king in the foot and on his deathbed Bran gave them his last instructions.

'Cut off my head and take it to London. Eventually you must bury it in state on the White Hill of London, turning my face towards France. But on the way to doing this you will be a long time on the road. First, spend seven years at Harlech where your music will be provided by the birds of Rhiannon. Spend the next eighty years in Pembroke; all this time my head will be with you, incorrupt. While you are there you must never enter or leave by the door on the south side facing towards Cornwall. If you open that door then you must immediately take my head and bury it in London.'

Ceremonially they cut off Bran's head and left Ireland hurriedly. When they landed in Wales Branwen had a moment to contemplate what had taken place; looking back across the waves at the land dimly distant which had brought her such grief, her heart broke and they buried her where she died. They continued on their travels, making for Harlech, and asked of the locals what had happened in their absence. Great unrest had broken out and of the seven men left in charge during the Irish campaign, six had been slaughtered by a king who had worn a cloak making him invisible so that his opponents could only see his flashing sword. The seventh, Caradoc, Bran's son, died of a broken heart when he saw his men slain.

Still bearing Bran's head, the seven continued their journey until they reached Harlech where they found ample food and drink. As they feasted on the grass the three small birds of Rhiannon appeared and sang to them the sweetest music on earth. Seven years later they left Harlech for Pembroke, and there awaiting them stood a great keep with a view over the water. Two of the doors gaped open invitingly and the third, on the Cornwall side, was firmly shut. Eighty years they stayed there, easy and rested and in pleasant congeniality, and Bran's head with them, undecayed and vital like a companion – until one man could not resist the temptation to open the third door. As he did so a sense of loss consumed them all and a sense of every hurt each had known, and a sense of every bereavement each had known, and a sense of every slight each had known. Immediately they felt compelled to leave and on the high White Hill of London they buried Bran's head facing France.

Back in Ireland the land had been ravaged and no men lived. Five women had survived, pregnant, dwelling in a cave since the awful warring over Branwen. These pregnancies brought forth five strong youths who understood the need to propagate, so each slept with the mother of another and thus the population renewed itself. When the men reached full maturity they divided the country into a province each – which is how Ireland came to have five provinces. They sowed, tilled and harvested and they dug for gold and found it, and they expanded peacefully and made the land prosperous again.

And so ended the long avenging of Branwen which began at Bran's Council, where thirteen elegant and orderly ships with satin pennants sailed in over the horizon from Ireland.

MANAWYDDAN, THE SON OF LLYR

In the campaign to avenge Branwen, Manawyddan was one of the seven who survived Ireland. He had a great capacity for gentleness and good behaviour and when he and his companions had buried Bran's head with ceremony and dignity, Manawyddan looked out across London and the distant hills and expressed immense sorrow.

He said to his friends, 'Do you realise that of all of you I am the only one who has no place to lay his head tonight?'

Pryderi of Dyfed, son of Pwyll and Rhiannon, said, 'But the new king of Britain is your cousin, is he not?'

'Maybe so,' replied Manawyddan, 'but as far as I am concerned Bran was my king, and that is how I still see it. I can't bring myself to accept hospitality from the man who has taken Bran's place.'

'In that case,' said Pryderi, a man with the same nobility of spirit as his late father Pwyll, 'go to Dyfed. My mother Rhiannon is yours. She is still beautiful, you know – and you may share in the authority she has over the seven divisions of Dyfed. Enjoy it for as long as you wish. And if after a while you feel you cannot relish that kind of jurisdiction, tell me and I will give you land of your own.'

When the party arrived in Dyfed, and Manawyddan found himself sitting beside Rhiannon at dinner, he felt more and more attracted to her. Pryderi had been right and during the meal Manawyddan called across the table to him, 'Thank you – I accept your offer.'

'What offer was that?' asked Rhiannon, sharp as ever.

Pryderi replied, 'Mother, I have taken the liberty of giving you to Manawyddan as his wife.'

Rhiannon replied, 'I'll gladly go along with that.'

At which point Manawyddan and Rhiannon got up from the feast and headed for bed.

When they returned Pryderi said that all must continue feasting but he himself had to make a journey – to see Cassvallawn, the new king of Britain. Rhiannon, ever informed, told him that as the king had gone to Kent he should wait until the royal entourage came nearer to Dyfed. Pryderi agreed and decided instead to tour his own counties of Dyfed and those territories of Annwyvn he had inherited through his father's old alliance. It proved a most enjoyable trip – the land had never looked better, stocks of fish ran high in the rivers, the meadows flourished, the hunting proved rich and exciting. He made one digression – to visit Cassvallawn who had reached Oxford. The king, cementing alliances in the wake of Bran's death, acknowledged the Lord of Dyfed with enthusiasm and friendship and, thus relieved, Pryderi returned home.

A new feast began – at Arberth, the very same place where Pwyll, Pryderi's father, had all those years ago met Rhiannon dressed in gold brocade riding on her white horse. On the opening evening of the feast, as servants cleared away the remains of the first course, Pryderi and his mother, now married, of course, to Manawyddan, took a walk with several friends to the same hill from which Pwyll had first observed Rhiannon riding by. As they sat on the grass, thunder rolled out of a clear sky. A mist fell like a sudden veil, so thick that none could see the nearest person. When the mist lifted, a brilliant light shone everywhere and the landscape had been stripped – no sign of herds or flocks of other animals, the courtiers had disappeared from the palace, not a soul could be seen in the empty landscape except for four of the immediate original party, Pryderi and his wife, and Manawyddan and Rhiannon.

Returning to the court they searched everywhere. Halls, rooms, kitchens, stables – all stood empty, ringing with that sound that only echoes in an utterly deserted place. Nowhere, in field or house, could they see any trace of the extensive domestic life they had enjoyed a few hours before. Recovering from the shock they tried to make the best of it and evolved a *modus vivendi*. In the castle larders they found enough food to make a new feast every day for a month, and when they had exhausted that supply they hunted and fished; in fact, they survived not only well but contentedly, as the land gave them wild animals and the bees gave them honey.

Within a couple of years, however, their situation began to pall. They grew uneasy and decided to leave Wales for England where, just across the border in Hereford, all four took up the trade of saddlemaking, at which they proved brilliantly successful. Manawyddan himself led the craft; he turned out the most beautiful saddle pommels, for instance, with blue enamel and hard, excellent leather. With, seemingly, magic in his hands, he effectively put all the other saddlemakers in the vicinity out of business. The locals ganged up, Manawyddan and his friends got a tip-off that they could run into difficulties and in a discussion swayed by Manawyddan – Pryderi wanted to stay and fight – they decided upon discretion and left Hereford.

In the next city, reluctant to persist with saddlemaking, they decided to manufacture shields.

'But do we know anything about shieldmaking?' asked Pryderi.

Manawyddan shook his head: 'But we'll give it a try.'

Of course they made superb shields, in striking colours, with tremendous defensive capacities and before long every warrior in the area, and many from outside, wanted a shield from them. Again they had a serious effect on their competitors who, like the Hereford saddlemaking fraternity, ganged up. They had to leave.

'Now what?' said Manawyddan in the next city.

'Whatever you say,' answered Pryderi, 'you're the one with the ideas.'

'Shoes,' said Manawyddan, 'because shoemakers are unlikely to be either militant or brave enough to take us on.'

They turned their hands to shoemaking, though with a bit more circumspection this time; for example, they bought their leather locally and, initially, commissioned local goldsmiths to make the buckles. Soon, though, they chose to do everything themselves and the same thing happened – their rivals gathered with intent to slaughter these strangers who had begun to put them out of business. So Manawyddan, Pryderi and their two wives left and returned to Dyfed. Reaching Arberth, they lit a fire and made a long-term camp. For a month or so they relished a minor reconstruction of their old life.

One morning, by now well organised with good hounds, the men set out on a hard hunt. The dogs, though, suddenly retreated from a grove of bushes and turned tail, whingeing, confused. As Pryderi and Manawyddan rode across to see what ailed the hounds, a large boar, with gleaming white skin, exploded from the trees. The men reined back, called up the dogs and sent them in pursuit. A stand-off ensued: the boar, sparkling in the sunlight, stood at bay, head down, as the dogs crouched, snarling and uneasy. The men advanced and the boar broke a second time, ran for a while, then turned and once more stood at bay, as if inviting them to follow.

The boar was deliberately leading them – to an extraordinary building, a fortress they had never seen before in that countryside they thought they knew so well. This keep, high and sleek and powerful, had a superior kind of stonemasonry foreign to Manawyddan and Pryderi. The dogs chased the boar inside the walls and then silence fell, not a bark, nor a grunt nor a whine. Pryderi, anxious to retrieve his hounds at least, set out to enter, but Manawyddan restrained him, saying that the architect of this building had something to do, he felt, with the spell over Dyfed that had taken away their old life. But Pryderi could not resist, and urging his reluctant horse, he rode forward.

He reined in just inside the high black shiny walls, looking around – no dogs, no boar. But ahead of him, right at the centre of the vast, empty courtyard, stood a marble rock. On top of the rock stood a fountain-pedestal, surmounted by a bowl of thick gold, and from this flowed four chains of great light and beauty ascending endlessly out of sight to the skies above. The entire object, possessing compelling beauty, lured Pryderi over and he dismounted in order to run his hands over the golden bowl. His flesh stuck to it, immobilising him. His speech too had gone – he was a silent prisoner unable to call out for help.

On the grassy bank outside, Manawyddan waited, walking up and down restlessly until the sun began to move round to the west. Then he mounted and rode slowly home to be greeted by Rhiannon in their own courtyard.

'Where is Pryderi?'

First she looked aghast, and then rebuked him.

'If you don't find your friend I will,' and Rhiannon saddled up, riding off to look for her son and his hounds.

Reaching the castle with still some daylight to spare, she rode through the open gate and saw Pryderi standing there stuck fast to the golden bowl. Rhiannon moved warily around looking at him, asking him what had happened and receiving no answer. Then she too dismounted, touched the bowl and likewise could not move or speak. She stood there, wordlessly facing Pryderi, and the endless chains stretching far upward into the sky. As night fell they heard thunder: a thick mist rolled in like a ball through the open gate of the castle, and the bowl, the fountain, Pryderi and Rhiannon all vanished.

Back at the empty court of Dyfed, Manawyddan had for company only Pryderi's wife, by now greatly upset at the disappearance of her husband; neither did she appear too sanguine at the idea of being left alone with Manawyddan. He, though, assured her of his protection and friendship; this soothed her and in their unease at the disappearance of the other two, they decided to get out of Arberth and head for England and take up a trade. Exactly the same pattern emerged as before: Manawyddan, proving an excellent craftsman – shoe-making again – incurred the envy of the local guild who threatened to kill him and he, despite the encouragement of Pryderi's wife to stand and fight, opted to flee and return to Dyfed once more.

This time Manawyddan had proved prudent enough to buy several bushels of seed wheat. On their arrival back at Arberth he planted this wheat and in due course tamed the land that had grown wild all around the long-deserted court. The wheat promised to make a truly splendid harvest – Manawyddan watched it daily as it grew fat and gold. As the time for reaping drew nearer, he walked among the stalks every day, feeling and smelling them, gauging, as any practised farmer would, the absolutely appropriate moment. A good husbandman knows the precise moment when a corn crop must be cut, and soon, in one of the holdings, Manawyddan decided that the time had come, that tomorrow would see a long and fruitful harvest day.

In the morning tragedy greeted him. Of his fine crop of fat ears on high stalks nothing remained – all the stalks had lost their heads and stood naked and forlorn, the morning breeze whistling through them like a winter wind. He went to the next farm which fortunately had remained undamaged, so he decided that the following day should see it reaped. Overnight, however, the misfortune repeated itself – the morning brought stalks with not an ear among them. When it happened on a third acreage Manawyddan, desolate, had to do something.

On the fourth farm, he sat up, concealed in a headland coppice, and watched, his sword across his knees. At midnight he heard a noise like the roar of a huge wave and over the hill poured innumerable tides of mice. They inundated the cornfield: a mouse ran up each stalk, snapped off the ear and ran away with it, an incredible sight and one which Manawyddan could do nothing to halt. A last mouse, however, failed to get away, too heavy and too greedy. Manawyddan caught the mouse and popped it in his glove.

Back at the court Pryderi's wife asked him what he had in the glove.

'I have caught a thief,' said Manawyddan and told her what had happened to his corn.

'I know that what you have seen probably counts as a marvel,' she said, 'but are you, a proud man of noble birth, going to demean yourself by killing a mouse? Furthermore, the thought of you doing it makes me somehow uneasy, as if there is more to this than we can see.'

'Without question I am going to hang him,' replied Manawyddan. 'This mouse thieved from me. The punishment for theft is hanging. If I could have caught them all I would now hang them all.'

No matter how the woman begged and reasoned and drew upon her intuition, Manawyddan remained set on his course.

On the highest hill he could find, the hill at Arberth where Pwyll and Rhiannon had met, where the enchanted mist had cast a spell over Dyfed, he rigged two forked stakes to set up a gallows. As he did so he saw coming towards him an old man in poor clothing who introduced himself as a beggar returning from England where he had been singing for a living. He, like Pryderi's wife, also chided Manawyddan for stooping so low as to hang a mouse, and he even offered Manawyddan money from the alms he had begged in England. Manawyddan refused, even though the man put considerable pressure on him not to degrade himself. Meanwhile the mouse lay a prisoner in Manawyddan's glove.

As the scaffold neared completion up rode a holy man on a fine horse, a man with trappings of wealth.

'What are you doing?' he asked of Manawyddan.

'I caught a thief. The punishment for theft is hanging. I am hanging the thief.'

'A man of your noble stature? Stooping so low to pick up so little? A nobleman hanging a mouse?' The priest made incredulous noises, and he too offered to buy the mouse, or even to pay Manawyddan good money to desist. He got nowhere.

As Manawyddan tightened the cord around the mouse's neck, a bishop with a large entourage rode up the lane under the overhanging trees to the summit of the hill. He also offered Manawyddan a large sum of money, and then kept increasing his offer.

'I caught a thief,' came the monotonous but determined reply. 'The punishment for theft is hanging. I am hanging the thief.'

But Manawyddan sensed that this man had a vested interest of a particular kind – his demands seemed too urgent for a passing, uninterested stranger.

Finally the bishop said to Manawyddan, 'Name your price.'

'I want my noble friend Pryderi, and his mother, my wife, Rhiannon, released.'

'Certainly. Now let the mouse go.'

'I also want the spell lifted off Dyfed.'

'Certainly. Now let the mouse go.'

'I want to know who the mouse is.'

'She is my wife,' said the bishop. 'Now let her go.'

Manawyddan asked, 'Who are you and how did all this happen?'

'I am Llwyd and I have been attacking Dyfed in revenge for the man with whom Pwyll, Pryderi's father, played Badger-in-the Bag. Remember the feast where Pwyll disguised as a beggar came to reclaim Rhiannon?'

His soldiers, he said, had begged him to let them destroy the land of Dyfed, so he turned all his retinue into mice and they attacked the corn. The one mouse who could not run fast enough was his, the bishop's, wife. Pregnant, she was too slow and heavy to escape.

Manawyddan, in a strong bargaining position, negotiated some more favours – that never again should a spell be cast on Dyfed; that no further revenge should ever be taken on Pryderi or Rhiannon or himself; that before he released the mouse he should see Pryderi and Rhiannon.

They materialised at that moment. Manawyddan greeted them with tremendous enthusiasm and relief, and when they had settled down he released the mouse from the noose. Llwyd, 'the bishop', took out a magic wand and the mouse changed into a lovely woman, heavily pregnant. At that moment too all the lands and courts of Dyfed around them reappeared in their old and prosperous state, the animals and workers and farms and lanes; all of life stirred itself, as if after a long, long sleep. The sun came out.

There the story ended and the sweet ways returned to Dyfed.

MATH, THE SON OF MATHONWY, LORD OF GWYNEDD

or much of Pryderi's reign over Dyfed, Glamorgan and two other counties, Math, the son of Mathonwy, ruled Gwynedd. A man of principle and tradition, he had no peace of mind unless his feet nestled in the lap of a virgin, thereby protecting her virginity, and he observed this custom unless distracted by war or hunting. The particular virgin in whose lap Math liked to rest his feet at this time was called Goewin, a sweet girl from the Pebin valley, known for her beauty.

Math's retinue in those days included his sister's two sons, Gilvathy and Gwydion, and, not surprisingly given her looks and proximity, Gilvathy fell in love with the virgin Goewin. So hard did the bolt of love strike him that he lost his appetite, then his colour, then his lively demeanour. His brother Gwydion noticed this listlessness and thoughtfulness.

'There's something bothering you. You're paler, quieter.'

'I am not at liberty to tell you,' Gilvathy said, 'for the simple reason that, as you know, Math has this magical gift of hearing all that is said, even in the most intimate of murmurs.'

'I've got it,' said Gwydion, 'I'll say it for you. You've fallen in love with her, you've fallen in love with the virgin. Haven't you? With Goewin.'

Gilvathy's sigh gave the game away.

'Right,' said Gwydion, 'how are we going to get her for you?'

He conceived a plan and the two nephews called upon Math. Gwydion addressed him.

'My lord, may I draw your attention to something bizarre?'

The Lord of Gwynedd gave him permission to speak.

'My lord, on the south coast people have witnessed the arrival of curious beasts. Nobody has ever seen anything like them.'

'What are they?' asked Math.

'They are called pigs,' said Gwydion, 'or swine. Much smaller than cattle, round and fat, but succulent and with a lot of flesh.'

'Who owns them?' asked Math.

'I believe they belong to Pryderi, son of Pwyll, and he got them as a gift from Arawn the Lord of Annwyvn. Do you want some?'

Math asked, 'How do you propose to get them?'

'I will disguise myself as one of a company of twelve bards and we will ask Pryderi for them.'

'And if he refuses?'

'My lord, I don't intend to come back here without those pigs.'

With Gilvathy and ten others, Gwydion rode south to a session of Pryderi's Council in Cardigan where, as men of learning and culture, the twelve 'bards' received a most enthusiastic welcome. Pryderi cleared a space on his right hand for Gwydion and asked him to tell a story.

All night Gwydion told stories, good and beautiful and bad and funny and tense and involved, long stories, short stories, that made them weep and laugh and wonder, and the assembled court talked aloud his praises – in short, he charmed the legs off them. Pryderi, immensely taken with him, then monopolised Gwydion in conversation.

Then the moment came for the request to be made.

Pryderi responded, 'In normal circumstances and particularly as you have entertained us so brilliantly, I would with the greatest of pleasure give you the pigs, but I have undertaken to my people that I shall not let any go either by sale or by gift until they have bred twice as many as they are at the moment.'

'Fair enough,' said Gwydion, seeming to accept this in a most understanding way. 'Neither say "yes" nor "no" just now, give me the night to sleep on it.'

Then he and his companions hurried into conference. They analysed the words Pryderi had used that neither 'by sale or gift' could he part with the pigs.

'But what about exchange?' suggested Gwydion.

He called down his magic to provide them with irresistible objects in favour of which Pryderi might be persuaded to exchange the pigs – a dozen superb black stallions bridled and saddled in pure gold, a dozen black greyhounds collared and leashed in pure gold, and for the warriors that would ride these stallions and hunt these hounds a dozen shields, conjured – Gwydion, by the way was a master of illusion – from mushrooms.

Though struck by the beauty and generosity of these gifts Pryderi still had to consult his court. After short deliberations, in which they took the point that an exchange, as distinct from a gift or sale, would not break Pryderi's word, Gwydion's cleverness paid off – he got the pigs. However, he had neglected to tell Pryderi – and he only revealed it to his companions when they had safely left Pryderi's court – that his magic had finite boundaries and would wear off almost before they got back to Math's palace in Gwynedd. They herded the pigs at a furious pace across country, riding north as hard as anyone could thus handicapped. Through Powys and Rhos they went, to Harlech because by now, as Gwydion assessed accurately, Pryderi had mustered his troops and sought revenge for the trickery which turned the shields back to mushrooms.

When they had safely built an enclosure for the pigs they rode on to Math's court where they found preparations under way for the raising of a huge army. Word had reached Math that Pryderi had mustered armed support from twenty-one counties, so high had his anger risen. Gwydion and Gilvathy and their companions took up arms too and pretended to join the march to Penarth. They came back, though, to the palace from which all the men had left on this mission of arms, cleared the women out of the chambers at swordpoint and that night Goewin the virgin, however unwillingly, had to sleep with Gilvathy.

Next morning Gwydion and Gilvathy rejoined Math's great troop which had fortified two towns and soon Pryderi arrived. The battle raged mightily, with Pryderi the first to give way. Math's forces, his nephews prominent, pursued them and other battles broke out. Pryderi, buying time, asked for a truce and offered twenty-four hostages. As the truce kept failing, they decided in negotiations that the matter should be settled between the two main protagonists, Pryderi and Gwydion.

Math gave his consent to the single combat, the armies withdrew and in the event Gwydion's magic carried the day. He killed the great Pryderi, a man who should have been allowed to die gracefully in his own bed and not at the hands of a trickster. His sad armies returned to Dyfed, beaten, depleted and leaderless. Gwydion and Gilvathy went on a victory tour of Gwynedd to accept the plaudits and their uncle returned to his castle to rest.

As Math raised his feet to rest them once again in Goewin's lap she drew back.

'My lord, I am not eligible for this honour any more. You must find a virgin.'

'But you are one.'

'No. Not any longer.' By now Goewin was in tears. 'Your nephews returned on the eve of battle and forced me into your bed where Gilvathy, assisted by Gwydion, raped me.'

The furious king sent out an order that nobody should give food or drink to the two nephews, still on their lap of honour around the kingdom. When eventually they returned to the castle he drew his wand on them. He turned on Gilvathy and with a fierce blow of the wand transformed him into a hind and Gwydion into a stag.

'Animals you are, and animals you shall be,' and Math drove them off to mate in the woods with an instruction that they return to the castle in exactly a year.

On that appointed day, Math in his chambers heard the castle hounds barking madly and sent a servant to find out the cause. The man reported back that a stag and a hind stood outside with their fawn. Math strode out to the castle green. He waved his wand over the three animals and turned the stag into a wild boar, the hind into a wild sow and the fawn into a human boy. He told the pair to go away and breed, and return in exactly a year, took the boy into the castle and gave him the name of 'Haydn', meaning 'deer'.

The next year when the boars returned with a young one he turned the nephews into a wolf and she-wolf, having changed the young wild pig into a boy whom he called 'Hwychdwn', meaning 'boar'. And when the wolves came back he took the cub they had bred, turned it into a boy called Bleddyn, so that now in the castle he had three boys whose names reflected their origins as a young deer, a young boar and a young wolf. Then Math restored the two nephews, Gwydion and Gilvathy, to human form, pointing out how disgraced they stood, two men who bred children off each other; they had been punished enough for the rape of Goewin. Muted and respectful they took their place in the castle alongside their uncle.

As they sat down Math asked them to choose a virgin for him, as he now needed to rest his feet. They suggested their sister, the king's niece, and Math sent for her.

'Are you a virgin?'

'As far as I know,' she replied.

Math reached downwards, bent his magic wand against the floor and said, 'Then step over that and we shall soon know.'

The girl did, but from her dropped a fine child with golden hair, who yelled. The girl, hearing the yell, ran towards the door and on the way dropped another little bundle which Gwydion, before anyone could tell what it was, grabbed, wrapped up and hid in a chest in his own chambers. Math, meanwhile, took the first yellow-haired child and gave him the name of 'Dylan', meaning 'the sea'.

That night Gwydion awakened to the sound of a baby crying, and in the chest at the foot of his own bed he found an infant boy. Gwydion arranged to have the child wet-nursed and within two years the boy had matured so rapidly he could attend the court unaided. At all stages of his development he equalled those twice his age and he formed a deep and loving parental relationship with Gwydion.

One fine day, as Gwydion left the court to go for a walk, the boy followed him and they came to the house of Gwydion's sister, the woman who had failed Math's virginity test. She questioned Gwydion as to the identity of the boy following him. He revealed that it was her son – to her distress, because she felt shamed.

'Why?' asked Gwydion. 'You should feel proud – look at him, a fine boy.'

'What is his name?'

'None as yet.'

'Then he'll not have a name until I give him one.'

'What a bitch, eh? He will get a name. I'll see to that. You're annoyed because you can never again call yourself a virgin.'

And Gwydion, furious, returned to the palace.

Next day he called the boy and took him for a long walk by the sea at Menai. Out of the sedges that grew along the banks of the straits, and out of the seaweed that piled along the shore, Gwydion used his magic to make a fine ship with great leather sails. They sailed this round the coast and at the entrance to the harbour where his sister lived they stopped. Gwydion knew that she would be watching from the castle and would recognise them, so he altered their appearance by magic. At the same time, he began to entice her by making shoes no woman could resist.

The woman sent messengers to ask for a pair; Gwydion made a

pair too large. She paid him but asked for a smaller pair; he made them too small. She complained, and he sent back a reply to the effect that he would make no more shoes until he saw and measured her feet.

His sister came down to the harbour herself and went aboard the ship, where she found the disguised man and boy cutting out shoes.

'Why can't you make shoes that fit?' she asked.

'I can now,' he replied.

At that precise moment a wren landed on the prow; the boy threw a dart at it and hit it in the leg. The woman cheered and said, 'Hasn't the fair-haired boy a hand of skill?'

'You've given him his name,' said Gwydion. 'You've named him Llew, the One with the Skilful Hand,' and that instant the ship turned back into seaweed. Then Gwydion changed back to his old self and changed the boy back too, to his sister's fury.

'He may have a name,' she said, 'but he'll never carry a weapon until I arm him.'

Years passed. The boy Llew grew up marvellously, big and powerful and an excellent horseman, but obviously deprived of feats of arms. Gwydion set out to alter that fact and one day took the boy on a long ride along the shore until they reached the gates of the coastal town where his sister lived. As they approached, Gwydion used his magic to change them into different men and told the watchman that two distinguished young bards from Glamorgan had come on a visit. Gwydion's sister sent for them, arranged a feast and had much good conversation with the older of the two 'bards' before everyone retired for the night.

Gwydion rose before anyone else and magically raised an illusory fleet, all shouts and trumpets, to threaten the harbour defences. This put the entire castle on alert including the two 'bards', both of whom Gwydion's sister asked for help. Gwydion advised her to prepare her defences rigorously, every hand to the ramparts. She called her servants and they equipped Gwydion and the boy with suits of armour and full weaponry.

'Are we armed?' asked Gwydion.

'You are,' replied his sister.

'But is he armed?' Gwydion pointed to the boy.

'He truly is.'

'Well done, madam,' said Gwydion and revealed himself and the boy.

The woman, angrier than ever at having been fooled, now swore an oath that the boy would never find a wife of any race that dwelt anywhere in the world. Gwydion cursed her for her evil and swore a bigger oath that the boy would get a wife and a good one. He went to Math, told him the whole story and Math, greatly taken with the boy's beauty and strength, joined his magic to Gwydion's. They created a girl out of the flowers of oak, broom and meadow-sweet, a wonderfully lovely young woman whom Llew then wed and bedded amid great rejoicing. At the celebrations Gwydion prevailed upon Math to give the boy some land, and so the couple got off to a good and prosperous start in life.

One day, not long after they settled in their castle, young Llew set out to pay Math a visit of homage. That afternoon his wife saw a stag-hunt racing by so impressively that she sent messengers to find out who hunted so brilliantly.

'Goronwy, Lord of Penllyn,' reported the messenger, and when the hunt turned for home late that evening, the wife invited them in. She and Goronwy fell for each other; all through dinner they gazed in each other's eyes and that night they got up from the table and went to bed together, Goronwy occupying the place of the absent Llew.

He slept there the next night, and the next – she would not let him go. He suggested that by pretending affection she might find a way of killing Llew so that she could then marry Goronwy. After three nights together he finally left, lest Llew came home and caught them together.

When Llew did return his wife gave him a warm welcome, but in bed that night she proved unusually taciturn and withdrawn.

'Are you all right?' he asked her.

Eventually she said she had been preoccupied with the fear that he might be killed.

'Nonsense,' he said, touched by her concern. 'I'll tell you something you don't know and see if it puts your mind at rest.'

He proceeded to give her details of how difficult it would prove for any enemy to kill him – because of where and how his only vulnerability lay.

'I cannot be killed on horseback or on foot. I can only be killed with a spear that a man has spent a year making. I cannot be killed indoors or outdoors.'

'But this is marvellous,' she said. 'Are you telling me that there is no way an enemy can kill you?'

'I can only be killed in one way. A bath has to be made for me on the bank of a river, with a thatched roof over it. Then a goat has to be brought alongside. The only way I can be killed is if I am caught with one foot on the goat's back and the other on the rim of the bath.'

'That,' observed his wife, 'is a situation you can probably avoid.'

'Exactly. That way, you see, I would neither be on foot nor on horseback, nor indoors nor outdoors.'

His wife then sent this detailed information in secret to Goronwy and they began to conspire.

A year later, during which time Goronwy had devoted his energies to making the special spear, Llew's wife said to her husband, 'Remember how you described to me how you could only be killed with one leg on a goat's back and the other on the edge of a thatched bath? Shouldn't I know how you stood like that so that I could protect you in case of an attack?'

He explained to her again that with one foot on a goat's back and the other on the rim of a bath he stood neither on dry land nor in water.

'I'll show you tomorrow,' said the innocent Llew.

The wife then made her arrangements. She chose a river-bank destination, collected every goat her servants could lay hands on and sent a message to Goronwy to hide nearby. Servants picked out the biggest buck goat of all and led it forward. Llew balanced himself by this thatched bath with one leg on the rim and the other on the spine of the standing goat, an unsteady posture.

'See?' he said with a smile to his wife.

Goronwy, standing up in the rushes on the far bank, needed only a second. He flung the poison-tipped spear, which penetrated Llew beneath the rib-cage and stuck there quivering. Llew screamed in agony and before everyone's eyes changed into an eagle and flew high into the air; circling rapidly, it then flew away. Goronwy and his new woman went arm-in-arm back to Llew's castle, to bed, and on the following day, to new conquests of Llew's old dominions.

The story reached Math and Gwydion. After a respectful period of mourning and head-hanging, Gwydion asked Math's permission to leave the palace of Gwynedd and find his beloved nephew Llew. It proved a long quest, through the brightest and darkest parts of the land, asking here, seeking there, enquiring hither, searching yon.

One day at Penarth Gwydion dismounted at the house of some peasants and asked for a night's shelter, which they gave him with a glad hospitality. During the course of the evening the swineherd came in from the hill and his master asked him if the sow showed anything unusual in her behaviour. The herdsman replied that even though she returned to the pigsty every evening the sow disappeared every day, mysteriously and unstoppably, and he could never trace her journey. Gwydion sensed that there might be something in this for him.

Next morning, fresh and mounted, Gwydion watched as the swineherd opened the pigsty. The sow came out like a rocket and galloped up the hill by the river and over the crest down into the next valley. There, under some trees, she halted and began to snuffle and eat. Gwydion reined in at a distance, then walked silently over to observe her. Her diet consisted of worms and rotting flesh; even more puzzling it seemed to fall from the sky. He looked up and on the top branch sat an eagle, shivering and unwell. Every time it shuddered flesh fell from it, into the sow's mouth.

Gwydion, applying his magic, recognised the eagle. He began to sing to it as sweetly as a bard or a nightingale and enticed the bird down off the tree, down further and further, until it sat on his knee. At which point Gwydion tapped the bird with his magic wand and there in front of him lay Llew, pitiably reduced physically and psychologically, a walking skeleton, sunken-cheeked and mumbling.

Gwydion gathered him up and took him gently back to the castle. Math, Lord of Gwynedd, rallied his physicians and after a year of aromatic and herbal care, Llew stood upright again and began to look his old beautiful self. In conference with Math and Gwydion he discussed revenge upon Goronwy. Regiments were raised and trained and they marched upon Goronwy and his woman, Llew's former flower-wife.

She escaped first, taking all her waiting-women of the court in a mad dash across country, making for a hidden court in the mountains, Gwydion on their heels. The women, unaccustomed to pursuit and terrified, kept looking backwards and thus fell into a huge lake. All drowned, except their leader – who had to face Gwydion.

'I will not kill you,' he told her. 'I will do worse than that. I will turn you into a bird, but not an ordinary bird. You have behaved in the most shameful way to a good man, Llew, my beloved nephew. Therefore, you are never again to associate with the daylight and all it brings. I am turning you into a bird that only comes out by night and whom all the other birds regard with hostility.'

He turned her, the flower-wife, into an owl.

Goronwy had marched to Penllyn to retrench. He sent out diplomats to see whether Llew would accept terms, including generous compensation. Llew refused and told the messengers that Goronwy must return to the spot where he threw the poisoned spear and let Llew now hurl the spear at him.

They met on the bank of the river, at the very place where Llew's flower-wife had set him up for the fatal spear-throw. Goronwy proved cowardly. Initially he had asked whether any one of his men would face Llew for him. They had all refused, and even now he tried to talk his way out of it by saying to Llew that they, as men, should not be misled into mortal danger by the tricks of a bad and faithless woman. Llew disregarded him and as one last plea Goronwy asked if he might stand behind a large rock nearby as Llew threw the spear. Llew agreed, knowing it would make no difference, and the spear went through the rock, straight into Goronwy and snapped his spine.

The stone still stands, to be seen to this day – Lech Gronw, the Stone of Goronwy, with the hole through it.

Llew returned to his lands and also took over those Goronwy had ruled. He reigned wisely, much loved, and in due course succeeded Math, son of Mathonwy, Lord of Gwynedd.

THE DREAM OF THE EMPEROR MAXEN

In the days of ancient Rome the Emperor Maxen, a man of wisdom and tolerance, had an extraordinary experience.

One morning, announcing that he wanted to hunt, he and a bunch of companions rode to the Tiber valley north of Rome. Rarely has a hunting-party had such illustrious membership – no fewer than thirty-two crowned heads, all client-kings, tenants of his empire, all offering the most explicit allegiance to Maxen. From such glorious groupings around him Maxen took his real pleasure (much more, it has to be said, than from the actual hunting).

The day, as it does along the Tiber, grew very hot and sleepy and the emperor's attendants arranged a shelter around him. They did this by hanging all the party's shields on their spears until they formed a kind of tented roof, and they pillowed him with an imperial gold shield. Honoured and protected, he slept well, and then came the beginning of the strange experience – because Maxen had a dream, a colourful, journey dream.

He dreamt that he left the space where they had all now gathered and travelled to the far end of the valley where a high mountain rose, the highest on earth, its tip as high as the blue sky itself. When he climbed this mountain, a wide and beautiful plain lay beyond. Several broad shining rivers flowed down the mountain across this plain to the sea, and he joined the widest one of these, travelling downstream until he came to the river's huge mouth. Within this bay stood a city, protected by a great castle, distinguished by many multi-coloured towers. Beneath the castle walls, riding at anchor on the water, Maxen saw the biggest fleet he had ever encountered or even heard of, with a flagship so magnificent that the planks on deck alternated from gold to silver and the gangplank had been made from the ivory of walrus tusks. In his dream Maxen saw himself walking along that ivory plank, and when he had embarked the mariners hoisted sail; the ship sailed out of the harbour across oceans to an island that, he felt, must be the most exquisite and lush anywhere.

He traversed this island on whose furthermost side stood insurmountably tall and jagged peaks; and then came another island, where in another wide bay stood another great castle. Maxen entered this gigantic building, walking into the high hall of the keep.

He looked slowly all around him in amazement. The roof of this hall had been made of gold, the walls inset with jewels, the doors gold too, and golden couches beside silver tables. On one such seat two young golden-haired boys played a board game; they wore clothes made of jet-black satin and brocade, thin headbands of gold studded with shining gemstones and brilliant leather shoes strapped to their feet with bars of pure gold.

At the foot of a pillar nearby Maxen saw an ancient man with copious white hair. He sat on a large ivory chair on which had been carved in gold the twinned figures of eagles. Wearing gold armlets and rings as well as a thick gold torc round his neck, the old man seemed most distinguished by virtue of his bearing as well as his dress. He sat carving pieces for the same type of board game that the young boys were playing.

Across the room from the elderly man Maxen saw a girl, sitting in a gold chair, and her beauty dazzled him like the sun. She wore a bodice of white silk with gold brooches, a gold brocade cloak fastened by a gem-encrusted brooch; her hair stayed in place under a band of gold studded with rubies and she wore a wide, deep belt of gold. She greeted Maxen, embraced him and drew him down to sit beside her, her arms wound around his neck.

But at this moment, as Emperor Maxen slept amid his hunting-party in the Tiber valley, the heat of the afternoon made the animals moan restlessly, and the wind made the shields rattle and clang where they hung high on the spears. The emperor woke up.

After that dream Emperor Maxen never had an easy moment; he could not get that girl out of his mind. He grew listless, withdrew from occasions he had previously enjoyed tremendously, indulged no longer, for example, in wine or music. He gave his courtiers the impression that he wished to sleep all the time – true, too, because then he could dream uninterruptedly of this woman in the hall, with the boys in the black brocade and the white-haired man on the ivory throne with the carved eagles.

Eventually one of his most senior officials approached the emperor.

'Sir, your kings are most upset,' he said. 'They are even turning against you.'

'But why?' asked the listless Maxen.

'Because you show no leadership, you give them no imperial tasks to carry out, they feel they have lost their emperor, they can neither speak to you nor hear from you.'

'Call all the wise men of Rome, and I will tell them the truth of what afflicts me.'

Maxen stood before them with something like his old verve and told them of his dream, and of how the girl in it had captured not just his heart but his soul too. Then he asked for the benefit of their collective wisdom. Having conferred they advised him that he should send messengers to all three parts of the world for three years, who would surely bring back news of this woman.

To begin with, this failed, and after a year Maxen fell into deeper despair. Then one of his most senior kings suggested he take up the beginnings of the journey himself and sure enough Maxen found the place on a river-bank where his dream journey had begun. His best messengers were summoned once more, their robes folded in special ways to guarantee them safe passage – by arranging their caps and sleeves they made it clear that they were messengers and therefore not to be molested. Step for step, river for river, island for island, they traced Maxen's dream journey.

A day came when, near Mount Snowdon, with the island of Anglesey visible in the distance, they found the girl. She was just as Maxen had described her – simple and glorious to behold, in the golden hall near the boys in the black satin and brocade, seated across from the white-haired old man on the ivory throne.

They knelt and addressed her as 'Empress of Rome', a greeting which irritated and then intrigued her. To her queries they replied by telling her that the Emperor of Rome had dreamed of her existence and sent them to bring her his love and his invitation to return with them. She, though beguiled, instructed them to tell their master that he should come and make these offers himself. They left, without even halting for refreshments, and helter-skelter rode back the way they had come.

Maxen, having prepared just in case they had found her, left immediately with them. He brought his armies too, and they conquered all before them, including Britain. At each stage of the journey he confirmed, from the details of his dream, the rightness of the messengers' direction. Arriving within sight of the final destination in Wales, he knew they had well and truly found the place of which he had dreamed.

In a state of almost unendurable excitement Maxen entered the golden hall. He shivered to see them all once more, his dream-people, this time in real life. Walking with his full emperor's grace to the place where the girl sat, he raised her to her feet, embraced her and greeted her as Empress of Rome. She accepted him.

And so to bed. In the morning, pleased that his dream had found a virgin for him, he made her an offer of any dowry she wished. She chose Britain as a gift to her father, claimed three large islands for herself in her capacity as Empress Helen and three fortresses to be built for her – at Arvon, Carmarthen and Caerlion. Maxen granted all these gifts with pleasure.

In the company of his wife, and in the enjoyment again of all the pleasures of life he held dear, hunting and music and wine, Maxen stayed seven years in Helen's land. By doing so he ran the risk of forfeiting his empire; the Romans had allowed a tradition to evolve whereby any emperor, no matter how distinguished or godlike, who stayed abroad for seven years for any reason, even on a campaign for the empire, must relinquish the Purple. Thus, Maxen received a message telling him that his throne had been usurped, and to stay away from Rome.

Riled, he set out to return, and en route conquered part of Gaul, but his siege of Rome proved ineffectual in terms of taking the city. His wife, however, came up with the strength he needed; she had brought with her, led by her brothers, a band of devoted soldiers, men who would have risked anything, undertaken any task for her.

The brothers and their officers, all experienced soldiers, analysed Maxen's strategy at the walls of Rome. They agreed that cunning might prove more effective than the hitherto fruitless frontal attacks. So they measured the height of the walls in several places and then, out of sight of the garrison of Rome, set carpenters to work making scores of scaling ladders.

The informal rules of engagement permitted both emperors a two-hour break each early afternoon to eat and rest. The contingent led by Helen's brothers decided to take advantage of this, so they fed their soldiers more copiously in the morning. When the break came, with the soldiers inside the walls resting, up went the scaling ladders and the attackers had captured and killed the usurping emperor almost before he knew what had happened. It took three days to subdue the rest of the garrison, and only when the entire city had been completely taken did they allow Maxen to enter in triumph, his empress, Helen, beside him.

Overcome by gratitude, Maxen offered Helen's brothers the services of his entire army to gain such lands as they wished. They interpreted this liberally, and in their long years of campaigning killed every man in every territory they annexed.

As a final insurance, they cut out the tongues of the women; from now on the future generations of those they had conquered would speak a language that only they, the conquerors, understood – their own.

And so ends the tale of the Emperor Maxen and his Dream.

THE STORY OF LLUDD AND LLEWELYS

When Beli, the Great King of Britain, died he left four sons, of whom one, Lludd, succeeded to the throne and reigned prudently over Britain. He refurbished all of London, strengthened the city walls, raised more and better watchtowers and obliged the citizens to build houses to a higher standard than existed in the known world. He loved the city and through his influence upon it London got its name, a corruption and extension of the word 'Lludd'.

Among his brothers, Lludd loved Llewelys much more than either of the others; the two men had an intimate relationship, each being the other's confidant.

When news reached Llewelys that the King of France had died, and that the only heir to the kingdom was a daughter, he wondered whether she might require a husband. Llewelys naturally discussed with his brother the suitability of marriage to this Frenchwoman, both nationally and familially – certainly it would bring prestige to Britain. Lludd encouraged him and put at his disposal a fine and decorative fleet that soon sailed for France with Llewelys in the flagship. The mission proved immediately successful; after a minimum of deliberation the French court advised their young princess that this would prove a good match, and it did – Llewelys, guided by his brother's advice and goodwill, also grew into a wise and firm sovereign. Thus the brothers ruled Britain and France.

Some years later, Lludd's kingdom fell victim to three simultaneous and utterly puzzling plagues for which the Britons could find no cure. The first arrived in the shape of an invading race of people, the Coraniads, who, by magic, could overhear every conversation throughout every corner of the island, high and low, dark and bright. This gave them an intolerable advantage in every department of life. No redress could be obtained against them because as soon as discussion took place on any such topic they overheard it, even if those conferring whispered at the bottom of a deep hole or high on the outstretched peaks of a mountain. Furthermore the Coraniads undermined the economy with their currency – they used faery money, which could be exchanged in the form of coins, but which if kept or saved turned to mushrooms.

The second plague occurred once a year and drove people crazy. On the night before Beltaine, on May's Eve, an indescribable screech rang out across the entire land, a high and awful scream and all who heard it felt threatened with derangement – some even succumbed. Brave men turned pale and hid indoors, women fell ill, children never recovered from the terror, which also scared the animals and stripped the trees of their leaves.

Plague number three struck deep into the life of King Lludd himself. The storekeepers at his courts and temples, even those in London, no matter how high and securely they piled their provisions at night, found their shelves and warehouses empty next day – even if they had laid in a year's store.

As these plagues intensified not a person in the kingdom remained immune and they turned to King Lludd for guidance and release from their torments. He, poor man, though anxious to do the very best for his subjects, made no headway. Finally, at one major council of his advisers, somebody suggested that the king's own brother, King Llewelys of France, might bring an objective view to all of this and Lludd set sail, though in secret.

Llewelys received information that his brother had been seen on the high seas approaching France and having divined the reason went to greet him. In mid-Channel they detached their flagships from their large fleets and sailed singly forward to meet each other with warm greetings. Llewelys told Lludd he guessed the reason for his visit. Then they both realised that the wind would carry their discussions back to the Coraniads and Llewelys devised a means of speaking to each other without being overheard. He ordered a long bronze trumpet, like an elongated hunting-horn, to be made and through this he and Lludd would converse. Unfortunately when they began this conversation whatever they said at one end came out the other end as abuse and vilification.

Llewelys soon grasped that a devil dwelt within the long bugle and had his servants blow wine through the horn, which rinsed out the demon. In the ensuing conversation Llewelys told Lludd how to banish the eavesdropping Coranaids. He gave him a large supply of a particular type of insect not found in Britain, some to be kept for breeding purposes should he ever need them again, and the rest to be pulped and the pulp dissolved in water. On his return Lludd should call a major conference of every man, woman and child in the country, and spray this watery mixture over them all. His own people would feel no ill-effects other than a little discomfort, but the Coraniads would all die of poisoning.

Lludd then outlined the problem of the second plague, the May's Eve scream.

'Caused by a dragon,' said Llewelys down the brass trumpet, 'under attack from a dragon attempting to invade your country. Your own dragon resists the attack every year but screams terribly. Now what you do is this.

'When you get back, survey the island mathematically, measure it precisely from coast to coast, from the four farthest points, and when you have arrived at the exact centre mark the spot. Then dig a hole, a deep pit, soundly constructed, the sides shored up. At the bottom of this hole put a cauldron of your best mead which you then cover with a sheet of your best silk. Trust nobody else – stand guard here yourself next May Eve.

'Watch carefully. The fighting dragons will eventually lurch and roll over the countryside in your direction and the moment will come when, out of sheer exhaustion, both will fall directly into the pit and land on the silk covering the cauldron of mead – only by then they will have adopted the shape of a couple of pigs. They will sink, wrapped in the silk sheet, to the bottom of the mead and, out of thirst and greed, will then proceed to drink every drop. All you have to do then is haul out the sheet with the two in it, tie a knot, lock the lot into a chest made of stone which you will already have standing by, and bury the bundle in the most secure fastness you have in your kingdom.'

Lludd shouted down the bugle, 'And what about the third plague, the disappearance of the food?'

'Simplest of the lot,' called back Llewelys. 'A wizard is stealing your food every night. He casts spells over your dinner-table and when all of you nod off he steals the food.'

'But how do I stop him?'

'Stay awake,' shouted Llewelys. 'Don't fall for the spell. Order a tub of freezing water to be placed by your side and the moment you feel drowsy, jump into it and that way you will catch him and defeat him.'

Lludd embraced his brother, thanked him, set out home again and began to carry out every instruction Llewelys had given him. First he pulped some of the special insects into a watery mixture. Next, he called all the population, including the Coraniads, to a huge conference where he sprayed the mixture over everyone. The Coraniads rolled to the ground, squealing in agony, and died. Then he found the centre of Britain – at Oxford, as it happens – where he dug a huge and secure pit, put a large cauldron of the very best mead at the bottom and covered it with a sheet of glorious silk. All night he sat up, and sure enough the dragons came and fought in the air high above his head. When eventually they shrank with tiredness to the size of a pair of small, weary pigs, as Llewelys had said they would, they fell on the silk sheet and sank down into the mead, which they then slurped up with a sleepy vigour. Lludd tied them up securely in the silk and locked them in a stone chest deep beneath Snowdon. Nobody ever heard such a scream again.

As for the third plague, Lludd ordered up a feast and had a man-sized tub of iced water placed by his elbow. As the night wore on the speech of the revellers grew ever more slurred; as their songs grew more halting, they began to nod and fall asleep, heads on the table. Lludd found himself following suit and had just enough presence of mind to jump into the cold tub and keep himself awake. He crouched quietly to see what happened next.

The doors opened and in came a huge figure of a man, well-armoured and carrying an enormous basket which he began to fill with food and drink. The basket expanded to accept every scrap of food in the place, and, having swept the tables bare, the giant left the sleeping hall.

Lludd ran after him, ready to do battle. The giant put down his basket and unsheathed his sword. They fought mightily, heaving to and fro, rocking the walls of the keep; sparks flew in streams as Lludd's ferocious blows struck the giant's armour. Eventually the giant capitulated, asking Lludd to spare his life.

Lludd only did so when the giant promised to make restitution for every theft he had ever perpetrated, remain loyal to Lludd and his people and never misbehave again. Lludd accepted this, and with the last of the three plagues finally cured, Lludd received the lasting gratitude and esteem of his subjects in Britain, which is how they came to name London's highest hill after him – Ludgate.

THE TALE OF CULHWCH AND OLWEN

he famous King Arthur had a cousin called Culhwch whose early life had peculiar twists in it. When Culhwch's mother became pregnant her nerves gave way, and she could tolerate no company nor stay under any roof all during the pregnancy; she left the palace and began to wander through the kingdom. However, at the moment her confinement began she grew sensible again – until she found herself near the home of a swineherd. A violent antipathy to pigs threatened to bring back her nervous condition, and even though this agitation induced the birth, she fled once the child had been born. The swineherd knew who she was, took immediate care of the baby and shortly brought it to court, having already given it the name of Culhwch, which means a place where pigs run and snuffle – in other words he named the boy after his birthplace, not an unusual practice in those days.

The boy had not long settled into his childhood at the court when his mother died. On her deathbed she said to her husband the king: 'I fear that you will want to take another wife and I don't blame you. But such a woman might disinherit our son, Culhwch, Arthur's cousin. Please, therefore, do not marry again until you see a briar with two heads of blossom on my grave.'

The devious woman then summoned her own holy man to whom she had always confessed, and instructed him to tidy her grave very frequently, cropping every bush that looked as if it might grow two flowers.

For seven years the monk carried out the dead queen's wishes; for seven years the king sent a court lackey every month to check whether any roses grew on the queen's grave. After each inspection, owing to the monk's alertness, the servant reported no trace of any flower. Then the monk, at heart a dilatory fellow, forgot, and the king himself as it happened, while out hunting, saw the grave and sure enough a thorn bush with two roses on it had sprouted. Not a man to delay, the king began the time-honoured system of enquiry as to where he might find a wife. Soon his advisers revealed to him that King Doged had a wife who would make the king an ideal partner, so he set off with an army, killed Doged and captured his wife, daughter and territories.

One day, the new queen, out for a walk near the palace, encountered a toothless crone. Sensing that this meeting had been arranged by fate, the queen asked the crone some questions.

'I have seen no children at the palace.'

'The king has no children,' replied the crone, a shifty creature at the best of times.

'Why did I have to be chosen by a childless man?'

'It won't always be that way. He will have a child by you.'

'What else?'

The crone, who had been lying, ceased her deviousness and said, 'He already has a son.'

The queen rushed back and said to the king, 'Why do you hide your son from me?'

'Fair enough,' the king replied, 'here he is.'

The queen looked him up and down.

'Time for you to marry and you can marry my daughter. She's good enough for any man.'

'I'm not old enough to marry any woman,' said the lad.

'Then in that case,' said his stepmother, 'you can marry nobody unless you marry Olwen, the daughter of the King of the Giants.'

Amazingly, the lad trembled and blushed at this remark, as he felt a love pour through him for this girl he had never seen and of whom he had only, this moment, heard. His father told him to get his hair cut, and then visit Arthur, his cousin.

On a grey horse, bridled and saddled in gold, the boy rode off to Arthur's castle. His weaponry included a battle-axe, a hatchet capable of drawing blood from the air and a gold-hilted, gold-bladed sword. He dressed like a champion: two hounds loped beside him, each wore a collar studded with rubies and garnets, and he himself wore a voluminous purple cloak decorated at each corner with a crimson apple; an ivory hunting-horn joggled at his belt and his boots had been hammered from sheets of red gold. The light shone on his face as he rode down the hill to Arthur's gate.

The sentry would not let him in.

'The knife has entered the meat, the mead has entered the drinking-horn; feasting,' said the doorkeeper, 'has begun, but only for those invited.' Culhwch would have to stay like all unannounced arrivals, in the guesthouse, well fed, well watered, well entertained, well bedded. He could see Arthur first thing in the morning.

'No,' said Culhwch. 'If you don't let me in I will shout three times. Each shout will echo as far as the next island and as high as the clouds, and the noise will empty the womb of any woman carrying a child and make barren all those who are not.'

'I'll have to ask Arthur,' said the sentry.

Keeping Culhwch waiting outside, the man went into the castle and told Arthur that despite a long life of wondrous escapades in India and Norway and Africa and Greece he had never seen such a remarkable vision of manhood as the rider at the gate. Notwithstanding such an encomium, Arthur tried to enforce his rule of the guesthouse, but even as he spoke in rode the gleaming Culhwch.

He greeted Arthur effusively with a torrent of words and blessings. Arthur replied in similar vein and then offered the hospitality of the feast. Culhwch said he had not come for that, he could get food and drink anywhere – no, he had a favour to ask. If Arthur granted it Culhwch would praise him forever; if he did not, Culhwch would speak Arthur's shame everywhere.

'Anything,' said Arthur, reeling off a list of things he could give Culhwch, with the exception of his own weapons and wife.

'I want you to cut my hair,' said Culhwch.

As Arthur, with a gold comb and silver scissors, began barbering, he traced his kinship with Culhwch. On discovering how closely they were related, he was moved to say, 'Cousin, you can ask me for any favour you want.'

Culhwch replied, 'I want to marry Olwen, the daughter of the King of the Giants.'

Arthur, despite his glowing promise, showed some reluctance. To reinforce his request, Culhwch invoked the names of as many mythological personages and great heroes and heroines as he could find in Arthur's lineage and entourage. At the mention of these names the room grew silent. The burning love of Olwen so stimulated Culhwch that he had no difficulty in reaching back through the golden and glorious ages of Arthur's ancestry; in this way he gained moral and psychological support for his own quest.

It worked. Arthur there and then committed all his power to finding her and delivering news of her whereabouts to Culhwch. He immediately dispatched the royal messengers to search the known world and find this woman in order that Arthur's magnificent ancestry and associations would not be shamed. After a year, though, they came no nearer to finding Olwen, and Culhwch chided Arthur that everyone else's favours had been granted except his. Up spoke one of Arthur's lieutenants, Kai. 'That's not fair to Arthur. I'll go and look for her and you come with me. If this girl actually does exist we'll find her.'

He spoke with terrific confidence, as well he might: he could hold his breath for nine days underwater; he needed no sleep for nine nights; nobody could survive a cut from his blade.

Kai took with him a warrior called Bedvyr, the court guide, who knew every pathway, and the court interpreter who knew every language; the party even included a wizard who, in times of danger, could render them invisible. Off they went, Arthur's blessings and hopes with them.

Their first task proved almost a mirage – a great castle, the most magnificent building any of them had ever seen. But however hard they rode it seemed to get no nearer, puzzling them enormously. They also observed that in front of this castle a huge flock of sheep grazed the plain on all sides as far as the eye could see. From a hillock a lone shepherd surveyed these thousands of animals. He turned out to be a fearsome figure, proud of never ever having lost a sheep, unapproachable because the breath of his sheepdog – a huge and ugly animal, big as a horse – scorched everything it touched (except, presumably, sheep).

They tried to dispatch the interpreter to speak to this shepherd but he refused to go alone, so they all went, though only after the wizard had put a spell on the sheepdog. After some small talk the shepherd told them that the great fort belonged to the King of the Giants.

'That's our man,' they said to the shepherd, and told him that they wanted the King's daughter for Culhwch to marry, and that Arthur himself sponsored their guest. The shepherd gave them a look of profound pity.

Culhwch gave the man a ring as a sign of gratitude and later that day when the shepherd went home to his wife, he told her that soon, the owner of the ring would be stretched in front of her, dead.

It turned out that this woman was Culhwch's aunt, the sister of his mother. She went out to greet her nephew, but Kai snatched a lighted brand from the fire and shoved it in front of her, preventing her embrace. She grabbed the brand and bent it into the shape of a steel spring – as Kai had divined she would have done to Culhwch's ribs.

Inside her home the woman calmed down and told them the King of the Giants had killed twenty-three of her twenty-four sons. Her twenty-fourth, even though he had escaped, now spent his life terrified, hidden in a trunk – a pity, she said, for he had lovely curly golden hair.

When they told her they were pursuing Olwen as a wife for Culhwch, she jumped back in great alarm and insisted they leave before anybody from the castle found them. But when she understood their determination, she gave them some valuable information. Olwen, she said, came by every weekend to wash her hair and always left a ring or some personal effect behind her.

Olwen arrived next day, wearing a silk gown the colour of fire; around her neck a thick torc heavily encrusted with emeralds and rubies. The men, watching from behind a wall, were captivated; they admired her hands, delicate as the flowers of the forest; they marvelled at her golden hair, at her sea-spray-white skin and at the way in which her beauty touched all it encountered: everywhere she placed a dainty foot up sprang a clover flower.

As she sat down in the shepherd's house Culhwch came out of hiding and unleashed a passionate plea of love. Olwen replied by explaining why her father never wanted her to marry.

'You see – the tradition says that if I ever wed he must die,' she said.

'Leave with me now,' pleaded Culhwch.

'No. Go to my father, you're brave enough to risk that. Ask him for my hand in marriage. He will put to you a list of tasks. Accomplish them and I'm yours. Fail and you're probably dead.'

'Go for it,' the others said to Culhwch.

Next day they headed for the castle, and *en route* disposed of the nine keepers of the nine gates and their nine famously savage hounds. Olwen's father, the King of the Giants, asked his servants to raise his eyelids – so great they needed to be propped up with forked sticks – in order that he could look closely at these upstarts.

Culhwch declared his mission. The Giant told him to come back tomorrow, but as they left the hall the treacherous ogre seized a massive javelin with a poisoned tip and let it fly at their departing backs. Bedvyr grabbed it by the haft as it flew past him and used the momentum of the weapon to turn it round in mid-air and hit the giant on the knee. His roar shook the stones in the walls and he complained bitterly that he would never again walk without pain.

When the heroes rose next day they spent some time preening, so that they cut a dash. They travelled to the castle and confronted the Giant.

'Give us Olwen like any other normal marriage arrangement.'

The Giant said that he had to go and consult the senior women of the family, and as they turned to relax he threw another poisoned javelin at them. One of Culhwch's men caught it and threw it back so hard that it went straight through the Giant's chest and shot out the other side. He roared so loud that the birds flew off the roof outside in fright, and he complained bitterly that he would never walk without puffing, or ever again have a good appetite.

The heroes left, had something to eat and settled down for the night. Next morning they returned to the castle. They implored the Giant not to try any more tricks on them, but he threw another poisoned spear. This time Culhwch returned it, hitting him in the eye so hard that the point shot out through the back of the Giant's skull. The ogre complained bitterly that he would never again see without his eyes watering and they began to discuss his wounds with him, to see if they could dissuade him from causing further trouble.

When Bedvyr first hit the Giant with the first javelin, the Giant had likened it to the sting of a horsefly. When the second one hit him, he said it felt like the bite of a leech. The third one – in the eye – hurt, he said, like the bite of a mad dog. So, as and from next morning, he agreed not to throw any more.

Consequently he sat down with Culhwch to discuss the whole issue of Olwen and her hand in marriage. The Giant said, 'Fair is fair. You do what I ask and you'll get Olwen. And I'll accept my fate. Not that I'll have to, because you'll not even achieve one of these.'

'First task?' asked Culhwch.

The Giant produced a list of forbidding ventures, starting with a hill they could see outside the door which he wanted burned and crushed to potash and ploughed into the ground before the following dawn, a not insuperable task for a hero like Culhwch – but then came the rub.

In order to do this properly, Culhwch had to find a particular ploughman, named by the Giant, who would not voluntarily do the job; then a particular smith to provide the tools, who would also need compelling by force; then two famous oxen belonging to a particularly difficult character who would lend them to nobody without being forced at swordpoint; and various other oxen, two of which had been turned by magic from human form because of the evil they had done.

To all of these Culhwch agreed without a hint of qualm, even when the Giant wanted honey much sweeter than that of a first swarm's making, from bees who had no drones among them; even when the Giant asked for the goblet of a man who would never part with it because it held the strongest drink in all the world; even when the Giant asked for the famous food-basket which contained the favourite food of every person under the sun; even when the Giant asked for more and more and more – the list went on and on and on.

He wanted Culhwch to get him, for instance, an unattainable drinking-horn; a harp from which its owner would not part; the magic birds of Rhiannon; the magic Irish cauldron; a famous tusk off a living boar with which the giant would shave his beard, but the tusk could only be obtained by the son of the King of Ireland; a hag's blood from the hearth of hell, kept warm in the flasks of Gidolin the Dwarf; and fiercely guarded bottles in which no liquid ever turned sour.

Culhwch calmly answered 'no problem' to every task, no matter how impossible.

'Go on,' said the Giant, naming everything in detail, 'get me this scissors and comb, that young dog and the famous leash he needs; then get me the only collar that will restrain the leash and the chain that will strengthen the grip of both; then get me the only houndsman who can handle all of that, a man called Mabon, and nobody knows where he dwells; and then get me the horse that is as fast as the waves of the sea.'

Though Culhwch seemed unmoved, the jaws of his companions had dropped open in amazement and dejection.

The Giant went merrily on, reading out a list as long as his arm, and you know how long a giant's arm is. He demanded an extraordinary variety of people and objects, and the point was – they all interlocked, and the availability of each item always depended upon getting hold of another object, always seemingly unattainable. The task with which he ended his list was typical: Culhwch had to appropriate a sword from another giant – who could only be killed with that very sword.

'You'll not get one of them,' said the Giant confidently, 'and you'll not get my daughter.'

Culhwch replied, 'I have my cousin Arthur and all his powers and forces at my disposal.'

'Well, you know the deal,' said the King of the Giants. 'Get all of these and you get Olwen. Fail even one and that's you finished.'

Culhwch and his friends rode away. He had already decided to start at the end of his quest rather than the beginning, perceiving that the logic peeled backwards in that direction.

First of all, they found the castle of the giant who could only be killed with his own sword. Kai went forward to the gate, but the gatekeeper would not let him near the place. Oh, he offered him hospitality all right, but only in the guesthouse.

'You'll regret that,' said Kai, 'when your master hears the skills I have.'

'What skills are they?' asked the gatekeeper.

'No man in the world can sharpen and polish swords like I can.'

'I'll go and tell him,' and the gatekeeper came back with an invitation to Kai to go in and meet the giant and sharpen and polish his sword. The warrior sat in a chair opposite the giant, took a stone from his bag and first he polished one side and handed it back.

'Do the other side,' said the giant. Then he did the other side and handed it back.

'You're a competent fellow,' said the giant. 'Have you any friends as clever as yourself?'

'There's one outside the door this minute,' said Kai, 'and he has a real trick. He has a spear that flies by itself off its haft, attacks and then comes back again.'

'Bring him in.'

In came Bedvyr and before any questions could be asked Kai jumped up, and waving the sword over the giant as if to test it, cut off his head. The rest of the party slaughtered all round them, left the castle in ruins, took as much booty as they could comfortably carry and set off on the most difficult task of all – to find Mabon, the mastiff keeper, the man whose whereabouts and very existence remained in question.

But now Culhwch had to rethink his sequence, because in order to reach Mabon he found that he had to observe the chain of tasks in the order the King of the Giants had said them. For this they needed help and Arthur joined them with his multitude of warriors.

First of all they went after Mabon's kinsman, held prisoner in a heavily defended castle. The castle owner, fearing the legendary might of Arthur, handed over the prisoner readily.

Advised by this kinsman, the next leg of the quest found them speaking through the interpreter to the Blackbird of Kilgowry. The Blackbird told them that in all his long years, long enough to have pecked a blacksmith's anvil down to the smallness of a nut, he never heard of Mabon, whom someone had abducted when only three days and three nights old; the bird, however, knew of a creature who had been on earth even longer, the Stag of Rhedenure.

The Stag told them likewise, that he had in his long life, long enough for a single oak sapling to have grown to a giant with many branches then fade away to a small red stump, never heard of Mabon, whom someone had abducted when only three days and three nights old; then the Stag took them to someone even older than him, the Owl of Cawlwyd, so old his wings had dwindled to stumps; who sent them to the Eagle of Gwernabwy, so old that the stone on which he stood every night had now worn to the size of a pebble; and he sent them to someone even older, to a salmon he had once tried to capture, the Salmon of Llyn Llyw.

The Salmon let them sit on his back and ferried them upstream to Gloucester, where they came to a stockade from which groans emanated. Here Mabon had been imprisoned with more cruelty and injustice than anyone had ever encountered, and through the wooden wall he called to them that he could only be released by force. Arthur went home, mustered a full army, and with Kai and Bedvyr leading the raid from their perch on the Salmon's back, they freed Mabon.

Now they had acquired a major key to the chain of quests, and one by one they ticked them off successfully, sometimes making great journeys, always achieving great feats. For example, at Milford Haven they captured the two great pups of the great bitch, and to make the leash which alone in the world would restrain the two dogs, they snatched the strands of hair from a warrior's beard; they killed the boar to make the razor from his tusk that the King of the Giants had ordered. They even went to Ireland to gain the magic cauldron that could only be taken by force – hundreds were killed in the attempt before Arthur and his men returned with the cauldron full of Irish booty.

One of the major tasks involved gaining a comb and scissors from between the ears of a ferocious prince. It seemed impossible that anyone could even challenge this aristocrat, who dwelt with seven pigs and who possessed unbounded ferocity. Arthur got together his biggest army and took him on. He even embarked upon single combat himself, but could make no headway, except for killing one small pig, while the prince remained unmarked.

Arthur called up all the magic available to him. The wizard changed the interpreter into a bird, who perched beside the wild prince and tried to persuade him, or one of the remaining pigs, to negotiate with Arthur. They all refused and when the interpreter pointed out that Arthur's determination to get the scissors and comb from between the prince's ears would probably result in the slaughter of them all, the prince went on the offensive.

The remaining pigs launched themselves into the sea and swam across to Dyfed to invade Arthur's kingdoms. Arthur followed, appalled at the trail of death, burning and destruction wrought by the prince and his pigs. They roared through Milford Haven followed by Arthur, his huge armies and his best warriors, and every time a confrontation took place, Arthur suffered severe losses, including the slaying of his own beloved son.

This savage campaign raged through the countryside, down into valleys, by river banks, across foothills and farms. Sometimes the prince and the pigs went to ground, then roared out of cover and slew all in their path. Arthur appealed for help to try and contain or subdue this man and his pigs – he even sent to Brittany. Finally, with all the men of Cornwall, Devon and the south, they cornered the prince and the swine on the banks of the Severn at the mouth of its channel.

Arthur's forces attacked from several directions at once, but instead of trying to kill the prince with swords or spears, they knocked him into the river and held him down. Mabon rode in like a javelin and snatched the first of the objects, the comb, from between the man's ears. The prince struggled back to his feet, throwing off the warriors who festooned him, some of the strongest men in the world among them. The prince took off again, this time heading south towards Cornwall.

Once more they caught up with him and finished the job, grabbing the scissors from between his ears. Then they let him go and he was last seen running out to sea, defeated, in a towering but impotent rage.

One task now remained – the blood of the Hag of Hell. They found her in her northern cave, an awful sight, with a smell that bent the bushes. To fight ugliness with beauty, to fight darkness with light, two of the finest, freshest warriors went in. They came out again as quickly, bleeding where she had torn their hair out at the roots, naked and scratched where she had whipped off their armour, terrified and deaf where she had screamed death at them. His knights had to hold back the incensed Arthur. Two more grand young warriors went in – she destroyed them. All four had to be taken away, folded like sacks across the back of a docile old mare.

Now they could no longer restrain Arthur. He drew his broad knife, jumped into the mouth of the cave from a high rock overhanging one side, hit the hag right on the point of the breastbone so that she split down to the cracks of her toes, and her blood poured into the two tubs they had brought for the purpose.

Culhwch and the shepherd's son, now free to come out of the trunk he had hidden in, and any who wanted – not that a great many of the original party had survived – set off for the castle of the King of the Giants to declare comprehensive success and claim Olwen.

After the Giant had duly been shaved and barbered with the boar's tusk and the comb and scissors, he gave credit to Arthur for the great accomplishments of such an extraordinarily difficult series of tasks. Even though he knew the inevitable outcome of Culhwch's success, the Giant still cast his big lazy eyes around the castle, as if contemplating a way of taking on the warriors yet again. They all pressed forward and he saw that he had no chance, no option but to accept his fate – he had been completely defeated and therefore had no magic left.

He agreed with Culhwch that his end had come: the fates had always said that he would die when his daughter married. Culhwch turned to where Olwen stood and, claiming her, declared himself lord of all the Giant's lands. That night, after a big and noisy feast, during which the Giant lay tied up in a corner, Culhwch bedded his woman, who remained his for life.

The following morning, the shepherd's curly-haired son asked for permission to do the killing, in revenge for his twenty-three dead brothers. In the bright sunlight he caught the Giant by the hair, dragged him briskly along the ground to the castle cesspit, dunked him in it a few times, cut off his head and stuck it on spikes outside the gates.

And so, Culhwch won Olwen, the daughter of the King of the Giants – and secured the inheritance of which his stepmother had hoped to deprive him.

THE DREAM OF RHONABWY

ord Madoc, ruler of Powys, had a jealous brother, Irwerth, who resented being less powerful, less wealthy, less celebrated. He discussed his lot with his other kinfolk and his advisers and they said, 'Let us plead your case with Madoc.' Which they did, but though Madoc made Irwerth a generous offer of status and command, Irwerth refused, raised an army and took off into England on a rampage – not precisely what Madoc wished. So Madoc raised another army, of the best farming men he could find in Powys, and sent them off to find Irwerth.

One of these men, by name Rhonabwy, came, in the company of several others, to shelter at nightfall in a house so decrepit they could scarcely believe it. Acrid smoke and unpleasant smells drifted from the living-room – and no wonder – the potholed earthen floor, littered with the debris of cattle feed, stank with cowdung and urine.

In the hall of the household they found a crone tending an indifferent fire on which she burnt straw and chaff. It kept her warm, but the dust from it blinded everybody around the place. She did have in her possession, however, a comfortable-looking animal hide on which a weary man might grab a night's sleep.

Rhonabwy and his friends tried to engage the crone in talk, with little luck. Other householders arrived, equally unprepossessing: a sour little man with red flaking skin and no hair, and his wife, a tiny woman, skin and bone; she and her husband carried bundles of twigs for the fire. They barely observed the rules of hospitality: the food on offer would hardly entice a starveling, milk thinner than old gruel, sticky wet wheaten bread, cheese going sour. Rhonabwy and his friends quickly wondered whether they had chosen the best lodgings imaginable.

Outside the wind rose, and rain came lashing with it. They tried to sleep, putting up with the flea-hopping, dirty beds among the animal droppings. Rhonabwy, a man of some sensibility, could not tolerate these conditions and when the others had dropped off he moved on to the animal skin, which seemed at least half decent. He fell asleep and almost immediately began a glorious dream, full of more colour than he had ever seen in life.

He saw himself crossing a plain he knew well, towards a ford on the river Severn. Lost in thought and enjoying his journey with his friends, he shook his head when he heard a great noise directly behind him. Riding in their wake came a bigger man than any of them had ever encountered. Young, with curly hair and beard, he rode a yellow horse and wore an outfit of vivid yellows fringed with fir-green, with a sword of gold and a flying cloak of green silk. Alarmed, Rhonabwy and his friends spurred their horses, but he easily caught them up and seemed so threatening that they, though fighting men, begged for mercy.

'Who are you?' they asked.

'My name is Iddawc, and they call me the Churn, because I stir things up. I stirred up a row between King Arthur and his nephew – that led to the battle of Camlan. All because I pretended that Arthur had couched the message with which he entrusted me in the rudest of language. Still, I have repented of that.'

As he spoke, they heard another noise behind them, and galloping hard came an even more brilliant horseman, this time dressed in scarlet brocade trimmed and covered with broom-yellow silk, a shining man, whose weapons and horse and clothes seemed in the cleanest and most beautiful possible order.

Looking with some scorn at Rhonabwy and the others, he asked the man in green and gold for a loan of 'these little fellows'.

The first man replied, 'Why don't you befriend them, like me?'

'Fair enough,' said the second one and rode off. The first man told Rhonabwy and his friends that people called the man in yellow Rhuvawn the Shining.

Rhonabwy and his friends rode on accompanied by the first man, and when they reached the river Severn they saw a great festive camp, nearly a square mile in size, pennants and banners flying in the breeze above the striped pavilions. King Arthur himself sat on a small island in the stream flanked by courtiers, including a tall boy dressed in black and white. He had skin white as ivory under a cap black as jet.

The man in green and gold wheeled his horse and led Rhonabwy and his friends down to where Arthur sat. The king greeted the man cordially, though in a way which made Rhonabwy and the others feel slighted.

'Where did you find these small fellows?'

'On the road, my lord.'

The king laughed, though a dry laugh, then said, 'I worry that our kingdom only has such pygmies to guard it,' and turned away.

The man in green and gold said to Rhonabwy, 'Did you notice the ring the king wore?' Rhonabwy nodded.

The man went on, 'The stone in that ring contains a magical property which will oblige you to recall all you have seen since we met.'

Shortly afterwards Rhonabwy and his friends observed a marvellously colourful platoon of warriors riding at a canter towards them, and they asked their mentor, the man in green and gold, about them. He said they accompanied the other colourful horseman, the one in shining yellow – and as such, and indeed in their own right, too – they had access to every noble house in the land and they received the best of hospitality from the highest and the lowest. They wore nothing but red – nowhere on the person of any one of them did a colour shine without the reddest possible glow. They dismounted and their servants began to pitch their tents upriver.

Then another wonderful troop arrived, wearing brilliant white above the saddle and raven black below. Unheeding, one of them galloped across the river near where Arthur stood, splashing the king and his companions. The tall boy in the king's company, the one with the white skin under the jet-black cap, lifted his sword and scabbard together and brought them down fiercely on the horse's flank. The rider began to draw his own sword, but the boy refused it by pointing out to him indignantly that the man had splashed the king.

Rhonabwy asked his man in green and gold the identity of the headstrong rider.

'The son of Taliesin,' came the reply.

As the massed soldiers gathered in their ranks, a chieftain rose named Caradoc. He rallied them to fight in the forthcoming battle for which, after all, they had gathered here. He seemed eager to goad Arthur, whom he accused of unwillingness to fight. The king replied to this man's taunts of hesitancy by calling upon all troops there and then to begin their march to the battlefield. While the massed ranks reined their horses around in the right direction, and rode across the river at the ford, Rhonabwy looked up the Severn valley and saw coming down towards them three further divisions of mounted soldiers, the third of which wore brilliant white edged with black. Even the horses had snow-white hair, except for jet-black legs.

Their appearance stunned Rhonabwy, who asked his mentor about them.

'Norwegians,' Iddawc said, 'the white troops of Norway.' Behind them came a troop dressed in exactly the opposite arrangement of colours, all black, fringed with snow white.

'Denmark,' said Iddawc, 'the black troops of Denmark.'

By now the front of Arthur's great army had reached the ridge overlooking the valley of Bath, the newcomers catching up with the rear of the columns. Rhonabwy and his friends, simply because Iddawc led them, followed the march without question. As the armies descended the ridge into the plain, a terrific fuss broke out ahead, with horses plunging in a wild mêlée. Rhonabwy and his companions tried to figure out what was happening and at that moment a rider came in from the far edge of the hill at a cracking pace, dressed in red and white armour which caught the light.

So fiercely did the commotion rage that Rhonabwy wondered whether Arthur had sounded a retreat or something; instead, as Iddawc pointed out, the confusion attached to the armoured rider, one of the greatest of all Arthur's followers, called Kai, so fine that one half of the army at the outside spurred their horses inwards to see him and those inside tried to get out so that he would not trample them. The panic grew so huge that Arthur had to instruct his armourer to rise and call for order by waving Arthur's golden sword. This terrified all who saw it, with its twin tongues of flame springing from either side of the blade like scorching serpents.

'Who is that man waving that terrible sword?' Rhonabwy asked.

Iddawc replied, 'Cawder of Cornwall – he arms Arthur on the morning of battle.'

Arthur's chief servant appeared, a burly, taciturn man with red hair. He unpacked his saddle-bags and laid on the ground Arthur's magic cloth made of quilted satin with an apple embroidered at each corner; this cloth, when he wrapped himself in it, concealed Arthur from everybody but allowed him to see them. A gold chair followed, and then a board game to which Arthur challenged a man called Owen.

Owen, though an excellent player, needed to concentrate against such a brilliant exponent as the king. As he began to do well, a blue-eyed, yellow-haired messenger appeared from the tent that had red and white stripes topped by a serpent's head. The man, who wore yellow satin and yellow-green hose, with a black leather scabbard containing a golden-hilted three-edged sword, told Owen that the king's attendants had begun to harass Owen's ravens in their cages. Owen asked Arthur to call off his men. Arthur only indicated that Owen's turn in the game had come.

A short time later, another messenger walked over from the yellow pavilion which was topped by a bright red lion. An auburn-haired man, large-eyed, cleanshaven, dressed in yellow with white hose and black boots, he wore a scabbard made from the hide of a red deer. He addressed Owen:

'Lord, the king's servants are tormenting your ravens in their cages, poking and stabbing them. They've even killed some.'

Owen said to the king, 'Lord, tell them to stop.'

'Play on,' said Arthur.

They began another game and this time from a spotted yellow tent that had been surmounted with a huge eagle's head in jewelled gold, came a golden-haired boy wearing green and gold. He held a yellow spear in his free hand, with his other he spurred the horse hard, hauled it to a rearing jump beside the board game and, furious, told Owen the king's men had practically wiped out the ravens.

'Play on,' said the king.

'Go,' said Owen, 'into the thick of the ravens' difficulties and raise my flag to whip them up.'

He did and the ravens went berserk. They flew high in the air, rested awhile on currents of warm air and came tearing down into the attack, gouging out eyes, tearing off ears, breaking noses with their harsh beaks.

Not long after this the fight reversed with Owen's men attacking Arthur's ravens. Three times the scene repeated itself. Messengers approached Arthur – one, wearing armour and a gold helmet with a leopard crest, sat on a beautiful grey horse swathed in thick crimson linen; another came on a white horse with one black leg, horse and rider covered in green and yellow mail topped by a gold helmet with the crest of a lion; a third rode up in flecked armour wearing a yellow helmet. All three carried weapons, tall spears dripping with ravens' blood; all three told the king of the havoc being wrought by Owen's ravens, and on each occasion when Arthur asked Owen to call off his tormentors, Owen said 'Play on.'

When the board games had been concluded, it transpired that the enemy upon whom the king's armies were marching had made an offer of peace. Arthur rose from his gold chair, settled on his magic cloth as he did for all important conferences and called his many advisers. They came from far and near, from Greece and Ireland, from Norway and Denmark, from France and Powys, and in the end after much consultation they agreed the terms of a truce. The chief adviser seemed too young to be included in such a convocation but, as Iddawc explained to Rhonabwy and his friends, no man in these lands gave more accurate counsel. At which point people arrived to pay tribute, among them two dozen men from the Greek islands leading two dozen donkeys, each of whom bore two baskets, one pannier full of silver, the other of gold.

Kai had the last word, calling upon everyone to go to Cornwall in Arthur's honour and to return to these fields in six weeks for the ending of the truce. At which point Rhonabwy awoke from his colourful dream and when he told it to his friends the dream made him famous.

Of his own adventures, in the armies of Powys pursuing Irwerth, we know nothing, and can only presume they were not as interesting as his dream.

THE COUNTESS OF THE FOUNTAIN

itting in his royal suite on the banks of the river Usk, on cushions of brilliantly coloured brocade, King Arthur was surrounded by his warriors, including Owen and Kai. There too sat Cunon, a fine soldier and an even finer storyteller. Arthur took a sleep; Kai poured the drinks and prevailed upon Cunon to tell a story. Cunon began, and told this tale.

As an only child, immensely talented and spoiled, Cunon learned every feat of arms and skill that could be taught, and then, as a man should, set out to travel the world in search of adventure. One day, riding carefully down a ravine, he came out into a glorious valley full of trees whose uniform loveliness gave a most stabilising appearance, and a wide river that had the look of sweet silver. By the river ran a well-tended path, often used by horses and waggons and oxen. Across a wide red and green plain, on a distant height, stood a fine castle.

Cunon rode up to the sward that lay before the castle and there he saw three figures, a pair of boys and a man. The boys, obviously training to be hunters, carried the most exquisite weaponry. Each held a longbow made of carved ivory and deergut bowstrings; each arrow had been fashioned from ivory, with gold tips and flights of peacock feathers. The boys also carried knives of gold with ivory hilts – these they had stuck in the ground a little way off, and for target practice they aimed to hit the gold blades with their gold-tipped arrows. They wore outfits of saffron brocade, and the saffron head-bands on their foreheads signified them as young warriors. The man supervising them had a distinguished presence; he too wore saffron, threaded and fastened with gold with a gold lace collar.

The man hailed Cunon and by turning with him indicated that Cunon should accompany him to the castle. In a hall beyond a high stone arch, sat two dozen women, each of dazzling beauty, making a long tapestry. As Cunon and the man stood at the door the women rose from their work and divided themselves into four groups of six. Of the first six, some led Cunon's horse away to be fed, watered and rested and some helped the warrior himself to sit down, easing off his high boots. Of the next six, some polished Cunon's armour until it shone like white gold and some sharpened his sword until the point caught the light of the sun streaming in through the high windows. Of the third group of six, some shook out a long and wide cloth of stiff white linen and laid it on the table while others served the food. Of the final six, some helped Cunon off with his clothes and others brought forward large silver bowls of scented water in which he washed; they handed him towels of green and white linen. Helping him to don linen shirt and trousers, tunic and short cloak of saffron brocade, they led him to cushions of crimson linen and served a lavish meal in vessels of gold, silver and ivory.

The strangers in this great hall did Cunon the courtesy of not plying him with talk until he had first satisfied his obviously great hunger. He misinterpreted this, took it for a lack of real conversationalists in their society and complained – upon which the men chided him gently by pointing out the courtesy they were doing him. However, now that the talking had begun, the man from the sward felt free to ask Cunon the purpose of his journey and what had brought him this way. Cunon replied that he had committed himself, as a matter of honour, to finding his equal in warriorhood.

'And is that all?' enquired his host.

'That's all.'

'H'm,' said the man. 'Well, I could easily point you in the right direction – but no good would come of it. In fact, nothing but harm would happen.'

Cunon looked crestfallen and the man changed his mind, but with some caution.

'All right. If you insist on looking for the evil in life, I will tell you what I know – where you may find what you are looking for.'

He directed Cunon to set out next morning and go back a little to a wood through which Cunon had already ridden.

'Take the right hand fork of the main road through the wood; this will lead you to a wide clearing in the trees, so wide you could call it a field. Now in this field you will see a high hillock, a kind of mound, and sitting upon this will be a large man of a black visage, larger and blacker than anything you have ever come across.'

'How black?' asked Cunon.

'Black as jet. He will jump up when you approach and then you will see that he has only one leg and one wide foot, centred in the middle of his body. As you draw near you will see that he has only one eye, right in the middle of his forehead. The iron spear he carries in his one hand would weigh down several normal men. He will swivel his eye towards you and growl, but do not be put off by his threatening appearance. He guards the forest, he is responsible for all the animals and you will notice that however wild they may be, they will sit and graze unalarmed near him. Now go up to him, and ask where to go next. He will shout at you and seem very threatening, but that will be the worst of it.'

After a night spent sleeping on linens and the skins of tender young animals, Cunon set off next morning and found everything exactly as the man had said, only to a much bigger degree. The wild animals numbered three times as many as he had been led to expect; the black man much larger and blacker, the spear in his hand much heavier, his manner much more truculent. When Cunon inquired as to the power he held over all the wild animals, the giant reached out with the butt of his spear and struck the largest stag Cunon had ever seen. The stag bellowed and immediately, from the woods and hills, even more animals came running until the whole wide field teemed with deer and antelope and lion and snakes – every conceivable beast and reptile stood there.

'Feed,' shouted the black giant and they lowered their heads in an obeisant manner and began to graze.

Cunon asked the giant, as he had been told, which direction to take. The enigmatic nature of the question caused no problems. The giant, still truculent, asked Cunon in return which way he wished to go and Cunon replied by repeating his quest – to find a man his exact equal in warriorhood. The giant told him to take a pathway that led up out of this clearing. From the peak of this climb he would look out across a great valley in the middle of which he would see a huge, spreading, evergreen tree. Underneath the tree a fountain bubbled, and on a great wide marble stone beside it stood a silver bowl held by a chain so that the bowl could not be removed.

The giant told Cunon to fill the bowl from the fountain and pour the water on the white marble. He would hear a wild and thunderous noise shaking the earth beneath his feet; this would be followed by an icy shower of huge hailstones stripping all the leaves off the trees. Flocks of birds would descend and begin to sing the sweetest songs, but at the very moment of their highest and most exquisite notes, Cunon would hear a new noise, a high long moan. Coming towards him he would see what he wished for – a man dressed in stiff black brocade with a black pennant fluttering from his spear, who would immediately launch an invincible attack on Cunon.

The warrior took in the black giant's words and rode out of the clearing, picking his way through the legions of animals still grazing. He found everything as described: the valley, the tree, the fountain, the bowl and chain and the marble slab. Cunon, as instructed, filled the bowl from the fountain and emptied it on the slab. The thunder roared louder and the rain and hailstones fell heavier and icier than the giant had led him to believe – in fact so devastating did the hailstones become that Cunon had to cover both his horse and himself with his shield and armour, otherwise their flesh would have been stripped to the bone.

Sunshine and the singing birds followed, and just as they had begun to soothe the pain caused by the hailstones, a loud moaning began and out of the distance materialised a horseman in black with a black pennant fluttering from his spear.

Cunon attacked him and immediately found himself unseated. The stranger took Cunon's horse and rode away with it. Cunon retraced his steps and found himself back with the Keeper of the Wood, who laughed humiliatingly. Cunon continued on foot and by nightfall reached the palace where he had spent the previous night. There, they gave him a horse with a red mane and he returned to Arthur's court where he now sat recounting this story.

'I still feel the shame of it,' he told his listeners, 'and I only tell you because somewhere, right here in Arthur's realm, without his knowledge, this has gone on.'

They began to argue – at times quite heatedly – among themselves as to whether they should find this knight, and eventually, unobserved, Owen armed, saddled and rode away.

He rode the same long journey as Cunon had ridden, and saw all the same sights, the same youths, the same man, the same castle, the same women. He found the black giant, Keeper of the Woods, rode to the green tree, threw the water from the silver bowl on the marble, experienced the same weather sensations, heard the birds and the moans – and along rode the black knight.

Owen attacked, the stranger countered – a fierce battle. Owen overcame him, struck a deadly blow through the man's helmet, and the stranger, turning his horse, rode away at great speed. Owen pursued him, could never quite catch him. Ahead, a city materialised, walls, battlements, towers, turrets, shining in the morning light. The stranger spurred his horse over the sward in front of the castle, the gate-keepers raised the portcullis for him and he galloped through. As Owen rode hell-for-leather after him they dropped the pointed portcullis which sliced Owen's horse in half just behind the saddle, killing the animal and throwing Owen to the ground. They also dropped an inner gate, trapping Owen between two enormous defences which he knew he could never breach.

As he stood there, at a loss, he saw a woman in a yellow satin dress walking down the lane of houses that led up to the main castle. He called out to her and she, clearly smitten by the handsome warrior, offered, speaking through the bars of the inner gate, to help. She told him that the black knight looked as if he would surely die as a result of the wounds Owen had given him, and that the men of the castle now wanted Owen's blood. She gave him a ring from her finger and told Owen that as long as he held it in the palm of his hand he would be invisible.

In due course, she declared, he should wait for her by the knights' mounting-block. She returned to the castle and when the black knight's colleagues came to kill Owen, trapped, they believed, in the space between the two gates, they found only the remains of the dead horse. As they opened the gates, the invisible Owen slipped through and went to the mounting-block where the girl waited, the sun shining on her yellow clothes.

He laid a hand on her shoulder and she led him, unseen by anyone at court, indoors to a large and beautiful room. In this chamber, with walls of red and gold, the girl lit a fire, heated water and in a silver basin bathed Owen's wounds, drying them with linen towels. On a table of solid silver covered with yellow linen, she served him dinner, a champion's portion all to himself. He and the girl sat there talking as Owen ate and drank his fill. Her name was Luned.

Suddenly a loud cry rang out through the castle and the city. In the course of the evening it happened twice more. On the first occasion the girl explained that the owner of the castle, the black knight, had just begun to die. At the second cry he died. The third meant that they had begun the funeral. Upon hearing this Owen rose from his comfortable couch and looked out of the window.

The streets teemed with people of all kinds, rich and poor, walking and riding. They moaned and mourned and shook their hands and wept as they moved along the narrow stone streets in a huge procession behind and around a white funeral cart lit by candles and escorted by noblemen. Walking in a space made for her directly behind the bier came a woman dressed in saffron brocade with multicoloured shoes on her feet, who tore her hair out and wept. Owen nearly fell from his window perch at the beauty of the woman and inquired about her from the girl at his side.

'They call her "The Countess of the Fountain" and she is the widow of the black knight you killed.'

'But I have never seen a woman I love more.'

'She is my mistress,' said Luned, 'and I can assure you that she has no love for you.'

She led Owen away from the window and sat him down on a chair by which she had prepared a table with shaving bowls and razors. She washed Owen's head and face and shaved him with an ivory-hilted, gold-riveted razor, served him another superb meal and sent him to bed. Then, she went to press his suit with her mistress.

When she entered the lady's rooms she had difficulty in penetrating the atmosphere of grief. At last she spoke to such purpose that her mistress responded angrily and quarrelsomely. The girl finally settled the row by saying:

'Whether you like it or not you now have to consider how the kingdom of your late husband is to be defended, and whether you like it or not, despite your grief which I do not disrespect, your kingdom can only be defended by a man with superior feats of arms who can protect the Fountain. Now the only place on earth where it is likely you will find a man who can defend the Fountain is at the court of Arthur, and if you wish I will go there and find one.'

Having secured the Countess's agreement, Luned pretended to set out for Arthur's court. But she actually went only to her own chambers, where Owen still resided. When she had stayed in the room as long as if she had been to Arthur's court and back, she began to dress Owen in beautiful clothes. So that he would be acceptable at court she gave him saffron, with collars of gold lace; his shoes had gold buckles in the shape of lions. Together they walked into the body of the castle to meet the Countess of the Fountain. Luned even introduced Owen as the warrior who had killed the black knight and therefore, logically, a superior defender of the Fountain. She managed to persuade the Countess, grieving aside, to consider this new man. The Countess promised to think it over and sent the two away.

The Countess convened her court and told them that the Fountain had to be defended by a man who could not be overwhelmed, and asked whether they would offer one from their own number, or should she seek elsewhere? Unsurprisingly they told her to look elsewhere – which cleared the path for her to introduce Owen and, quickly, to marry him. He, in turn, solemnly undertook the guardianship of the Fountain and, as good as his word, effortlessly routed all who came near it.

Three years passed at Arthur's court and Owen had not returned. Arthur, of whom Owen had always been a favourite, grieved at the warrior's absence. He shared his grief with the others who suggested to him that they go in search of Owen. Arthur himself led forth an army of the best and fittest knights.

They found the fortress, and the boys at target practice presided over by the man in saffron and the beautiful serving-girls who tended them throughout the night.

Next morning Arthur's party set off to trace the footsteps of Owen and came upon the same experiences – the black man, Keeper of the Woods, the high hill, the green tree and inevitably the bowl, stone and fountain. Kai told Arthur that in a flash he had just understood what all this signified and implored his king to be allowed to have first tilt at everything. Kai threw the water on the stone and immediately the heavens were rent and in the devastation that followed several of Arthur's most loving attendants were thrown from their horses and killed. In the now leafless tree, the birds sang to a clear sky. Up rode a black knight, who promptly threw Kai.

Next morning Kai, with Arthur's reluctant permission, faced the black knight again, and this time the knight seriously damaged Kai, splitting his skull and fracturing it. Each of Arthur's men then felt obliged to take on this knight, and each one lost. Only one stood between the knight and Arthur, the knight called Gwalkmy, who thundered into battle. For three days he and the black knight jousted; three days they rode back and forth, and neither could unhorse the other. On the afternoon of the third day they hit each other simultaneously so hard that they broke each other's girths and fell to the ground. Heavy in their armour they rose to their feet and lurched at each other, swinging huge swords. They swung and they cut and they cut and they swung and at last the knight hit Gwalkmy such a blow that he split his helmet revealing, for the first time, Gwalkmy's face. At the same time Gwalkmy had hit the knight such a blow that he cut away the front of his helmet disclosing the knight's face – Owen, whom they had come to find and, in fact, Gwalkmy's cousin. Neither wished to claim victory over the other, which enabled Arthur to greet them as equals and welcome Owen back to the fold.

Next morning, Owen, still tired from the welcoming celebrations, persuaded Arthur to linger and enjoy some hospitality. The feast which followed took three years to prepare, three months to eat and three weeks to recover from. At the end of it all, Arthur invited Owen to return briefly so that all of Britain could hail him. The Countess of the Fountain gave Owen her blessing but with the proviso that he return within three months; Owen, however, carried away with it all, stayed three years.

During this absence Owen had an unfortunate encounter with a woman. The stranger, riding from the west on a bright horse with a long curling mane, wore gold brocade and all her harness-pieces had been made from the best of beaten gold. She turned her horse up the slope near the castle and reached Owen. As Owen took the hand she held out in greeting, she whipped the ring from his finger, saying, 'Cheat! Liar! Deceiver!' and rode away.

This affected Owen profoundly. He languished and soon took off on a long solitary journey. All the grand appearance of knighthood fell away from him and he merged with the wild. His appearance became like that of the small animals; he shrivelled and foraged with them in the undergrowth.

Eventually his travels brought him to the estate of a noblewoman who saw this creature running half-naked and whimpering along the grass. He had become so emaciated that the blood in his veins could be seen, and his matted hair covered most of his body. The noblewoman found in her medicine chest a precious ointment and sent a handmaiden to leave the ointment and some decent clothes near this creature who, she felt, must once have been a man. Owen rubbed the ointment all over his body and immediately a physical and emotional improvement began to take place. He recovered sufficiently to wear the clothes, and then approached the girl with enough morale to begin to make sense of his life. The girl brought him to the castle to convalesce.

One day tremendous commotion broke out in the castle and the servants rushed around handing out swords and daggers and shields. When Owen inquired what was going on he was told that the castle periodically fell under siege to a neighbouring nobleman who thought he could overthrow this undefended gentlewoman. They had beaten him off each time, but now it had become a matter of how long they could hold out. This enemy had already seized two of the woman's largest estates nearby.

Owen told them of his knighthood, and they gave him a horse, armour and some weapons. He rode out of the castle gate and from the highest point on the sward could see that he faced a huge army. Scouts marked for him the position within this assembly of the attacking leader. Owen rushed forward, grabbed the man and dragged him back to the castle, slamming the gate behind them. Now he had a means of bargaining, and even though all the vast regiments of the enemy surrounded the castle, Owen forced them to negotiate in return for their leader's life. In this way the noble-woman who had befriended Owen won back the possessions which her enemy had plundered, and Owen paid back his debt of gratitude and hospitality.

Next morning he saddled up and despite the tearful protests of the noblewoman rode away. Not even the promise of her vast lands could keep him – he still had journeys to make.

He travelled for days and as he ended the crossing of a wide desert and rode up into the foothills of a mountain range, he heard a wild cry, then another, then another. Where huge cliffs rose out of a forest clearing, he saw a strange sight – by a cave-mouth a large white lion was trying to kill a great-fanged snake. When the lion finally acknowledged that it could not kill this creature, and tried to get away, the snake prevented it. Owen dismounted, and tiptoeing forward cut the snake in two with one slash of his sword. Then he mounted and rode off, and when he looked back he saw the lion loping along behind him like a household dog.

As night fell Owen made camp – not that he had much to do; the lion gathered huge amounts of firewood, then ran off and killed a stag which he dropped at Owen's feet. An expert with the skinning-knife, Owen prepared the stag for eating and as he sat down to enjoy the venison chops with the lion, something groaned in the air. By careful enquiry and not a little magic Owen released the owner of the voice – the same girl, that young noblewoman, Luned, who first befriended him at the court of the Countess of the Fountain. She had been imprisoned in a stone tomb under the ground for defending Owen's name against his detractors in her mistress's castle – they had called Owen a deceiver for staying so long when he went back to Britain with Arthur. Furthermore they had threatened that unless Owen came back to release her by a certain day – tomorrow – they would kill her. Owen freed her and they spent a happy night exchanging their experiences since they had last met.

Luned advised Owen that he should travel to a nearby castle owned by a most hospitable knight. She expressed a desire to stay behind by the fire in the meadow, but begged Owen to return the following day, as she still feared for her life. Owen gave her his promise and then he and the lion rode up to the drawbridge. They received a great welcome from the chieftain who, though exquisitely hospitable and accompanied by a girl of really extraordinary beauty, presided over the most mournful feast Owen had ever seen.

With the lion at his feet Owen asked the reason for this melancholy. They told him that the castle lay under continuous threat from a savage giant cannibal. Only the previous day he had seized the chieftain's two sons while out hunting, and had threatened to eat them unless the chieftain handed over this beautiful young woman, his daughter, who sat sadly at the table.

Owen said, 'You have been hospitable to me, and my code of honour includes repaying hospitality. Let me deal with the cannibal.'

'I wish you would,' said the chieftain.

Early next morning a huge roar announced the arrival of the cannibal – a giant, dressed in black and brown, and looking filthy. In each hand he held a son up by the hair.

Owen went towards him and the cannibal dropped the young princes in order to begin fighting. The lion joined in, most effectively.

'Call that fair?' roared the giant. 'I'd fight you if you had no lion.'

Owen ordered the lion back to the castle, but inside the drawbridge it whined and roared when it smelled Owen in danger. Eventually the lion could take no more; it jumped on the battlements, ran along the ramparts, launched itself on the cannibal, and with a single paw, tore him apart from shoulder to groin. Owen restored the two boys to their father and rode back to collect Luned.

He arrived just in time – two youths had picked her up and were swinging her towards the campfire. He asked why they intended to kill Luned in the fire and was told that Owen had failed her, therefore she had to die. Owen, concealing his true identity, offered to stand in for the man they named, this Owen, who had failed the girl.

A fight began. Like the cannibal, the young men complained that they could not fight Owen with the lion in attendance. So Owen locked the lion and the girl up in a prison of the thickest stone and went back to the fight. The two young men, however, proved more than a match for him and he began to give ground. The lion, behind the wall, smelled this and, tearing a hole in the stones, came roaring out and killed the two men.

Owen then took the girl up on his saddle and they rode away, back to the court of the Countess of the Fountain. Owen stayed there long enough to pay his respects, before taking Luned back to Britain, to Arthur's court, where he married her and remained faithful to her evermore.

He had many more adventures while at Arthur's court, deeds and exploits in which he defeated appalling enemies and rescued women who had been hurled into brutal captivity after their noble husbands had been cruelly slain. His fame spread with his prowess and Arthur made him his chief-of-staff. Eventually Owen inherited his grandfather's estates, and amid much nostalgia and fond farewells he left Arthur's court with a retinue of knights and a flight of ravens, to take over his hereditary lands.

As for the lion, he stayed with Owen until the last great enemy had been overcome, and then with a smile loped away, presumably to get on with his own life.

PART FOUR

The legends of Arthur, of Cornwall and Brittany, with their chivalry and bright colours, sound the last shouts of the great Celtic stories. Having much in common with the Red Branch cycles of Ireland – the knights, debts and obligations of honour, kings of noble disposition, extraordinary birth and human frailty, beautiful and deceiving women – they illuminate the last centuries of Celtic monarchy in Britain.

Abroad, the continental Celts had faded but their great history, though never written down, remained in the oral tradition, ready to be transcribed, fragmentarily, in the slowly spreading literacy. In Britain Sir Thomas Malory, in jail, told from earlier sources stories of knights and great deeds, and of the extraordinary boy-king Artorius, who had come like a Messiah to lead his people in their darkest hours. Malory himself was a knight, with much battle experience, though by no means as chivalrous as those he wrote about – he rustled cattle, poached deer and conspired in attempted assassination and assorted thuggery.

The Arthurian cycles and the related romances, connected with Cornwall, Wales and Brittany, served a number of cultural purposes. They rewrote a black period of history in the frightening and uncertain power vacuum caused by the Roman departure from Britain; they gave a 'bible' of sorts, a moral code, by which a new aristocracy could learn. Above all the tales kept alive the glorious past that the hard-riding Celts, 'the fathers of Europe', had inspired.

How might the Celts have developed had they united to defeat or survive the Western Empire of Rome? In the tales which only touch on the Arthurian tradition great inspiration abounds; passion and style were made available – as Wagner demonstrated – on a truly operatic scale. The story of the famous lovers Tristan and Iseult, just one of a varied cycle, and perhaps the least coloured by Christianity, retains as powerful a place today in the body of Celtic legend, and thereby in the culture of Britain and western Europe, as it did when it first appeared in a twelfth/thirteenth-century French poem by Beroul.

TRISTAN AND ISEULT

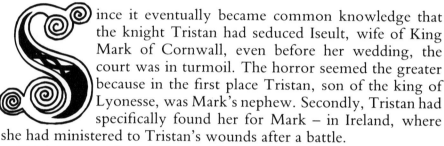

Since it eventually became common knowledge that the knight Tristan had seduced Iseult, wife of King Mark of Cornwall, even before her wedding, the court was in turmoil. The horror seemed the greater because in the first place Tristan, son of the king of Lyonesse, was Mark's nephew. Secondly, Tristan had specifically found her for Mark – in Ireland, where she had ministered to Tristan's wounds after a battle.

On the voyage from Ireland to Cornwall, while their ship stood on the sea becalmed, the couple, mistaking it for good wine, drank the love potion that Iseult's mother had prepared for her daughter's forthcoming nuptials. The potion bound Tristan and Iseult to each other.

Among the courtiers and knights Tristan had always stimulated envy – so accomplished, so stylish. Those who most disliked him had always kept an eye on his private life and soon discovered his passionate affair with Queen Iseult. Pretending righteousness, they told Mark who, though disinclined to believe them, felt obliged to exclude Tristan from the inner circle of the court. Tristan, however, continued to meet Iseult at night in the castle orchards.

Mark learned of this arrangement too. A malicious hunch-backed dwarf from Tintagel led the king to the trysting-place where he hid in an apple tree to eavesdrop. Iseult saw the king's reflection in the water and managed to give the impression of distressed innocence, by the way she spoke to Tristan. She swore she loved him honourably, and only as the king's favourite nephew who had found such a beloved husband for her; and yet these evil rumour-mongers had tried to sully such a friendship and pollute the king's good opinion of them both. Tristan, catching on to her ploy and having also seen the king's shadow, answered her in similar vein. So touching did they make their pleas of honour sound, oh! how vilely had they been misrepresented, that King Mark swore vengeance on the dwarf, who promptly fled the court.

The king then went to see Iseult, by now back in her chambers, who repeated her expressions of woe at the falsehoods of their slanderers. Mark, now completely deceived by his wife, embraced and forgave her, dried her tears and, foolish man, sent for Tristan to rehabilitate him in the royal affections. Tristan returned to the court with the grave, dignified air permitted to those who have been seen to suffer grievous misjudgment; with a show of reluctance he accepted the king's forgiveness. Thereafter, with the king's blessing, Tristan had all the access he could have wanted to Iseult's bedroom. They deceived the poor husband night and day, day and night.

The affair, however, became too blatant for several of the courtiers – the open copulating in the garden under the trees, the sprawling, naked and laughing, in the king's own bed. A delegation of knights approached Mark.

'My lord,' they began, 'it is a fact that your nephew Tristan and your wife Iseult are having a passionate affair.'

Mark lowered his head, unable to look them in the eye.

'My lord,' they went on, 'it is so open that anyone you ask will tell you about it. It is the talk of the place.'

Mark looked away, unable to look them in the eye.

'My lord,' they became emboldened by frustration, 'as long as you turn a blind eye to it, you are colluding with an undermining of the court's moral code. If you do not put a stop to it – and the way to do that is to banish Tristan – we can no longer serve at your court.'

Mark grasped the implicit politics of this – these men, powerful barons, supplied him with arms and men in times of strife. He turned to his courtiers.

'My lords, you know me, I am your king and I have no wish to act in a way that would cost me your support and friendship. But what am I to do? He is my nephew, she is my queen.'

'You need a plan, my lord,' they replied. 'But you need a plan with out-of-the-ordinary provisions and details. The best person to draft that is the dwarf who fled you in fear of his life, though he was, as you now know, telling the truth.'

'Get him back here,' said the king, beginning to acknowledge that he had no choice in the matter any longer.

The dwarf arrived, an evil-minded little wretch, but cunning as a serpent and with the gift of second sight. He persuaded the king to a plan: Tristan was to be sent on a long journey to bring a letter to King Arthur, but with instructions – not given until bedtime – to set out the following dawn. This would impel him to want time that night with Iseult. In order to establish whether Tristan would go to the queen's bed, the king should rise at midnight and leave the royal chambers. If Tristan, who, loyal knight, slept at the foot of the king's bed, did not immediately join Iseult, then the king could execute the dwarf along with the courtiers who had advised this course of action. Mark agreed to the plan.

The dwarf went out and bought a bag of white flour. That night he scattered the flour between the beds of the king and queen. At midnight the king rose and left. Tristan, desperate to get to Iseult, was shrewd enough not to step on the flour; instead he jumped from one bed to the other, but in the effort he reopened a hunting wound on his leg. Unheeded by him in his passion, it spouted his red blood all over the queen's bed.

The dwarf, hovering around outside, peeped in through the window and saw the lovers, flagrant. Behind him, squinting over his shoulder, stood the courtiers who had laid down the law to King Mark. They fetched the king: Tristan, hearing them walk up the stone passageway, went back to his own bed and generated a heavy snore. The subterfuge proved pointless: even Mark could not resist the evidence of the blood on Iseult's sheets and on Tristan's leg, and a hint of bloodied footprint on the flourstrewn floor where Tristan's foot had slipped in his hurry back to his own bed. With great sorrow Mark gave orders for Tristan and Iseult to be taken captive.

Next day the word spread throughout the kingdom of Cornwall – Tristan and Iseult had been found entwined in the king's bed and the king had thrown them into prison, awaiting execution. Mark, for no-one turns like a man who is forced to, had developed a sudden fierce hatred for the lovers and ordered a huge funeral pyre to be built on the clifftop. He denied the lovers the privilege of dying together – Tristan would burn first.

They led him out, by a halter round his neck as an animal to the slaughterhouse. Dragging him to the pyre, in full view of the king and court and by now a huge assembled crowd, they had to pass a small chapel set atop a sheer drop down to the ocean. Tristan pointed out to his executioners that the most vile of murderers is allowed time to make peace with his God and asked to be permitted a moment's prayer. Since the chapel had only one door they untied him and began to shepherd him inside. He asked to pray alone, and when they had closed the door the young knight bounded on to the altar, opened the stained-glass window behind it and jumped out, over the edge of the cliff.

Half-way down this sheer drop he landed on a wide projecting stone and the powerful updraught of the sea-wind balanced him and helped break his fall. His next jump took him down to the sand, soft enough to break the second stage of the leap. He landed safely, looked back up to see the shaking fists and the smoke from the pyre high above, and ran along the shore, out of reach of any immediate pursuers. At the same time his squire, Governal, and his followers, afraid that one of them would be chosen in Tristan's place, wheeled their horses hard and rode out of the court precincts. Bringing sword, armour and a spare horse, they caught up with their master miles down the coast. Determined to rescue Iseult, Tristan led them back towards the site of the intended execution.

King Mark, enraged at Tristan's escape, tightened security around Iseult and grew even more vengeful towards her. Despite the outcry at her appearance when they dragged her out by her tightly bound wrists, Mark showed every intention of burning the much loved queen. Prominent courtiers threw themselves at Mark's feet interceding as the executioners hustled her to the pyre; he all but spat on them. Even when they swore they would never serve him again, or contribute to his alliances, he ignored them, told them they could leave if they wished – and many did.

The clifftop pyre had grown huge with flames, the sparks from the thorn logs phutting and shooting into the air. Iseult, though she had been dragged along the muddy path, maintained a regal dignity. Dressed in a simple grey tunic with a cloth-of-gold border, her long hair caught up loosely with gold thread, she stood as erect as the ropes would allow, distinguished despite the mud and dishevelment. Tears slipped down her face as she listened to the weeping and pleas of her adoring citizens. Mark remained viciously impassive.

Near the court a sizeable leper colony had grown up over the years, attracted by the ocean air and by the reputation of Mark's courtiers for alms-giving. The leader of this colony, a man called Ivan, of a character as unsavoury as his physique, saw a lewd opportunity in the afternoon's events. The fracas caused by Tristan's escape had given Ivan and a hundred of the colony's men a chance to get close to the pyre. Just as the executioners led Iseult forward, Ivan had the effrontery to beat his leper's wooden clapper as loudly as he could and shout, 'Stop! Stop!' Only then did people notice how close the lepers had come and what a vile crew they looked – rampant sores, fingers rotting at the knuckle-stumps, one or two with an eye half-hanging out or a nose melting away in slime. The hidden parts of their bodies did not bear thinking about.

Mark turned towards Ivan who, not giving the king a chance to express his anger, quickly shouted again:

'My lord! My great and noble lord! I can suggest a much harsher punishment. If you throw the lady on the pyre she will only burn. Her punishment will soon end. However, if you give her to me and my men – whose condition has long denied all of us any lusty enjoyment – then you can take pleasure from our pleasure. We will keep her alive, I assure you. But daily she will pay for the dishonour she has done you. Think of it as a new kind of alms-giving.' At which his awful crew cheered.

'I have had to contain my lust for years. It has now grown so great that no female creature on earth could bear it. Multiply that by a hundred, one for each of us.' He waved a hand to indicate his colleagues. 'Think of the fine meats and wines of the court to which the queen has been accustomed. The crumbs from our begging-bowls is all she will now get. See what an appropriate punishment I propose!' More cheers from the lepers.

Mark sat on his horse, deep in thought.

Iseult screamed, 'Lord, burn me! Burn me!'

The people continued to cry, 'Mercy! Mercy!'

Finally Mark waved a hand to the executioners, indicating that Iseult should be handed over. Slobbering dreadfully the lepers pressed around her, shouting and pawing; Ivan had difficulty in clearing a path to lead her away. As the evil group disappeared from sight down the long leafy lane, the crowd outside the castle subsided and slowly dispersed.

The lepers' good fortune did not endure. Within about a quarter of a mile from the castle they had to pass through a thick grove, which by then had been occupied by the returning Tristan and his friends. The knight galloped out of the bushes, his coat of mail gleaming in the afternoon sun. The lepers thought to fight for their prize and, brandishing their staves, took up aggressive postures – some even swung at the horses of the other knights. Ivan could not be persuaded to let go the grip he still had on Iseult; a blow from an oak staff carried by one of Tristan's companions changed his mind. Tristan grasped Iseult round the waist and with one hand raised her to his saddle. They rode like the wind and that night made a secure and warm camp in the woods near Truro.

★   ★   ★

Back at court, the dwarf got drunk. The remaining knights, always jockeying for position in the retinue, observed that the dwarf often had long conversations with the king. Since knowledge is power, some of them resolved to try and discover what the odd pair talked about. They grabbed the dwarf in his drunken state and flattered him.

'Yes, I have a secret of the king's with which only I am entrusted. The king, you see, trusts me.'

'But you can trust us,' they said.

'Very well. Though I will not tell you the secret. I do not want to be accused of breaking my confidentiality. However, if you take me to the Ford of the Perils, I can tell my secret to the hawthorns there.'

They all rode off together to the ford near the rapids on the Par river. The dwarf turned his back and put his head through a hole in a hawthorn hedge; this way he could pretend he was speaking to the bushes. The knights nonetheless heard him utter the secret: 'King Mark has the ears of a horse.'

When they returned to court they told the king what the dwarf had said.

'True. I have horse's ears,' said the king, 'and he, the dwarf, gave them to me in a wicked spell. So he has told you, has he? Well, that's the end of him.' And the king, with one sweep of his silver broadsword, cut off the dwarf's head. This act went some little way towards restoring the kingdom's high regard for Mark – many people had heard of, and loathed, the dwarf's role in the downfall of Tristan and Iseult.

To begin with, the lovers in the woods, protected by their close followers, lived idyllically. They dined off the food of the natural world; Tristan's skill with the bow brought them tender young venison garnished by the berries in season. When the sun shone, no more pleasant place than the forest could be imagined, with the light dappling the leaves and shoots on the woodland floor. When the wind blew and the rain fell, Tristan took Iseult to a private cave that had a snow-white interior in which veins of gold and diamonds winked – not even the band of followers knew the location of this lovers' grotto.

One fine day, as they rode back from a hunt, they found themselves outside the hut of Ogrin, a hermit. He gave them bad news – that Mark had placed a price on Tristan's head: a hundred pieces of silver for Tristan dead or alive. The lovers shivered, and the priest tried to persuade Tristan to repent. The knight refused and told the friar the story of the love potion, which Iseult then confirmed. The priest pressed and pressed, but Tristan said he would rather live the life of a hunted vagabond, dependent upon the produce of the wild wood, than give up Iseult. She, in tears, agreed.

They rode away: this meeting took place on the very day that Mark had publicly proclaimed the reward on every building in Cornwall. Soon, however, the lovers received a pleasing bonus. Tristan's favourite hound had pined for its master since the day the knight had escaped. Tied to a bolt of wood in the castle courtyard he whined ceaselessly and excited the pity of the squires in the retinue. They pleaded with Mark who finally set the dog free. The animal fled the court like an arrow from a bow and, nose to the ground, traced every one of Tristan's steps – even the leap from the chapel window to the sand far below – until many, many hours later he bayed his way into the lovers' hearing deep in the woods.

His arrival, however welcome – and he overwhelmed his master with his wet nose – gave Tristan cause for concern lest the dog's barking attract a search-party. Iseult came to the hound's rescue with a story she had heard – how a forester over in Wales had trained a dog to follow a wounded stag so silently that the stag never knew; then, when the stag rested, the dog would pounce. They resolved to train Tristan's beloved animal the same way – it took only a month and many a time the hound gained them food with his noiseless preying.

The life in the forest eventually took a heavy toll. In truth they rarely had enough to eat, because no matter what they killed, the food was tough and stringy; they missed the delicacies which both had enjoyed at court. But at least they felt a little secure, and then one day something occurred which made them feel even safer.

Governal, out hunting, rested and watered his horse at a stream. Suddenly he heard hounds and from a hiding-place behind a tree he saw a hunt race by. The huntsman, ahead of his friends, proved to be one of the knights who had plotted Tristan's downfall, a deadly enemy of whom they had often talked. Watching the route the hunt was taking, Governal raced through the wood to get in front of the man and as the knight drew level, Governal sprang out and cut off his head. He hacked the body apart and when the rest of the party found it they quit, terrified. Thereafter everybody, including the bounty-hunters after Mark's reward, avoided that part of the wood.

Governal brought the head back to the lovers' camp and Tristan felt much reassured at the removal of one of the men he had most feared.

One sunny day Tristan returned exhausted from a stag-hunt. Iseult prepared a bed of leaves and gentle fresh branches for him and the pair lay down. Despite the heat she kept on a light gown and he kept on his trousers. He laid a sword between them and they fell asleep with arms and faces touching, but not bodies.

A forester, puzzled by some tracks on the ground, found the bower and recognised the famous royal lovers. In repose the privations of the forest life showed up clearly; Tristan had lost that untroubled look, Iseult looked undernourished, with thin limbs; her rings, for instance, were loose on her previously voluptuous hands. In the hot afternoon, when the birds had fallen still and only an occasional rustle of a small animal stirred the undergrowth, they slept deeply.

The forester stepped back silently, ran as hard as he could to his horse, then rode to the palace, his head full of the reward he would get. Court was in session, but the king, seeing the unkempt man enter the hall with an air of urgency, found a reason to slip away from the deliberations and, swearing the forester to silence, rode out on an errand 'both private and urgent'.

They arrived at the bower where the lovers still slept – Governal and the others had stayed out on the hunt. Mark, his sword un-sheathed, drew back the leaves covering his wife and nephew and looked down. Unexpectedly, their vulnerability touched him, and though he raised his sword he stayed his hand. He found himself confused by the fact that neither lover was naked – it seemed to confirm the precious innocence they had always protested. On this account he assumed – wishful thinking in any case – their love to be sacred rather than profane.

Mark had on his finger a ring Iseult had given him on their wedding-day; she wore the one he had likewise given her: the king swapped these rings. He saw how the sun burnt her fair skin, so he arranged his gem-studded gauntlets to throw a shadow protecting her face. Finally he replaced Tristan's sword as it lay between them with his own gold-hilted one. Then, threatening the forester with instant death should he ever divulge the nature of these transactions, Mark rode back to court.

Soon after this the lovers, owing to a dream which frightened Iseult, woke abruptly. Tristan, in a reflex action, grabbed the sword. He saw the gold hilt and recognised it at the very moment Iseult noticed the different ring. They jumped up in alarm: Mark had seen them, and they assumed he had gone back for reinforcements. So the lovers fled, heading north-west towards Wales, a territory where Mark's rule did not run, where vagabonds and renegades frequently took shelter. But they had to make long, exhausting rides and by the time they felt they could rest comfortably, their condition had appreciably deteriorated.

A major development now took place, which had a bearing on the plight of the lovers and on their future lives. The love potion began to wear off. It had been intended to last three years, long enough for newly-weds to put down firm roots of love.

Tristan, out hunting, stopped in mid-stride as the potion ebbed from his veins and asked himself why he had subjected both of them to such hardships. He especially regretted the way in which the queen had been reduced to frugality and hiding. That night he and Iseult resolved to seek Mark's forgiveness so that she could resume the life of a queen and he the life of a knight – to be spent in the service of King Mark; but if the king would not have him, he would emigrate to Lyonesse or Brittany.

They rode back to the hermitage of the friar Ogrin and he, overjoyed at their repentance, wrote a letter on their behalf to Mark. That night, while Iseult and the priest held their breaths, Tristan rode to the palace. As he laid the letter on the king's window-sill, Mark saw the hand and called out, 'Who's there?'

'It's Tristan. I am leaving a letter for you, but I dare not stay to talk to you.'

'Wait! Wait!' Mark cried. But Tristan had gone, returning safely to the hermitage.

The king called his chaplain and handed him the letter. When the chaplain had read it aloud the king almost wept with joy that his beloved queen wished to come home. The letter had been quite specific – if Mark did not have Iseult back then Tristan would take her to Ireland where she would be made queen of her own country. Furthermore, if anyone doubted Tristan's account of events, let them fight him. And if Mark did not forgive Tristan the knight would seek service under another king.

When Mark's courtiers heard the contents of the letter and Tristan's challenge to them, every baron there advised Mark to take Iseult back, but not Tristan. The chaplain wrote a letter to this effect and it was taken, as Tristan had requested, to the Red Stone Cross. Tristan collected the letter that very night and took it back to Ogrin and Iseult. The priest read it and gave the couple their instructions.

Three days later, as the king's letter had requested, Tristan and Iseult, not without sadness, rode to the Ford of the Perils. They exchanged gifts – she gave him a ring of green jasper which thenceforth would signify, if he sent it to her, a request from Tristan which nobody on earth would prevent her from fulfilling; he, at her request, gave her his hound. They rode forward, Iseult despite her long hardship in the woods, looking every inch a queen—the hermit priest had gone to Saint Michael's Mount and purchased for her the most beautiful clothes he could find: purple silks, white linens, gold brocade, ermine.

All Cornwall had come alight with news of the royal reconciliation and Mark had had the nobility to treat the occasion festively. On the banks of the river, by the ford, royal attendants had erected a huge camp of brightly coloured pavilions. At first sight of the camp, Iseult turned to Tristan urgently.

'My lord and my love. I do not know how the king will treat me from now on. He may wish to punish me. He may be goaded by our enemies. Please do not leave Cornwall – whatever the king says – until you are sure that I am safe. There is a forester, Orri, who will hide you, and I will send you messages.' Tristan agreed.

The king and his closest courtier rode forward. Tristan led Iseult's horse towards them, and addressed Mark.

'My lord. Here is your queen. I have never loved her dishonourably. I have never behaved towards her less than chivalrously. In your retinue I see you have some men who say otherwise. But they have never said it to my face, nor ever allowed me to challenge them in combat. I beg you – give me a chance to clear my name in front of your court. If your court finds me guilty you may burn me alive.'

Mark indicated that he needed time to think about this and drew to one side, both to greet Iseult and to confer with his courtiers. Eventually he was persuaded to a course of action that would banish Tristan for a year, long enough to prove Iseult's fidelity as a wife; then Tristan could return. Refusing all gifts Mark offered, Tristan took his leave, and Iseult returned to the castle.

The streets had been hung with silks and tapestries; brilliantly coloured silk banners billowed down from the walls. Silk paved the streets – wherever it seemed likely that Iseult would put a foot, someone had spread a silk rug. The queen's return was marked by a great feast, with the king bestowing patronage and largesse. Tristan, meanwhile, though pretending to leave the kingdom, had ridden back to the woods to hide in the cottage of Orri the forester.

★   ★   ★

As the months went by, three of the original conspirators who had poisoned Mark against Tristan and Iseult – their names were Baron Godwin, Baron Gwenlon and Baron Donelan – began their whispering again. One day, as the king watched some of his tenants burn brush off a moorland, the three sidled up.

'Listen, my lord. Have you thought about this: the queen has never really explained her actions, has she? Never really defended herself against your accusations of her affair with Tristan? Don't you think she should be obliged to? That's what people are saying.'

Mark, to their surprise, turned on them.

'What is this you're trying to do? Have me banish my own queen, my own beloved wife? I have already banished my dearest knight Tristan, my own nephew, on account of your malicious remarks. Curses on your foul mouths. Just for that I'm going to invite Tristan back. Clear off and don't ever let me hear you say any of these things again, do you hear?'

They fled, and reconvened a little way off to consider their next approach. This time they tried a more honeyed line, but Mark still routed them and they rode off. But the king, returning to the castle, felt uneasy: these three barons had considerable value to him as allies, and as enemies they had enough power to make his kingdom uncomfortable. When Iseult saw Mark, so distressed did the king seem that she mistakenly thought Tristan had been found. Never revealing her fear she questioned Mark. He wrung his hands.

'They're saying you have not entirely vindicated yourself, not entirely explained what exactly went on between you and Tristan.'

'But I will if you want me to,' she said.

'I think I do want you to.'

Iseult, for the first time in her husband's company, lost her temper.

'I told you that within months someone here would stir things up against me. All right. Let them. But I'm telling you now that I will face any court or tribunal or judge, I will undergo any trial by ordeal, no matter how painful. All they have to do is name a time and a place and I will be there. One condition, though – this has to take place in front of King Arthur himself and his Knights of the Round Table: if that doesn't silence this malice, nothing will.'

Mark, somewhat chastened at this outburst, agreed. He issued a proclamation calling every man, woman and child to Iseult's vindication fifteen days ahead. Iseult sent a messenger, Perinis, to King Arthur, but en route he was secretly to call on Tristan in hiding at the forester's hut. The letter he brought asked Tristan to come to the convocation, but disguised as a leper with a wooden beaker in his hand. He was to stand at the end of a plank bridge leading over a marsh and ask for alms.

The messenger set off to find King Arthur and his knights, who greeted him with great expressions of concern for Iseult. Perinis, a trustworthy man, and a supporter of both Tristan and the queen, explained Iseult's unusual vulnerability to her enemies.

'My lord, she is an Irishwoman and she has therefore no relatives and few supporters at court, where most of the retinue are Bretons or Saxons or Normans. The king, though a thoroughly decent man, takes his opinion from the last person he heard speaking, or to put it another way, he is easily swayed. My lady the queen feels that if you attend the hearing of her explanations, your august presence will lend power and weight and at least guarantee her a fair hearing.'

Arthur, a great admirer of Iseult, wept and assured Perinis that without fail he and his knights would be at the Ford of the Perils. Not only that, one by one his knights, Gawain, Gerflett and Evan, spoke up to claim rights of combat against each of the three poisonous barons, Godwin, Gwenlon and Donelan.

Arthur bade his men prepare most diligently for this event, instructed his attendants to give Perinis the greatest care and hospitality the castle could provide, and then bestowed upon him the great honour of riding a little of the way to bid him farewell. Non-stop, Perinis then galloped to bring to Iseult the good news of Arthur's – and Tristan's – agreement to her plans.

Tristan looked the part. No shirt, a rough brown smock, broken shoes, a dirty black cloak, he seemed a churl as well as a leper. He had artfully painted his face with hideous mud and woad to look like pockmarks and lumps, and he carried the wooden clapper and beaker Iseult had specified. He had instructed his squire Governal to ride ahead and hide nearby with spare horse, weapons and armour at the ready.

As a leper seeking alms, Tristan received an arresting view of human nature. Some travellers hit him severe clips across the head with their staves; others hurled abuse at him; a few gave generously – meat and drink from noblemen; peasants tossed him coins. At times he could hardly contain himself in his disguise, especially when he chose to rout with his crutch the particularly offensive ones, some of whom he thumped hard, drawing blood.

As they pressed forward over the marsh to the place where Iseult would stand tomorrow for her questioning, the throng never for a moment recognised Cornwall's most famous knight. Suddenly the crowd parted and riding up the slope like some brilliant troop came Arthur and the Knights of the Round Table. Oh, they looked wonderful! Each horse had been groomed as if for a ceremonial procession, each knight had a new shield with his coat-of-arms more gleaming than ever before, each man dressed in abundant silk. Tristan, beginning to enjoy this game of his, begged Arthur for his gaiters, saying his leper's legs were freezing. Two knights pulled them off, Arthur gave them to the 'beggar' and the glorious retinue rode on.

King Mark appeared and again Tristan begged a gift; the king dropped his fur hood into the 'leper's' hands and engaged him in conversation.

'Where are you from?'

'I'm the son of a Welshman and I come from Caerleon.'

'And what happened to you? Have you been long . . . afflicted?'

'My lord,' croaked Tristan, 'I've been like this for three years. I used to have as my lover a noblewoman, and I owe my pockmarks to her.'

'How is that?'

'From a disease she gave me in the bed.'

'I suppose your thoughts towards her are less than tender now?'

'Well, my lord, she was very beautiful. In fact there is only one woman more beautiful than her.'

'Who's that?'

'The lovely Queen Iseult, my lord.' At which Mark roared with laughter and rode off; he never recognised Tristan either.

Where Tristan stood – the place was called Mal Pas – every traveller got muddy. Up rode the three malicious barons and asked the 'beggar' for directions via harder ground. He pointed towards a seeming firm stretch of ground, in reality a quicksand, and the moment they rode into it down they went, flailing around in the mud. Their horses panicked, the men shouted and Tristan on the mound above them yelled 'advice' to them, calculated to make their positions worse.

Just then Iseult rode into view and had a fit of laughing when she saw the three mischief-makers in the swamp. Not only that, Tristan now held out his wooden stave to the worst of them, Baron Donelan, and just as the man appeared to be getting hauled out Tristan let go, pleading infirmity, and the baron fell back, deeper in than ever. The crowd watching, including the two kings, Mark and Arthur, laughed hugely at this comical beggar baiting these pompous, unpopular courtiers covered in slime.

By now everybody but Iseult and the 'leper' had crossed the marsh to the place where Iseult's case was to be heard. There they stood arrayed in vivid colours, an enormous crowd with, in the foreground, Arthur and Mark and their respective retinues of knights. Long coloured pennants fluttered in the breeze and trumpeters sounded. Mark's chief courtiers, including his nephew André, had offered to wait and help Iseult across, but she refused. From the other side of the marsh they called to her, wondering how she would avoid ruining her clothes in the churned-up mud. Iseult was wearing the most beautiful white silk trimmed with ermine-tails, and a gold ring on her head kept in place a white linen scarf edged with gold.

She approached the 'leper'.

'I wish you to carry me across the marsh.'

'But I am a diseased man.'

'I won't catch your disease. I will sit astride your shoulders and you can walk across that plank to the other side.'

Tristan bent down, leaning on his crutch. The people on the far bank interpreted Iseult's move as part of a penitential statement – she would arrive to be questioned in as humble a fashion as possible, and what could be more humble than a foul-smelling, hideous leper for a mount?

She had fun with Tristan. She berated him for being fat and ugly and made him turn his face away. He smiled, delighted at the chance to see and hear his beloved Iseult again. She climbed on his back and, with a leg either side of him, rode him across the marsh, then in front of Arthur and Mark slid down. As the 'leper' turned away Arthur wanted to reward him, but Iseult said that the man had already begged a houseful of things – as she sat on his back she had felt huge numbers of alms, food and clothing and money under his cloak. The 'beggar' slunk away across the plank to the other side of the marsh and disappeared into the woods.

There, Governal waited. He had provided two excellent horses and had brought along the richest of the knight's regalia that he and his master could wear. They changed under the trees. Governal dressed in white, covering his face and head with a white silk scarf so that only his eyes could be seen. Tristan wore black serge under black armour; his black horse wore black trappings and each man wore a sword and carried a shield and a lance: on the end of Tristan's fluttered a favour Iseult had given him a long time before. They rode out to join the ceremonial jousting that Arthur had ordered by way of entertainment before the serious business of the trial, which was to begin the next morning.

The other knights saw the strangers riding in and went towards them. They engaged Tristan first – Mark's nephew André tilted at him, but ended up on the roadway with a broken arm. Governal suddenly spotted the forester who had led Mark to where the lovers slept in the wood: the man died instantly, Governal's sword going straight through him. Iseult, who recognised the two strange and brilliant riders, gave a silent cheer. While the Round Table Knights were contemplating what to do, the two rode away, melting so quickly into the woods that Arthur wondered whether they were ghosts.

The kings rode to their pavilions, Arthur escorting Iseult of whom he was very fond. The great camp settled down for the night with conversation and flute music and excellent food. Anticipation, like a thrilling cloud, hung over the tents.

At dawn everyone rose quickly. Distant thunder rolled, the mist cleared, the sun soon grew hot. Every Cornish citizen of any note had turned out, and now they hurried to the most advantageous positions in front of Arthur's tent. Attendants, with visible reverence, spread a wide grey cloth of silk over the grass; on this they heaped every relic in Cornwall, healing-stones, amulets, statuettes, reliquaries. One by one the three principals appeared at the doors of their pavilions, Mark, then Arthur, then Iseult – at whose beauty the crowd gasped.

Arthur spoke.

'King Mark. You were misled about your wife. You are too quick to believe the words of mischief-makers. We should never have had to hold this meeting and you allowed yourself to be goaded into it by men with poisoned mouths. They should die for their trickery. I wouldn't mind hanging them myself. Let us make this much clear: when Iseult has been vindicated those men must never speak against her, or you, or Tristan again.'

Mark, though a little stung, replied.

'My lord king, I agree with you. Maybe I was foolish. Maybe I listened to men who had ulterior motives, or who merely disliked the queen. Their envy of Tristan was already plain. But don't you understand that once the story had been told at all I had to kill it stone dead, and this seemed the best way. I agree with you. Once Iseult has made her declaration, let no man speak against her, or Tristan, or me again.'

Arthur then instructed Iseult to come forward. With Gawain in close attendance to keep watch, he bade her hold her hand over the relics on the grey silk cloth and swear that she had never loved Tristan with anything other than purity and honour.

Iseult, who had been standing between the two kings, holding a hand of each, stepped forward, paused, then looking in turn at each of the principal men, Arthur, Mark, Gawain, she spoke. Her low voice carried quite clearly on the morning air, and everybody heard what she said.

'My lord Arthur, my lord husband, respected gentle knight – I swear by the relics on this cloth and by all the relics in these holy lands, that the only men ever to come between my thighs have been two – my beloved husband King Mark of Cornwall and the foul leper who carried me over the marsh to this place.' She spoke her oath so powerfully and peacefully that tears stood in the eyes of the assembled crowd.

Arthur, moved almost to silence, stood forward beside the queen. Raising his noble head he spoke as if proclaiming.

'Hear that. Any man who ever again reviles the name of this good woman will die. At my own hand.'

His head swivelled until he fixed the three knights, Godwin, Gwenlon and Donelan, with a bitter look. They took the hint and rode away as the first cheers began to ring out.

Arthur bestowed upon Iseult the great honour of his personal guardianship. Mark stated that if ever again he heeded calumnies uttered against Iseult he would take all the blame. The camps disbanded and as Arthur rode north Mark and Iseult returned to their palace united as king and queen.

Tristan, though never fully restored to Mark's court, stayed in Cornwall. And it must be admitted that, yes, when Mark went hunting, Tristan called on Iseult, and it has to be admitted that, yes, the two became lovers again. This fact became known to a grubby little man who, in the old days, had acted as a spy for Godwin and the other two. Now he rode to them and told them his new information.

'Are you sure?'

'Certain.'

'How do you know?'

'I saw them, with my own eyes.'

'Where?'

'Through Iseult's window.'

'No.'

'Yes. He had his sword buckled on and he carried his bow and a handful of arrows.'

'No.'

'Yes, I tell you.'

They arranged that if he instructed them as to how and where one of them could see Tristan and Iseult in bed together, he would be well rewarded. He gave them full details – how to slip through a gap in the garden fence, how to sharpen a long twig with which to twitch away the curtain gently, how to see without being seen.

Godwin went first, and chose a time when all Cornwall knew the king had gone on a journey. Iseult had sent a message with Perinis inviting Tristan to the castle. On his way there he actually saw Godwin, who then disappeared over a garden hedge. Then Donelan arrived and Tristan beheaded him so quickly Donelan hardly knew he had been attacked. Tristan also cut off two large locks of Donelan's hair and, hiding the body, proceeded to Iseult's room.

Just as he began to take off his cloak, Iseult, rising to embrace him, saw a shadow at the window.

'My dear knight, how the king would have liked to greet you himself,' she began, 'but he is away, and I must make you welcome.'

He began to catch her drift, especially when she asked him how good was his bow, how true were the arrows, and beseeched him to demonstrate.

'Fit an arrow to your bow and show me,' and in a lower voice she whispered, 'outside the window. Godwin. He is trying to spy on us. If he gets away we are ruined.'

Like lightning Tristan spun on his heel, releasing the arrow in the same movement. As if his head had been a soft fruit the arrow pierced Godwin through the eye and into the brain, and he fell dead.

It said that they explained these killings as Tristan's revenge, but that Mark, suspicious anyway, found the lovers together and, while Tristan sat playing a love-song on his harp to Iseult, Mark killed the knight by impaling him on the point of a poisoned spear.

Others tell a different end to the tale of Tristan and Iseult – that after this Tristan fled to Brittany, where he aided a king but then insulted him by refusing to marry his daughter, also called Iseult, of the White Hands. The brother of this Iseult threw down a gauntlet, but Tristan explained that his love for the first Iseult remained so great that no woman could supplant her.

Upon which he and the brother returned to Cornwall to try to see Queen Iseult. He had to leave without meeting her, but two years later he tried again, this time approaching the court openly, though pretending to be mad. He cut off his hair, scratched his face extensively, changed his clothing to motley and reversed the letters of his name, calling himself Tantris.

When finally, unrecognised, he confronted Mark at the court, Tristan played a clever game of word, subterfuge and jest – with enough truth to put Mark's nerves on edge. For instance, he dropped into the conversation a hint regarding the day Mark saw the lovers sleeping.

'I, good king, the son of walrus, will give you my sister in exchange for your queen. I will build for her a house of flowers high in the air. I have already dreamed of the love potion she and Tristan drank and I have already had Iseult in my arms.'

'That's enough joking for one day,' said Mark, a little nettled.

Tristan, becoming reckless, pressed on.

'I am a dreamer. I am a fool. Do you recall how you shaded the queen's face with your gem-studded gauntlets that day in the woods?'

Iseult, sitting nearby, lowered her eyes, and the king said uneasily, 'You're mad. I wish you had fallen overboard on your way here.'

Tristan, pretending more than ever to be mad, uttered passionate intentions towards the queen, but in his statements spoke to her in a code by which he hoped she might recognise him – or at least be sufficiently intrigued to want to see him again. The knights, growing uneasy, encouraged the king to terminate this meeting and they left the madman in the hall, while all went hunting and the queen retired to her chambers. She then sent her maid to find the fool and Tristan revealed to the maid his true identity. The maid led Tristan by the hand to see the queen.

Iseult refused to believe that this madman with the cropped hair and torn face was her beloved. He began a recital of the events of their lives – how he had saved her life when an evil knight abducted her; how he had been cured of a poisonous wound by her hand; how he had brought her from Ireland to marry King Mark; how on board ship they had mistakenly drunk the love potion; how he had leapt from the chapel; how he had rescued her from the lepers; and he mentioned the names of their friends, Governal and Perinis. To all of this she merely replied that somebody had tutored this madman extraordinarily well.

But two proofs remained possible. In a corner of the vast room sat the dog, Tristan's beloved hound, whom he had given Iseult on the day of her reconciliation.

'If you release that dog,' said Tristan, 'he will come straight to me.'

'Nonsense! that dog will come only to me until the day his master, my beloved knight, returns.'

'Release him. You have nothing to lose.' The maid untied the dog who rushed at Tristan like a rocket and nearly knocked him to the ground with wet kisses and barks and joyful licks. Iseult was astonished.

'But you have enchanted him. You are a sorcerer, that's it. You're a magician.'

'No, madam. Here is my final proof.' He held out his hand and opened it. In his palm lay the green jasper ring she had given him, and which she had said must always be the final proof of a messenger direct from Tristan. Iseult fainted.

When the maid revived her, the queen embraced the knight and would not let him move until she had kissed him five hundred times. Regardless of whether the king might return early they went to bed.

Inevitably, with sad parting, Tristan had to return to Brittany. There he became embroiled in a family feud defending his friend, the brother of the other Iseult, who was having an affair with the wife of a neighbouring knight. In a swordfight at the cuckolded knight's castle Tristan received a terrible wound – the swordsman had cheated by putting poison on his blade. As before, only one person could cure such a poisoned gash, his beloved Iseult, and he sent a messenger with the jasper ring to fetch her. He gave the messenger instructions that if Iseult agreed to come, the ship bearing her should sport white sails – if not, black ones.

Weeks passed, with Tristan's life slowly sinking. Then one afternoon – the ship, the ship! But were the sails white or black? The other Iseult, the one Tristan had refused to marry, looked out of the casement, and, driven by jealousy, told a lie.

'The sails are black, my lord.' And Tristan quietly died.

Iseult landed within minutes, rushed to the house, cradled him in her arms, anguishedly hoping to breathe life back into him, but too late. She, overcome, died too.

A great fleet of craft surrounded the ship taking the lovers' bodies back to Cornwall. Mark, though confused between jealousy and bereavement because he had truly loved both wife and nephew, rose to the occasion and gave the lovers a ceremonial funeral, burying them on either side of the nave in the castle chapel at Tintagel, high above the white Atlantic waves, above Merlin's cave. The kingdom mourned.

Within a year yew trees had begun to sprout out of each grave. Mark had them cut down, but they grew again. Three times they grew and three times he had them cut, but eventually he desisted and allowed them to grow. At their full height they reached their branches towards each other across the nave and intertwined so intensely they could never be parted.

Local people attributed the strength of their intertwining to the ancient love potion drunk all those years ago by Tristan and Iseult.

SELECT
BIBLIOGRAPHY

Bushnaq, Inea, (transl.): *Arab Folk Tales*; Penguin, London, 1987.

Byrne, John Francis: *Irish Kings & High Kings*; Batsford, London, 1987.

Campbell, Joseph: *The Masks of God*; Penguin, London, 1976.

Cross, T.P. & Slover, C.H.: *Ancient Irish Tales*; Harrap, London, 1937.

Crossley-Holland, Kevin: *British Folk Tales*; Orchard Books, London, 1987.

– *Folk Tales of the British Isles*; Folio Society, London, 1985.

– *The Norse Myths*; Penguin Books, London, 1982.

Dillon, Myles, (ed.): *Irish Sagas*; Mercier Press, Cork, 1968.

Dillon, Myles: *Early Irish Literature*; Univ. of Chicago Press, 1948.

Dunn, Joseph: *The Ancient Irish Epic Tale, Tain Bo Cuailgne*; David Nutt, London, 1914.

Ewert, A., (ed.): *The Romance of Tristan* (from Beroul); Basil Blackwell, Oxford, 1939.

Faraday, L.Winifred (transl.): *The Cattle-Raid of Cuailgne*; David Nutt, London, 1904.

Fredrick, Alan S., (transl.): *The Romance of Tristan* (from Beroul); Penguin, London, 1970.

Gantz, Jeffrey (transl.):

– *The Mabinogion*; Penguin, London, 1976

– *Early Irish Myths & Sagas*; Penguin, London, 1981.

Glassie, Henry, (ed.): *Irish Folk Tales*; Penguin Books, London, 1987.

Goetinck, Glenys: *Peredur – A Study of Welsh Tradition in The Grail Legends*; Univ. of Wales Press, Cardiff, 1975.

Gregory, Augusta: *Cuchulain of Muirthemne: The Story of the Men of the Red Branch of Ulster arranged and put into English*; Colin Smythe, Gerrard's Cross, 1970.

Grant, Michael: *Myths of the Greeks & Romans*; New American Library, New York, 1986.

Green, Miranda: *The Gods of the Celts*; Alan Sutton, Gloucester, 1986.

Guest, Charlotte (transl.): *The Mabinogion*; J.M. Dent, London, 1906.

Hatto, A.T., (transl.): *Tristan*; from Von Strassburg, Gottfried; Penguin, London, 1960.

Jackson, K. H.: *The Oldest Irish Tradition: A Window on the Iron Age*; Cambridge Univ. Press, 1964.

– *A Celtic Miscellany*; Penguin, 1970.

Jacobs, Joseph, coll.: *Celtic Fairy Tales*; The Bodley Head, London, 1970.

– *English Fairy Tales*; The Bodley Head, London, 1968.

Jackson, Kenneth (transl.): *A Celtic Miscellany*; Penguin, London, 1971.

Jarman, A.O.H. & Hughes, G.R. (eds.): *A Guide to Welsh Literature*; Vols. 1 & 2; Christopher Davies, Swansea, 1976 & 1979.

Jones, Gwyn & Jones, Thomas (transl.): *The Mabinogion*; J.M. Dent, London, 1949.

Kavanagh, Peter: *Irish Mythology: a Dictionary*; Goldsmith, Kildare, 1988.

Kinsella, Thomas: *The Tain*; Oxford University Press, 1970.

Knott, E. & Murphy, G.: *Early Irish Literature*; Routledge & Kegan Paul, London, 1966.

Luke, David, (transl.): *Jacob & Wilhelm Grimm: Selected Tales*; Penguin, London, 1982.

Mac Cana, Proinsias: *Celtic Mythology*; Newnes, London 1968, revised 1983.

MacCulloch, John Arnott: *The Religion of the Ancient Celts*; Edinburgh, 1911.

Malory, Thomas: *Chronicles of King Arthur*; (Revised, Sue Bradbury); The Folio Society, London, 1982.

Murphy, Gerard: *Saga & Myth in Ancient Ireland*; Three Candles Press, Dublin, 1955.

O'Driscoll, Robert, (ed.): *Celtic Consciousness*; Canongate, Edinburgh, 1982.

O'Faolain, Eileen: *Irish Sagas & Folk Tales*; Oxford University Press, 1954.

O'Flaherty, Wendy, (transl.): *Hindu Myths*; Penguin, London, 1975.

O'Hogain, Daithi: *The Hero in Irish Folk History*; Gill & Macmillan, Dublin, 1985.

O'Rahilly, Cecile: *The Tain*; Dublin Institute of Advanced Studies, 1967.

O'Rahilly, T.F.: *Early Irish History & Mythology*; Dublin Institute for Advanced Studies, 1946.

O'Suilleabhain, Sean: *Irish Folk Custom & Belief*; Mercier Press, Cork, 1977.

O'Sullivan, Sean: *Folk Tales of Ireland*; Routledge & Kegan Paul, London, 1966.

Owen, D.D.R., (transl.): *Arthurian Romances*; from Chretien de Troyes; J.M. Dent, London, 1987.

Parry, Thomas: *A History of Welsh Literature*; transl. by H.Idris Bell, Oxford University Press, 1955.

Piggott, Stuart:

– *Ancient Europe*; Edinburgh University Press, 1965.

– *France before the Romans*; Thames & Hudson, London, 1973.

Pollard, Alfred, W.: *The Romance of King Arthur*; Macmillan, London, 1979.

Rees, Alwyn & Brinley: *Celtic Heritage*; Thames & Hudson, London, 1961.

Rhys, John: *Celtic Folklore: Welsh & Manx*; Oxford University Press, 1901.

Rolleston, T.W.: *Myths & Legends of the Celtic Race*; Constable, London, 1985.

Sjoestedt, Marie-Louise: *Gods & Heroes of the Celts*; transl. Myles Dillon; Methuen, London, 1949.

Smyth, Daragh: *A Guide to Irish Mythology*; Irish Academic Press, Dublin, 1988.

Squire, Charles: *Celtic Myth & Legend*; Gresham Publishing, London; Undated.

Steel, Flora Annie: *Tales of the Punjab*; The Bodley Head, London, 1973.

Strachan, John (ed.): *Stories from the Tain*; Hodges, Figgis, Dublin, 1908.

Westwood, Jennifer: *Albion: A Guide to legendary Britain*; Paladin, London, 1987.

Yeats, W.B.: *Fairy & Folk Tales of Ireland*; Colin Smythe, Gerrard's Cross, 1977.

– *The Fairy Faith in Celtic Countries*; Colin Smythe, Gerrard's Cross, 1977.

INDEX

INDEX